WRITING THE DARK SIDE OF TRAVEL

D1570791

WRITING THE DARK SIDE OF TRAVEL

Edited by

JONATHAN SKINNER

Berghahn Books

NEW YORK • OXFORD

Published in 2012 by

Berghahn Books

www.berghahnbooks.com

© 2012 Jonathan Skinner

Library of Congress Cataloging-in-Publication Data

Writing the dark side of travel / edited by Jonathan Skinner.
    p. cm.
  Includes bibliographical references and index.
  ISBN 978-0-85745-341-9 (paperback : alk. paper)
  1. Travel—Psychological aspects. 2. Social problems. I. Skinner, Jonathan.
  G155.A1W75 2012
  306.4'819—dc23

                                                        2011037638

British Library Cataloguing in Publication Data

A catalogue record for this book is available from the British Library

Printed in the United States on acid-free paper

ISBN 978-0-85745-341-9 (paperback)

To Elizabeth Skinner (1931–2010)—our family compass—
who heard of this project though she could not see it,
but sadly was not here to hear of its completion.

I travel for travel's sake. The great affair is to move; to feel
the needs and hitches of our life more nearly; to come down off
this feather-bed of civilization, and find the globe granite
underfoot and strewn with cutting flints.

—Robert Louis Stevenson

Contents

▶ • • ✦ • • ◀

Illustrations

>••✦••◄

Acknowledgments

The majority of the chapters in this volume came together largely out of the sixth and seventh annual Oxford Travel Writing colloquiums run by Dr. Carl Thompson (Nottingham Trent University), Professor John Eade (University of Roehampton), and myself. We are grateful to St. John's College, Oxford, for hosting the 2008 colloquium, and to Queen's University Belfast and Dr. Dominic Bryan, Director of the Institute of Irish Studies, for hosting the 2009 colloquium. I extend my personal gratitude to Carl and John for their assistance in making these events so enjoyable and stimulating, and for advising on this publication. I am also grateful to the anonymous reviewers for their useful comments, and to John Skinner, David Kanter, and Veronique Altglas for their support and intellectual input into my Introduction. Finally, thanks are due to Barnaly Pande for vetting the manuscript, and to those at Berghahn Books for their dedication and help with this project.

Introduction
Writings on the Dark Side of Travel
JONATHAN SKINNER

Thursday, 11 August 2005. Killing time, I visit the Museum of Tolerance in Los Angeles. This is coming to the end of a tour of the Arthur Murray dance studios up and down the West Coast. It is a hot break after a month's dance fieldwork in Sacramento. Rather than fly back to Belfast from San Francisco, I opted for LAX and bookended my research with a personal journey driving up and down the state. I had gone up through Death Valley where I had solo hiked into the desert and made a souvenir vial of Death Valley sand. Then inland north to get through Yosemite, living in my rental car, sleeping in motels. Back south, I was sampling the dance studios along the coast—waltz in San Francisco, rumba in Hayward, foxtrot in Redwood City, tango in San Jose, salsa in chic Santa Barbara, merengue in Beverly Hills. Along the way, I was taking in the tourist attractions: the boardwalk in Santa Cruz where the movie *Lost Boys* was filmed; Cannery Row, Monterey, described long ago by John Steinbeck; Hearst Castle, which had inspired Orson Welles's *Citizen Kane*.

This was a self-driven pilgrimage of curiosity. It was a pre- and post-fieldwork treat to myself, a personal and intense journey; packed, busy, and part celebrity/celebratory. Before flying out, I was on a salsa weekend in Palm Springs, and the Beverly Hills dance studio, Crystal Cathedral for an atheist, and the Museum of Tolerance for a liberal were on the travel itinerary for Los Angeles. The Museum of Tolerance is a part of the Simon Wiesenthal Center, a monument to the Jewish Nazi hunter and Holocaust survivor with the aim of educating to prevent hatred and genocide. Its core is an educational journey through the Holocaust for visitors such as school children, with tests and *vox pop* audience samples. It also opens out debates to include local race riots, racial prejudices, and intolerance more generally.

I toured through many of the rooms, following a spiral staircase up and down the building. An old Jewish man shouts at us voyeurs and visitors, herding us through the exhibition rooms. Here a media image, there a group quiz and "What would you do?" test. In one display a vial—uncannily like one of mine—but of crematorium ash from a Polish death camp. Several afternoons a week, a death camp survivor acts as docent and narrates their survival story and holds a Q&A for the museum audience. I stayed around for this: an old man walked into our classroom, the school children hushed, and he told us—first hand, after showing us his heinous tattoo—about his deportation to Auschwitz, how he struggled to stay alive but lost his family before he was liberated by the Soviets and then the Americans, and how he came to live in Los Angeles, working in the restaurant industry, waking most nights from nightmares of his past.

The survivor teased us along his life journey, sometimes reading from his notes, mostly speaking to us, voicing his memories. We lost ourselves following his path, stumbling with him, dumbstruck by the immediacy of the Holocaust horrors. At the end, the school children returned to their present, to their easy embarrassment, and shied away from asking him questions. I took the opportunity and asked him about his religion: gone, that a God could allow such inhumanity. I learned that he remarried in the United States and divorced. That he lives in self-exile alongside other silent survivors but for their museum stints. His politics: Palestinians are Arabs, Arabs killed Americans in 9/11, Muslims are terrorists who should be shown no mercy. "Get rid of them! These are dark times!"

I recoil at the vitriol spat out by this gentle old man at the end of his testimony. It jars with what he experienced and spoke about, as well as the manner of his earlier delivery. It shook the audience. It confuses me. All of the scripted bonhomie was replaced with hatred and intolerance.

Lennon and Foley (2004: 21) include this Museum of Tolerance in Los Angeles in their explication on dark tourism. It is a venue where tourists view and experience artifacts, texts, and media representations of dark tourism. Unlike most dark tourist spots—Rojek's (1999) "fatal attractions"— Auschwitz (Poland), Checkpoint Charlie (Berlin), the Falls Road (Belfast), the Museum of Tolerance is not built on a site of atrocity (if we except the LA riots of 1992 and the Rodney King beatings). Furthermore, it is a museum with few original artifacts, relying instead on modern media images and technologies to represent issues to the visitor. For Lennon and Foley it is, nevertheless, still a dark tourism destination despite this lack of self-referentiality. It speaks where Auschwitz camp remains mute, the latter relying on piles of human hair and human material culture to make its impact. It is 'dark' in its topic and its lure of the visitor. In this fashion its remit is akin to that of the US

Holocaust Museum in Washington, DC, described here by its Director of Public Information:

> It's a counterpoint to all of these other museums and memorials that you see, they all celebrate humans—their technology and art and creativity and we're saying watch out there is another side to human kind and to what humans are also capable of doing. (Lennon and Foley 2004: 153)

This volume seeks to carefully explore the journeys to, from, and through the other side of human kind, with an attention to how to articulate and represent this—what some would refer to as—dark subject matter. This is a collection of chapters devoted to the subject of writers and artists struggling with the terrain of unsettling journeys—literally walks, pilgrimages and tours, but also dances, train rides, fieldwork, and personal recovery. How these personal and public trials and tours are and should be represented are in these contents. As a starting point, and as a way of raising the issues featured in this volume, I take a cue from the dark tourism/thanatourism literature and debates that can help inform our experiences, writings, and texts on the darker side of travel.

The darker side of travel can refer in part to the contentious "dark tourism" concept first proposed by Lennon and Foley in 2000 in *Dark Tourism: The Attraction of Death and Disaster* (2004). Dark tourism for them is the tourist and industry relating to death, disaster, and atrocity, a kind of secular pilgrimage for the late twentieth and early twenty-first centuries. It is a new sociocultural phenomenon: "a product of the circumstances of the late modern world" (3), "an intimation of postmodernity" (11) even as death becomes a commodity for consumption. For them, places such as Changi Gaol, Singapore; Pearl Harbor, Hawaii; the D-Day beaches and war cemeteries in France, are places associated with epic struggle of the human body and spirit. Included in these locations are routes turned into dark tourist attractions, "the commodification of the journey" (165). These can range from Titanic Cruises to the sinking place of the great liner, to live reenactments retracing by presidential limousine the final route through Dallas taken by JFK, or following the last route through Paris taken by Princess Diana in a similar black S-class Mercedes Benz. For Lennon and Foley, this variety of morbid tourist experiences has three contemporary characteristics: first, the place of global communication technologies in creating the initial interest; second, the dark tourism objects "appear to introduce anxiety and doubt about the project of modernity" (11); and third, there is an element of education and commerce/commodification associated with the destination.

Lennon and Foley do not explore the details of these three dark tourism facets in detail. If anything, they shy away from academic debate, writing about the dark tourism cusp between modernity and postmodernity (166), and that the features coincide with a late capitalist, late modern, and/or postmodern era—"[if] these features amount to late capitalism, or late modernity, then so be it" is their stance (11). More generally, the broad picture is one of sociological impact: the scope of bureaucratic rationality in the order of genocide, an ambivalence to science living in an atomic age of mutually assured destruction.

Certainly, Lennon and Foley articulate the tourists' attraction to liminal places where life tours death, the living look onto the dead as though each dark tourism Ground Zero—be it Hiroshima or 9/11—is a photo negative on humanity. Tourists have an appetite for horror and death, the "subtle, corrupting fascination" for Auschwitz identified by Steiner (1971: 30) but writ large to a global level. But they, including Rojek, are well criticized by Tony Seaton (2009: 527) who prefers the term *thanatourism* to dark tourism because it incorporates the tourists' "meditation on death and dying," the term for thanatopsis, a wider but more accurate delimitation. "Dark tourism is the travel dimension of Thanatopsis," Seaton explains. This phenomenon can thus be specifically defined. Seaton elaborates:

> Thanatourism is travel to a location wholly, or partially, motivated by the desire for actual or symbolic encounters with death, particularly, but not exclusively, violent death, which may, to a varying degree be activated by the person-specific features of those whose death are its focal objects. (1996: 236)

Thus, for Seaton, thanatourism belongs to the social science subdiscipline thanatology. Furthermore, Seaton (2009: 526) makes the point that our contemporary fascination with fatality is not a new post/modern phenomenon. Rather, it has evolved for millennia, specifically out of the Christian cult of death and preoccupation with pain and suffering for our sins. Christian shrines are examples of early dark thanatourism. Moreover, Seaton suggests that European Romanticism in the eighteenth and nineteenth centuries turned death into an aesthetic and imaginative sensibility (Edmund Burke propounded a sublime aesthetic of wild natural forces). As such, Lennon and Foley's dark tourism was born on the battlefield tours post-Waterloo and the visits to Pompeii while on the Grand Tour, and not out of the industrial and whole-scale mass slaughters of the two World Wars in the twentieth century.

Richard Sharpley (2009), one of the editors of *The Darker Side of Travel: The Theory and Practice of Dark Tourism* (Sharpley and Stone

2009b), introduces their volume suggesting that there is a sliding scale of dark tourism destinations and suggests that the allure of these sites can be in part explained as a reaction to the general sequestration of death in contemporary society. Dark tourism mediates the living with the dead (Walter 2009: 39), preparing us for what we hope is "the good death" (Stone and Sharpley 2008: 587), or at least a better one than those high-lighted around us. Dark tourist destinations thus function to bracket, to neutralize us towards the taboo topic of life's final frontier.

Sharpley's dark tourism scale is drawn in part from Stone's (2006) "dark tourism spectrum": Lightest—Lighter—Light—Dark—Darker—Darkest (cited in Sharpley 2009: 21). These "shades of darkness" (Sharpley 2009: 6, after 2005) are a typology moving uneasily from paler to darker depending upon the destination's purpose (its level of commodification), infrastructure, location, and authenticity and entertainment orientation (Sharpley 2009: 21): Alcatraz is lighter in shade than Robben Island because it is overshadowed by entertainment activities (Strange and Kempa 2003); York's "The Dungeon" is a dark fun factory and an example of "lighter dark tourism" (Stone 2009: 185) contrasted with Chernobyl tours that are so "unpackaged" as to be considered inappropriate—one of Rojek's (1993: 137) "Black Spots"? The dark tourism range or continuum has been typified and "troped" variously as hot or cold (Uzell 1992), paler/darker (Sharpley 2005), pure/impure (Seaton 1996). Whilst these tourism scholars will acknowledge the heuristic nature of their tourism poles, and that "dark tourism" is perhaps even sometimes "an unhelpful term" (Sharpley and Stone 2009a: 249)—particularly given that it is predominantly visual, experiential, and reactionary (Muzaini, Teo, and Yeoh 2007)—it is adopted for use by them wholesale.

"Labelling a site as 'dark' seems to be a complicated matter of perspective and privilege" (Bowman and Pezzullo 2009: 192). Just how dark are Strange and Kempa's Alcatraz and Robben Island if there are chinks of political light and seeds of hope and change to be found there? Are not all tourist sites potentially dark? Communications scholars Bowman and Pezzullo (2009: 189) make appropriate criticisms of tourism research into dark tourism that uses the "dark" trope, uncritically adopting this label with the "negative valence" and possible implicit prejudice attached to it. It is a shorthand we should be wary of adopting and careful and considerate in using. Moreover, "What is so dark about dark tourism?" Bowman and Pezzullo ask (2009: 189) before going on to draw attention to the ironic juxtaposition of dark tourism on the sunny holiday. Are there not different types of dark possible from levels of light, to moods of behavior, to historical periods? Does not the "lighten-ing" of the US Holocaust Museum's dark tourism status because it is not on authentic dead ground denigrate and marginalize the lives of the many emigrants who fled or escaped from the concentration camps? (See Bowman and Pezzullo 2009: 193.) Does not the dark tourism framework neglect the human actors and agents—the on-site "performers" for Bowman and Pezzullo (2009: 188)—by concentrating upon the dead at the expense of the living?

Sidestepping the mire of categorizing tourism destinations, Bowman and Pezzullo (2009: 194) argue that the tourists and those at the destination are co-performing at the destination: a dead stage with live bodies on it. The attraction to these locations might then be as a rehearsal for death, "spaces where we can try on reactions and imagine the subjunctive 'what if?'" (Bowman and Pezzullo 2009: 195). The tourists' motives and behaviors—for these "counter-experiences" from the everyday (Bowman and Pezzullo 2009: 198)—are thus far too nuanced, complex, and blurred to be neatly divided between tourism researchers' authenticity/commodification binaries: Bowman and Pezzullo (2009: 196) cite Edensor's tourists to the Taj Mahal tomb, showing them to be respectful but also playful at the same time, and thus more than just "dark tourists"; moreover, they also cite Slade's (2003) study of Australians touring Gallipoli more as nationalists looking for seeds of nation building than as dark tourists to further complicate the many spaces occupied by tourists. These tourist destinations are unstable performance spaces and the tourist tour an experimental journey of becoming.

That dark sites or dark destinations attract tourists is undeniable. Tourism and death are an attractive if unnatural combination, "an odd conjunction" for Seaton (2009: 521), one of surreptitious interest, public controversy, and intellectual curiosity in tourist motivation. The Auschwitz Memorial and Museum with its million-plus visitors, and the Holocaust and its museumification in the United States—also with its million-plus visitors compared with Rwanda's 30,000 tourists of "live" graves (Beech 2009: 223)—are an obvious case in point, one that illustrates many issues raised in the chapters in this collection. As we have just heard, one in particular is the difficulty, not least the appropriateness, of writing and representing such "darkness"—to use a term used by Sharon Hepburn (this volume) to describe the condition of atrocity, horror, evil. Is it possible to articulate or fathom the genocide of millions of Jews in World War II? The Shoah overwhelms our language and media (Rosenfeld 1980); it "negates any form of literature" (Wiesel 1960: 7); it is the end of poetry (Adorno 2003); it is so "unspeakable" that it cannot be trivialized by social theory (Steiner 1967: 163)—though I would suggest that Bauman (1989) and Arendt (1994) make disturbing but important warnings for us about the banality of the Holocaust and its testing connection with Modernity (specifically the modern nation-state and new mechanisms for social control).

"The Holocaust for some remains a vacuum that consumes all light intended to illuminate it" (Lennon and Foley 2004: 152). It is darkly fascinating, repulsively attractive for the tourist moths. Perhaps its ghoulish commoditization is necessary in our post-emotional society in which identification with the suffering and pain of others is becoming so difficult? The danger is that this commoditization erodes the impact of the history of the place, marketing the place with "euphemism and distory" (Dann and Seaton 2001a: 15)—or "dystory" in a dystopian sense. It is difficult to commemorate without compromise. Auschwitz is now a physical teaching tool in the Polish curriculum where it is obligatory for all school children to make the pilgrimage to the site and damning pictures of school children eating their packed lunches sitting on the crematoria have been circulated extensively in the public domain. Israeli anthropologist Jackie Feldman (2005) discusses failed tourist expectations in his study of educational visits to Poland for Israeli school children. These part-pilgrimage tours often fail because of a "cognitive dissonance" (Feldman 2005: 228; see also Dann and Seaton [2001b] on "dissonant" slavery heritage) between the tourists' expectations and the "authenticity" of the experiences. If the site does not look authentic, or the sensory envelope of the site is not all convincing and embracing, then the tourist experience does not succeed—the school children feel empty, let down, deflated, even betrayed.

Similarly, in a recent issue of *Journeys,* anthropologist Nigel Rapport (2008c) uses his walking tour of Auschwitz as a foil with which to connect himself with his readings about the place and its horrors—one of which is a reading of the German Anglophile writer W. G. Sebald (1998) and his meditative travelogue of an English pilgrimage, *The Rings of Saturn.* According to Rapport, there is an individual consciousness to walking journeys, one that develops from the body as movement precipitates identity. "Walking Auschwitz" though, Rapport feels disconnected between the experiences of history, which he wants to connect with, and the tourist role he feels himself acting out. His body movements are out of step; his identity out of context. He becomes the "resentful tourist" (2008c: 37) corralled along a scripted tour. The tour fails because it is like being on a film set or in a theme park—"an emotional abusement park" (Miller 1994). And yet this is hardly surprising given Rapport's thesis on movement and identity and his embodiment of the tourist visitor: visiting Auschwitz on a group tour, wearing tourist clothes (shorts and rolled-up shirt), and marking the "trip" with posed tourist photographs taken outside Birkenau (see Rapport 2008c: 38).

In visiting Holocaust displays or memorials, there is the danger that their commoditization results in their compartmentalization. The representation of the Holocaust from another time and another country in part consigns it to a historical position. It acts as a deflective move. The Holocaust Museum in Washington, DC, can also be interpreted to act as a reprieve for the US government in that the portrayal of genocide is distanced to mid-twentieth-century Nazi atrocity, rather than to the genocide of Native American Indians much closer to home. There is no slavery museum representing the iniquities and barbarity of that institutionalized slavery. Furthermore, Lennon and Foley (2004: 152) make the valid point that the dark fascination with the Holocaust exposed in a sanitized museum environment is not necessarily the logically appropriate way of warning "mankind." Is exposure to barbarism the antidote to that barbarism? They quote the travel writer Philip Gourevitch's (1993: 62) apt interpretation of the Holocaust Museum media show:

> One way history is doomed to repetition at the Holocaust museum is that day in and day out, year after year, the videos of the Einssatzgruppen murders will play over and over. There, just off the National Mall in Washington, the victims of Nazism will be on view for the American public, stripped, herded into ditches, shot, buried, and then the tape will repeat and they will be herded into the ditches again, shot again, buried again. I cannot comprehend how anyone can enthusiastically present this constant cycle of slaughter, either as a memorial to those whose deaths are exposed or as an edifying spectacle for the millions of visitors a year who will be exposed to them. Didn't these people suffer enough the first time their lives were taken from them?

Museums such as the Museum of Tolerance in Los Angeles and the Holocaust Museum in Washington, DC, involve survivors in their activities to personalize and dramatize the tourist's visit experience. The living connection with the past literally brings home the horror and lends authenticity to the uneasy representation of the Holocaust. Berman (1999) notes, though, the different orientations in the exhibitions: American representations are more humanistic in scope, "Americanized" in contrast with the more Zionistic, "Israelified" Yad Vashem (the Holocaust Martyrs' and Heroes' Remembrance Authority) living memorial to the Holocaust in Jerusalem. Cohen (2011) goes further by suggesting that Yad Vashem is a "darker" tourist experience because, though a secondary site to Auschwitz because it is based in Israel, it has greater "locational authenticity" (Miles 2002) than other Holocaust Museums; this concept comes from Miles's distinction between the Washington, DC, Holocaust Memorial Museum as a place *associated with* death and Auschwitz as a place *of* death and hence a darker destination. This makes it, by association, potentially a darker tourist experience — if shades of dark tourism or a spectrum or continuum running from lightest and palest to darker and darkest and ultimately "blackspots" are possible, helpful or indeed appropriate?

Anthropologists' reactions to Auschwitz and the Museum of Tolerance show how difficult it is to foster a balanced and respectful but disturbing representation of a darkness without causing offence or failing to elicit the appropriate response from the visitor. Accompanying a class of diverse university students around the Montreal Holocaust Museum with a Holocaust survivor, Rapport again senses a disconnect between tourist and guide, resenting the exclusivity of the darkness of the Holocaust story at the expense of the students' own trials. "His person and his narrative ... possessed more the aura of ritual relic than a truth relevant to the everyday here and now" Rapport (2008a: 161) explains.

In Mestrovic's (1996) post-emotional condition, where it is difficult to create empathy outside of the immediate family, inured and with death sequestered from life, we feel and react only from ever-more-risky or "edgier" pursuits (see Lyng [1990], and Bell and Lyall on the "accelerated sublime" [2002]). Death, Giddens's (1991: 162) "point zero" as the outer limits of our experience, is the new Ground Zero for the dark tourist. Only in the hyper do we gain the last of the authentic and come to live in the ecstatic present. In our modern risk society we become junkie zombies acculturated to the extreme—extreme travel pursuit, extreme leisure practice, extreme behavior. This is the subject matter of Graham Huggan's *Extreme Pursuits: Travel/Writing in an Age of Globalization* (2009) book about travel writers and their travel writings. In it, Huggan calls on us to expand our notion of travel and the travel text, specifically that compound "travel writing." These "travel" texts can include accounts of travel by Holocaust deportation and for migrant labor, and "writing" as film texts, ethnography, and audiovisual media. Entering the thanatourism/dark tourism debates, Huggan points out that whichever name is used, both dark tourism and thanatourism are compromised practices. They reflect a nostalgic authenticity by way of endangerment; in life-threatening times we feel alive, with representations of the life-threatening being the next best thing. That feeling of safety from exposure to atrocity elsewhere in time and space, Huggan (2009: 10) warns us, is "an illusory authority." There seems to be a degree of Schadenfreude and catharsis sought from extreme travel writing. Huggan's purpose in his new book is to examine our sociological desires and anxieties, and how they are salved and sorted in contemporary travel writing.

At the core of *Extreme Pursuits* is disaster writing. Like Rapport, Huggan considers Sebald's haunting writing, also the war reportage of Philip Gourevitch mentioned by Lennon and Foley. The current vogue for disaster tourism is a symptom of our modern reflexive risk society where death and disaster are the norm, the theatricalization of death for the male tourist especially living through a crisis of masculinity. This makes the disaster writing a cautionary literature, a witnessing at a safe distance of other people's pain. The text becomes a link between travel "too-far" (travel without return or the death of the traveler) and travel "not-far-enough" (a flirtation with death or aspiration of suffering) (Huggan 2009: 115). Whether book and/or film—Jon Krakauer's *Into the Wild* (1997) reconstruction of Christopher McCandless's failed Alaskan wilderness quest is one of the book/film text examples used by Huggan (2009: 111–17)—the travel text notes the passive nature of the "writer" as well as the reader. Both are consumers in their respective spaces. Furthermore, readers of Gourevitch's (1998) *We Wish to Inform You That Tomorrow We Will Be Killed with Our Families*—an account of the genocide in Rwanda written from a visit in 1995—will be familiar with how he struggles to imagine, let alone write about, the atrocities committed. How can one imagine the intent behind a genocide, and where does it go once the blood has been mopped up and the corpses rotted into aesthetically tranquil "fallen forms" (Gourevitch 1998: 19)? Gourevitch chooses literary narrative as his representational medium. Pelton, Aral, and Dulles (1998), in their guidebook *The World's Most Dangerous Places,* add graphic cartoons to their word text, by so doing taming and domesticating the violence they represent. This gives the disaster a thrill factor. Sebald (1998), by contrast, punctuates a traditional textual flow with occasional pictures, prints, and photographs to create an atmosphere of gloominess, difference, and dereliction. For Huggan (2009: 141), this last travel text is "a narrative of suffering—a martyrology of sorts." It becomes an outlet for neurosis, a space where all sorts of confusions can be faced: psychological, ontological, representational. Who am I? Where do I belong? Travel and its writing has the potential to create uncertainty but also to cure complacency. But more than anything, like anthropology, it encourages an intersecting of worlds—past and present, living and dead for Huggan (2009: 146), to which we might add in this volume the self and the other, and the near and the far.

Writing the Dark

August 1995: Exactly ten years earlier, and I am in my own dark place. Almost a year into ethnographic fieldwork on the small island of Montserrat in the Eastern Caribbean, and the 'previously thought' extinct volcano that first made the island begins to shake, rumble, and spew on the civilians beneath it. In July, "the Beast," as many came to refer to the volcano, had come back to life. I left the island to return to St. Andrews, Scotland, where I was completing my doctorate in Social Anthropology. There, I was angry, very angry. Talk about "fire in the mountain."[1] I felt like punching things and people. I felt that I could very easily lash out. The university town was exactly the same as when I'd left it, but I had changed, and with my sudden departure from Montserrat, I felt that I was still often mentally and physiologically back on the island. I felt guilt for leaving my friends and colleagues. I wanted to lash out at each comment about how exciting it must have been to have been in a volcanic eruption. And each time the floor shook in my landlady's house from the washing machine going into spin cycle, my heart raced as another tremor disturbed the island (see Skinner 2000). I knew that I was getting stuck in my isolating experience. And that I was either not able to express "where I was," or that it was not appropriate to do so. I needed to catch up with myself. We talked about this in the university counseling service for two sessions. The first was a nonjudgmental description and explanation of my unexpected return to St. Andrews. In the second session, we talked about counseling techniques. Several years later, I spent some of my own clinical practice as a person-centered counselor working for the same university service. Ten years on and "the ghosts in the head" (Skinner 2008a), "jumbies" for Montserratians, had been laid to rest with a return visit to Montserrat, and a life moved on into a very different research area.

Kali Talil (2010) writes that "trauma is a transformative experience, and those who are transformed can never return to a state of previous innocence." It can prompt change. And it can haunt the changed. Like the anthropologist's split subject position, the traumatized move between worlds and states characterized by some as between the normal and the abnormal. In far more extreme examples, the traumatized remain haunted by their experiences: "After Auschwitz, everything long past brings us back to Auschwitz," laments camp survivor Elie Wiesel (1990: 19). One difficulty with such trauma is that it can become "embodied in the neurophysiology of pain and fear rather than in words and images" (Young 1995:13). This makes it difficult to define and to work with, as Young (283) found in the case of posttraumatic disorder treatment of US Vietnam War veterans, dealing with the "wordless memories" as he put it. Stress levels and neural pathway damage sometimes relate to the politics of trauma more than to the patients, however.

Trauma has also been described manifest as "the fragmentation of the lived body" (Casey 2000: 155), of habitual movements broken into uncoordinated parts, divided and lacking integration and coherence. Such bleakness can be countered by positive body memories, by integrating and smoothing—acclimatizing—the trauma patient. For contemporary psychoanalyst Robert Stolorow (1999), the estranged and isolated condition he found himself in took six long years to "journey" through. He likens his personal journey to that of an anthropologist traveling through an alien culture; the absolute and normal, the predictable and comfortable—the sense of being-in-the-world—are all awry and out of kilter while he strays from his normal path. In Farrell's (1998: xii) terms, he has blundered outside "the magic circle of everyday life." Stolorow's phenomenology of trauma is perhaps an extreme version of Giddens's (1991) disembodied/disembedded reflexive self in Late Modernity, which might be difficult to understand while they inhabit their personal dark continent, though it is possible to access through their writings, creative expressions, blogs, poems, paintings, walkings, journeyings, dancings, and all manner of other narrative practices and self-articulations.

In his diatribe on postmodern ethnography, the Writing Culture School anthropologist Stephen Tyler (1986: 140) describes ethnographic texts as "a meditative vehicle" in the anthropological journey that we write. Here in this Introduction to this volume we have a personal and professional journey intertwined. For Tyler, though, our writing of reality is an imitation of that reality, a mimesis and poor one at that. Writing—the most powerful means of representation, an ideology of representational signification, and an ideology of power (see Tyler 1986: 131)—might be a magical act, but so too in this logos of writing we are strait-jacketed and imprisoned in our linguistic-based symbolic communications (see Bloch [1998] and Jameson [1972]). We are all doubly disabled in trying to understand the Other and then trying to represent them. "Language doesn't represent but constructs," Anna Banks (Banks and Banks 1998: 14) points out. This is one of the key challenges for anthropology—"the writing of the human" (Rapport 2008b: 230).

One consolation is that in this orderly composition of writing—"the logical-conceptual order of the text" (Tyler 1986: 132)—can come a therapeutic aesthetic integration of captured experience. In writing we try to gain control of our experiences. We write them together. And we write them out of ourselves. The limits of this writing are obvious (see also Archetti [1994] on the end of our "age of innocence" as text-studying anthropologists). Tyler calls on us, then, to "evoke" rather than attempt an impossible "representation." Sebald, we might say, evokes in a haunting fashion. Elsewhere, in *Holidays in Hell* for example, P. J. O'Rourke (2002) uses humor in his riff on the expression "acceptable level of violence" used to describe the state of Northern Ireland. He, and other travel writers, generally still opt for the descriptive turn in their writing.

Anthropologist James Boon draws a fine distinction between the travelogue and the ethnography as orderly compositions mentioned above: they are genres of writing, the former "a kind of writing-as-if-one had 'been there,' but briefly, *en passant*"; the latter, "a kind of writing-as-if-one had 'been there' longer, dwellingly" (1999: 48). Their rhetorics are to be read with a similar correspondence: "reading-voyage [as] fleet"—travelogue; and "reading-stay [as] participant"—ethnography. The ethnography, however, "genre-ally" has a particular disciplinary-based reading—and writing—community (Fish 1988).[2] Among anthropologists writing ethnography, the "1986" "new ethnographic critics" George Marcus and his colleague Michael Fischer (1986) encourage an ever-experimental moment of evocation, illustration, play, and dialogics in ethnographic writing. Julie Taylor, for example, picks up this challenge and problem with the nature of representation in her ethnography of tango in Argentina, *Paper Tangos* (1998). Concerned to "transmit the bodily knowledge of a dance form," Taylor (1998: xv) combines text with image, creating a flipbook of tango moves alongside a very moving ethnography. The steps seen correspond to the words read. The result is Taylor (1998: xix) "choreographing [a] paper tango" that pushes the reader to analyze, feel, and see the dance for what it is. Edwin Wilmsen (1999) uses metaphor and poetry in his *Journeys with Flies*, an evocation of life and long-term fieldwork among the tribesfolk of the Kalahari Desert, the fly standing as a metaphor for the ambiguities of life. In other ethnographic experiments, Mol (2002) splits her ethnography of medical diagnosis and treatment of atherosclerosis between a reported style of main text and a parallel academic discussion beneath. The reader heads north or south depending on their motivation. Rapport (1994) zigzags east/west and back again in his writing. Writing about violence in Northern Ireland, the anthropologist Allen Feldman (1991) sidesteps the problems with representation by focusing on the interviews he conducted with his body of informants. Fiction and the real are blended with literature, historical archive material, and literary theory by Michael Taussig (1986) in his eclectic study of terror and healing in Columbia, *Shamanism, Colonialism, and the Wild Man*. There, he uses Conrad's *Heart of Darkness* to draw the reader into "the greatness of the horror," "the mistiness of terror," "the aesthetics of violence," and the imperial, aggrandizing desires and repressions that are found from the heart of Congo and Columbia to the heart of man (Taussig 1986: 10). Evocative (nonrepresentational) faction (literary fiction with historical fact) becomes "impressionistic autoethnography" for Skinner (2003, 2004).

These are all techniques for developing the humanism of representation made by writers who are, after all, still "part shareholders in humanity" (James, Hockey, and Dawson 1997: 5). With all this in mind, Paul Stoller (1989, 1997) further complicates the problem with representation by calling for a sensuous anthropology that takes account of the lower senses and so discounts the ocular centrism of Western perception.

"The inchoate—the dark at the bottom of the stairs—which lies at the centre of human experience"—this is the subject of James Fernandez's (1986: xiii) anthropological project. Fernandez advocates the figurative, to analogy, "rhetorical devices of representation" (7) that we co-intuit. Metaphor, literally translating from the Greek as "change in motion" (Fernandez 1986: 37), allows for an expressive culture of rich tropes, ironic word plays, and imaginative figures of speech. One can be expansive, elusive and edifying in life, and hopefully also in text. Indeed, the cultural crossings and associations studied in trope theory are also at the core of travel writing journeys written about one place for people in another (see Fernandez 1991). However, I also take Judith Adler's (1989: 1383) point that travel and its writing generally serves a metonymic function with the brief encounter summing up "a culture." As Huggan has already shown us, the world is far more mobile now than ever before. Nomad thoughts of routes rather than roots may be with us, though much travel writing has still to catch up (see also Clifford 1997; Cresswell 2006: 43).

The existential anthropologist Michael Jackson makes a similar point when he compares "storying" and "journeying." Both practices involve crossing, breaching and blurring boundaries. "Storytelling moves us, transports us, carries us away, or helps us to escape the oppressiveness of our real lives" Jackson (2002: 30) opines. This echoes de Certeau's (1984: 115) comment that "every story is a travel story—a spatial practice." This comes out of de Certeau's *The Practice of Everyday Life* where there is the suggestion that the story is an everyday narrative form, which we can assume has a converse position of the trauma as an extraordinary state, one hard to narrate and give form to.

The story is not just about a journey, it is also a journey as emplacement and emplotment combine in the travel writers' narrative, Jackson (2002: 31) continues. Jackson exemplifies this in *Minima Ethnographica: Intersubjectivity and the Anthropological Project* that opens with the clause "I begin in the middle of a journey" (1998: 1). First Jackson writes the story. Then he analyzes it, making the point later on that storytelling is motivated by a need for self-expression and, further, that life stories are authored in collaboration between teller and listener. In other words, for Jackson, life stories are relational, "authored not by autonomous subjects but by the dynamics of intersubjectivity" (1998: 23).When told, they retain elements of that interaction with both actor and sufferer subject positions. When things fall apart, we spin a yarn to bring them together. When trauma intrudes and unsettles our daily habits and self-expectations, we recount and reimagine our situation. Put more graphically:

> If one's habitus is destroyed—by war, enforced migration, imposed social change, bereavement, debilitating illness, racist humiliation, unemployment or lack of recognition—then the capacities for acting, building and speaking that were developed in one's first and familiar lifeworld are suddenly invalidated, and this may lead to such a loss of confidence, satisfaction and enjoyment that one may feel that life itself no longer has any meaning, and is not worth living. (Jackson 2008: xxii)

Writing, narrating, storytelling that darkness, suffering, pain, brings it into relief and into some intersubjective shared light. This activity is one of mastery. It is about giving voice to pain, anger, violence, abuse, the darkness in the human pit. The human subject is a relational subject, for Jackson, requiring an "inter-existence" (1998: 3), interlocuting to find a voice, needing an object audience when subjected. But there are voices within the self: consciousness is dialogic. In addition to this, Jackson (1998: 2, 3) goes so far as to suggest that the "self has no reality except in relation to others," and that, after Sartre, "inter-existence is given precedence over individual essence." There is certainly an impulse "to connect" in a Forsterian sense, but Jackson's "inter-" is an add-on factor—inter-est, if you will. The individual is an expressive and performative being whether in solo or in duet.

One assumption here is that journeying and writing is a way of finding oneself, of becoming congruent. This is not necessarily a given. Musgrove (1999) articulates this when he looks at Freud on vacation, at Freud's travel writing texts, and notes that the identity of the journeying subject can be sent into flux and become as unsettled as the mobile body. Border crossings, and wavering between home and away worlds, can precipitate a loss of self (Musgrove 1999: 40), just as it can reinforce the self. They also have the potential to lead to a need to "possess" (colonize, describe, represent) the host environment in an attempt at regaining that sense of settlement, whether physically or figuratively. Faced with the monotony of the landscape of the northwest border of South Africa, travel writer Dan Jacobson (*The Electronic Elephant: A South African Journey* [1994]) grows increasingly anxious that the external emptiness before him might reflect his inner emptiness (Klopper 2005:

464). In fact, his travel north acts as a travel back into his past and reactivates difficult memories from his youth: an abandoned building comes to stand for his erased self, a rock sticking out from the veld becomes a jagged scab sticking up from his body. It is, as Porter (1991: 13) writes, as though "a foreign country constitutes a gigantic Rorschach test." The foreign plains act as a free association stimulus or projection field for the writer's dissatisfactions and desires.

Play and death are closer to each other than is commonly thought (Urry 2004), as evinced above in the dark tourism/thanatourism examples (see also Bowman and Pezzullo [2009] on the jazz funeral). So too is the tourism/terrorism distinction as travel and violence become increasingly interwoven—not just as Crick's (1989: 309) "suntanned destroyers of culture" but also in the travel interrogations, indignities, and suspicions we have to endure for our safety (Phipps 1999: 75). Taussig (2006), whose work covers many of the themes and issues discussed in this issue—violence, trauma, mimesis, representation, and intertwined personal and professional journeys—has written an academic crossover travel text about visiting *Walter Benjamin's Grave*, with the same title. One section opens, "'I am not making a pilgrimage,' I said to myself when I visited the graveyard at Port Bou in the spring of 2002" (6). Taussig is uncertain of himself and seems to be trying to convince himself of the uprighteousness of his activities, as though pilgrimages or dark visits are unseemly involvements for an academic. He continues:

> Indeed I was not even sure I wanted to visit the graveyard. I do not think this was entirely due to fear of cemeteries on my part. Nor was it because I am also attracted to them. It was more because I feel uncomfortable about what I discern as an incipient cult around the site of Benjamin's grave, as if the drama of his death, and of the holocaust, in general, is allowed to appropriate and overshadow the enigmatic power of his writing and the meaning of his life. Put bluntly, the death comes to mean more than the life. (2006: 6)

For Taussig, we are scared but tempted by death. It is the ultimate—excess, end point, edge, and even "authority" for the storyteller. Are we back to dark tourism again, the dirty little secret of the tourism industry, and if so, is it the dark more so than the tourism that is pressing against Taussig's sense of appropriacy?

In a perceptive article on the rhetorics of disaster and the imperative of writing, Michael Bernard-Donals uses the Shoah and museum tours by survivors to explore the limits of writing. He calls for us "to resist the idolatory of representation" (2001: 73), to recognize the limits of writing, in particular the impossibility of writing an event given that we cannot "write as knowledge" (74). Like Tyler, Fernandez, Gourevitch, and museum and tourism studies critics, Bernard-Donals maintains that whether we use literal or figurative language, an event or experience "resists *versimilitude*" (80, author's emphasis). Writing dissolves the experience and becomes an object in itself. Not only do events elude writing, but writing itself is an illusion, a sleight of hand. Writing is not a medium that represents. It is more a practice that haunts. Perhaps this goes some way towards explaining the students' disconnect with the docent in the museum? Reading a history of the Holocaust in the intransitive or experiencing the jar between personal testimony and historical fact can disorientate the audience. Bernard-Donals (2001: 85) cites a classroom experiment where the teacher used Art Spiegelman's classic graphic novel *Maus* to engage her compassion-fatigued students, to connect them to issues of minority status, intolerance, and dark acts in the past. The experiment to use a visual text "brought home" the Holocaust history, powerfully utilizing anthropomorphism over text or material culture. On occasion, such writing speaks to me more so than academic descriptive analytical attempts at representation. Bruner's (2005) anthropological examination of the conflicting interpretations of tourism experiences at the slave trader forts of Ghana—slaves disappearing through "doors of no return"—is less evocative, less touching, and hence less "representational" than Wideman's (1998) creative writing journey through the door—a trauma—a darkness smelling of slavery:

> We live in darkness, and, when they drag us up into the courtyard each day, there is no color in the light—it is like silver, glittering spears thrust into our eyes or the glare of hot sand when the sun burns fiercely. My eyes are swollen now, and water spills from them even after I've finished crying, but I remember the color of light in the village. (Wideman 1998: 6)

Nine Writings on the Dark Side of Travel

There are nine chapters in this volume. In their own ways, they all engage with the issues wandered through and wondered about above: the haunting dark, darkness, inchoate inner places, traumatized bodies and brains; mediums of representation and the nature of reading and writing; and travels and tourism, personal and professional journeys taken, often intertwined. These are all writings on the difficult and uneasy—the dark?—side of travel whether on the streets of Belfast, through Sebald's coastal East Anglia, absorbing the graphic novels on genocide in Bosnia, reading reluctant travel writers' visits and tours of Rwanda, on Camino pilgrimage through Spain, trekking along the foothills of Nepal, on dance retreat in the Republic of Ireland, on the train to a site of abuse in Australia, or accompanying tourists around World War I battlefields along the Western Front in France. In each, the examples are personal and particular, whether the academic ethnographer or travel writer, or the subjects being represented. You might say that there is a "tactile humanism" (Abu-Lughod 1993) about the ethnographic particularism in these writings. There is also a great deal of movement, of journeying be it the content of the text, the form of the writing, the mundivagrantations of the writers.

John Nagle considers Belfast, a city riven from its sectarian conflict. Belfast is an emblem of the Troubles, a people and a place traumatized by violence. Tourism has been one path forward out of the locked cycle, a counterinsurgency technique to peace. Yet the schism between Unionist and Nationalist drives well into the debate of what the tourist should see of the city, an illustration of the politicization of representation: protest and commemoration murals or industrial heritage, terrorism (dark) tours, or a more positive visit to the Titanic Quarter—itself built upon the name of an infamous shipwreck. Nagle's analysis of the city is by way of Freud, suggesting that IRA bombs traumatized the people, creating a void societal psyche. Tourism is a way of peace building, but the danger is that the dark tours given in the Black Cabs or the political walks through the Falls Road and Shankill Road continue to contain the city and its people within a traumatic paradigm, one that is *unheimlich* (uncanny) in its juxtaposition of the strange and the familiar, the safe and the dangerous. Here, regeneration is more than just economic.

In the second chapter, we turn from the collective to the individual with Simon Cooke's examination of the German (travel) writer W. G. Sebald's haunting journey through East Anglia, a book also tackled by Rapport and Gourevitch above. Sebald plays with his narratives and their mediums using memory, dream, history, photograph, and map to present a landscape full of foreboding. There is a pervasive darkness about his writing. It is everywhere. East Anglia becomes an area of darkness, but it is not an absence or nothingness or act of negation (see also Spurr 1994: 92–94). There is neither a negation nor a darkness as metaphor for the unconscious or uncivilized that you find in the writing of, say, Conrad. Sebald's unsettling work is an example of thanatourism, according to Cooke. Sebald avoids the danger of dropping his writing into an anthem to duty or example of commoditized titillation. Sebald does this by engaging with the text, bringing the reader into this reflexive site of suffering. Sebald ultimately resists the separation between the living and the dead: "the thanatouristic element is self-defeating in his writing" as Cooke argues. The incomprehensible simultaneity of bliss and horror are not restricted to a particular destination. Such sufferings, Cooke points out, have no discrete "place." They are all around us. Death is a part of—and not apart from—all of our journeys.

The graphic travelogue is examined by Tristram Walker in the third chapter in this volume. Specifically, Walker shows us how "adult comix" graphic novelist and artist Joe Sacco represents his travels in Bosnia and the Palestine. "Shock and draw" is the underground artist's modus operandi. But the violence of the cartoon panels is not gratuitous but informed social and political commentary based on first-hand observation. Sacco is a comix journalist who draws himself into his panels. These panels impel the reader/viewer forwards, sketching scenes of trauma that the reader has to link together. The form of representation is light and hinted at despite the weighty and dark subject matter. The blank gutter between the panels becomes important, a gap in the dark of the boxes, the terror of an unknown scene pending our visual arrival. The captions around the images are scattered about, fragmented, mimicking the scattered refugee families and reinforcing the impression that many events are going on at the same time. Walker concludes that Sacco's work is a witnessing and sharing of trauma that affirms life and hope in the face of bleakness, and reinforces the previous chapters' interpretations that these violent streets could be our streets around us.

In chapter four, Rachel Moffat compares and contrasts two travel writers and their accounts of genocide in Rwanda. Here, we return to literary criticism and the conventional textual medium of representation. Both Philip Gourevitch (see above) and Dervla Murphy are experienced travel writers with different identities and affiliations—the one Jewish, the other Irish—visiting postgenocide Rwanda. Both wrestle with their motivations and representations of their experiences. In *We Wish to Inform You That Tomorrow We Will Be Killed with Our Families: Stories from Rwanda*, Gourevitch (1998) deliberately set out to explore the logic and rationality behind such darkness on the cusp of a new century and millennium. He finds himself disturbed by his own curiosity. There is a moral ambivalence associated with both the writing and the reading of this atrocity, though in writing it there is also the potential to right it and to warn against it happening again. Much of this is captured in his walk at Nyarabuye with a Canadian Colonel: he hears a crunch and sees that the Colonel has accidentally stepped on a skull and broken it. His immediate reaction is to feel anger. This turns to guilt and complicity when he hears another crunch and feels a vibration underfoot as he too steps on the remains of another human being. Gourevitch's writing deliberately pulls the reader into the text. He elicits a reaction right from the very start of the book that he deliberately framed about a Shoah-like Holocaust, and deliberately titled after a written plea for help just prior to the bloodletting.

Murphy also takes care not to be seen to exploit a tragedy. Her work, *Visiting Rwanda* (1998), is an accidental narrative as Murphy is forced into reporter mode when her Zaire trekking vacation is curtailed by reports of violence in the areas she was intending to walk through. The reluctant reporter, Murphy did not seek out the accounts and testimonies from Rwanda. Sometimes she and her text turn away when Gourevitch felt obliged to account, record, and document with gut-wrenching precision. And yet Murphy is able to pick and choose her questions, and so give the reader a more "reader-friendly" travel in comparison with Gourevitch's probing investigation. Here we see the different travel writers' gaze on the horror, entertaining the reader but also warning them of the extreme suffering from which they are removed. There is a tactics at play in both the writing and the reading of these extreme travel texts, to return us to Huggan. Is this travel writing a reader's engagement with our new late/post/hyper-modern risk society? Here too we are left with the question of whether or not these travel writers are in fact just dark tourists using their accidental or deliberate writings to justify their travels.

Keith Egan, in chapter five, walks the Camino de Santiago in Spain, joining in and studying the pilgrims.[3] His approach is phenomenological, exploring their motivations and how the walk, pedestrianism, with its quiet reflective rhythms, becomes a therapeutic practice—walking therapy, a somatic mode of healing. Control of one's walk represents a regain of control in one's life whether wounded by loss—of self, other, or purpose—or suffering from illness or trauma. Sebald recognized this and walked, walked and wrote. In this piece, it is the person suffering and in an existential dark place: the dark terrain they walk through is on the inside rather than on the outer path. The walk is a way of moving out of their present condition, a physical and existential exposure and regaining of closure and coherence in their lifeworld. Many pilgrims have not reached a place in themselves where they can speak of their state. Here the body articulates the unspeakable for them. The Camino becomes a staged narrative practice of healing. And the stories that are told to Egan when the pilgrims do quite literally find their feet are often itineraries on the way, or personal journeys undertaken. John walks in the shadow of his sister who died while walking the Camino. He finds his vocabulary after reading her comments in the overnight guest books and talking to other walkers along the way. His is a bereavement journey. Overall, Egan's study, in which he also walks his own Camino, is a study of metaphorical expression in narrative practice, of personal hope and individual inspiration. Though old, this medieval pilgrimage route is still as supportive as it has always been.

The theme of shades of being is complemented by a chapter on the shades of darkness by Sharon Hepburn. In chapter six, Hepburn critiques the dark tourism thesis by painting a more nuanced picture. There are shades of darkness that have settled across tourist Nepal. These are not necessarily negative spaces, but they do have an absence in the culture of silence that pervades them. Moreover, tourists enjoying themselves in Nepal are often blind to the darkness—the fear, terror, killing—around them. Thus, it can be said that there is a tourism *in* darkness as well as a tourism *about* darkness. Hepburn adopts this dark tourism continuum, from paler to darker and dark, to characterize tourist and Nepali experiences—or obliviousness as is often the case for the former. Light and darkness are, respectively, concealed and revealed to the tourist. The tourist experience has been booked and paid for, and will be consumed regardless of its context.

Shades turn to dynamic shadings in chapter seven where Jenny Elliott presents both a medically traumatized state and a personal journey into retreat. This is all in the context of dancing mobile bodies representing the human condition. Elliott works with patients with severe brain trauma. Unlike the dark or pale tourist, these patients do not have the luxury of obliviousness to the dark. They have no escape from their personal traumas. Many are also silent, caught in an unresponsive body. This narrative is especially direct, poignant, and evocative. It is an embodied ethnography from a dancer choreographer who has access to her patients' states, uses dance to elicit patient responses, and does this all while also acknowledging her own existential condition and inner journey. Where Egan saw "hope" spring from his pilgrims, Elliott uses "creativity" in its raw and edgy practice to draw expression out from the members of her new dance company. This creativity is harnessed while on retreat through personal poetry, dance, and drawing before made public and released with resilience and vigor back in Nagle's broken Belfast in the form of a dance company performance. The two journeys running through Elliott's contribution converge on the stage. There, one of the patients, Micky, briefly escapes himself, standing before the audience before stumbling and losing himself. His stature, however, remains.

In chapter eight, Fiona Murphy journeys by train with an aboriginal woman, a member of the Stolen Generation returning to the institution where she and others suffered. Mary sighs as the train passes each bend ever closer to the place of her wounding, an anchor point which she has wrestled with and against all her life. The journey is a trope of a pathway to healing; the intention is that a reunion will result in reconciliation for the townsfolk where the aboriginal children were incarcerated as well as for the women themselves. This chapter presents a story crisscrossing the country, a "broken story" achingly public and private at the same time. Mary's life becomes a trauma trail. Mary's return enables a process of mourning but also draws attention to the politicization of trauma and its historical remembrance at personal, local, and national levels.

Chapter nine concludes this volume with Jenny Iles exploring the British memory banks found along the Western Front. The old battle lines are landscapes sedimented with history and meaning: bodies and biographies are literally embedded in this "Forever England." Specifically, Iles explores the British commemorations imposed upon the landscape of the Lochnagar Crater on the Somme, the bloodiest of battles. The crater, made by the detonation of a mine exploded under the German front lines, is an emotive topography of loss, a contemporary dark tourism destination and pilgrimage site that serves to bring the generations together. For Jenny, the unkempt rawness of the hole in the ground challenges her. So too the cemeteries nearby which bring the generations together as she comes to see the war as not the "old man's war" pieced together by grandfather's recollections, but a young volunteer's war of youthful sacrifice. Another writer struggles with representing the place and its history: "It's not big. It's huge"; "No words can capture this"; "This crater speaks louder than any words I could speak"; "I look at the hole, I think and then cry." Dark tourists and cultural critics are overcome by the starkness of the place, its size—devoid of the possibilities of language to make sense or describe such now unimaginable destruction and horror. It is an intense place, drawing in many repeat visitors to the crater. It absorbs relatives, tourists, and researchers alike. Even Iles finds her own personal biography becoming attached to the collective remembrance of the place. Her journey which spans the personal, the professional, and the emotional, is similar to those of other tourists touched by their engagement with a battlefield landscape. For her, the crater is a hole into the dark.

In writing on the dark side of travel and trauma, in traveling among the dead, through the dying, and alongside the suffering, the authors in this collection give us a tour of humanity's violence, miserableness, and awfulness. They look at those lucky enough just to be fleeting visitors to this extreme world. So too do we get insight into those caught, trapped, killed, or executed there. We explore the issues and difficulties of representing these places, people, and events. And finally, from this dark side—for want of a better expression—we also see the glimmers of great beauty and poignancy in the characterization of suffering (Moffat, Egan,

Cooke, Hepburn, Iles), and uplifting creativity in the cartoons, the wall murals, and the physical sketches of life (Walker, Nagle, Elliott, Murphy). We all hope that you are disturbed, touched, charmed, unsettled, and inspired by these contents.

Notes

This is a revised and updated version of an article that appeared as "Introduction: Writing on the Dark Side of Travel" in J. Skinner, ed., *Journeys: The International Journal of Travel and Travel Writing*, Special Edition, *Writing the Dark Side of Travel* 11, no. 1 (2010): 1–28.

1. Pattullo (2000) uses this expression as the title of her book about the Montserrat volcano crisis. It is also a line from an old slave song.
2. See also Wheeler (1986), and Stagl and Pinney (1996) for further discussion on the differences between ethnography and travel writing, and Skinner (2008b) for a rebuttal.
3. See also Coleman and Elsner (2003: 13–15) on pilgrimage as travel writing.

Bibliography

Abu-Lughod, L. 1993. *Writing Women's Worlds: Bedouin Stories*. Berkeley: University of California Press.

Adler, J. 1989. "Travel a Performed Act." *American Journal of Sociology* 94(6): 1366–91.

Adorno, T. 2003. *Can One Live After Auschwitz? A Philosophical Reader*. Stanford, CA: Stanford University Press.

Archetti, E. (ed.). 1994. *Exploring the Written: Anthropology and the Multiplicity of Writing*. Oslo: Scandinavian University Press.

Arendt, H. 1994. *Eichmann in Jerusalem: A Report on the Banality of Evil*. London: Penguin Classics.

Banks, A., and S. Banks. 1998. "The Struggle Over Facts and Fictions," in A. Banks and S. Banks (eds.), *Fiction & Social Research*. London: AltaMira Press, 11–32.

Bauman, Z. 1989. *Modernity and the Holocaust*. Cambridge: Polity Press.

Beech, J. 2009. "Genocide Tourism," in R. Sharpley and P. Stone (eds.), *The Darker Side of Travel: The Theory and Practice of Dark Tourism*. Bristol, UK: Channel View Publications, 207–23.

Bell, C., and J. Lyall. 2002. *The Accelerated Sublime: Landscape, Tourism, and Identity*. Westport, CT: Praeger.

Berman, J. 1999. "Australian Representations of the Holocaust: Jewish Holocaust Museums in Melbourne, Perth, and Sydney, 1984–1996." *Holocaust and Genocide Studies* 13(2): 200–21.

Bernard-Donals, M. 2001. "The Rhetoric of Disaster and the Imperative of Writing." *RSQ: Rhetoric Society Quarterly* 31(1): 73–94.

Bloch, M. 1998. *How We Think They Think: Anthropological Approaches to Cognition, Memory, Literacy*. Oxford: Westview Press.

Boon, J. 1999. *Verging On Extra-Vagance: Anthropology, History, Religion, Literature, Arts... Showbiz.* Princeton, NJ: Princeton University Press.

Bowman, M., and P. Pezzullo. 2009. "What's So 'Dark' about 'Dark Tourism'? Death, Tours, and Performance." *Tourist Studies* 9(3): 187–202.

Bruner, E. 2005. *Culture on Tour: Ethnographies of Travel.* Chicago: University of Chicago Press.

Casey, E. 2000. *Remembering: A Phenomenological Study.* Bloomington: Indiana University Press.

Clifford, J. 1997. *Routes: Travel and Translation in the Late Twentieth Century.* Cambridge, MA: Harvard University Press.

Cohen, E. 2011. "Educational Dark Tourism at an *In Populo* Site: The Holocaust Museum in Jerusalem." *Annals of Tourism Research* 38(1): 193–209.

Coleman, S., and J. Elsner (eds.). 2003. *Pilgrim Voices: Narrative and Authorship in Christian Pilgrimage.* Oxford: Berghahn Books.

Cresswell, T. 2006. *On the Move: Mobility in the Modern Western World.* London: Routledge.

Crick, M. 1989. "Representations of International Tourism in the Social Sciences: Sun, Sex, Sights, Savings, and Servility." *Annual Review of Anthropology* 18: 307–44.

Dann, G., and A. Seaton. 2001a. "Slavery, Contested Heritage and Thanatourism," in G. Dann and A. Seaton (eds.), *International Journal of Hospitality and Tourism Administration* Special Issue, "Slavery, Contested Heritage and Thanatourism." New York: Haworth Hospitality Press, pp. 1–30.

———. (eds.). 2001b. Special Issue, "Slavery, Contested Heritage and Thanatourism," *International Journal of Hospitality and Tourism Administration.* New York: Haworth Hospitality Press.

de Certeau, M. 1984. *The Practice of Everyday Life.* Berkeley: University of California Press.

Edensor, T. 2001. "Performing Tourism, Staging Tourism: (Re)producing Tourist Space and Practice." *Tourist Studies* 1: 59–81.

Farrell, K. 1998. *Post-Traumatic Culture: Injury and Interpretation in the Nineties.* Baltimore: Johns Hopkins University Press.

Feldman, A. 1991. *Formations of Violence: The Narrative of the Body and Political Terror in Northern Ireland.* Chicago: University of Chicago Press.

Feldman, J. 2005. "In Search of the Beautiful Land of Israel: Israeli Youth Voyages to Poland," in C. Noy and E. Cohen (eds.), *Israeli Backpackers and their Society.* New York: State University of New York Press, 217–50.

Fernandez, J. 1986. *Persuasions and Performances: The Play of Tropes in Culture.* Bloomington: Indiana University Press.

———. (ed.). 1991. *Beyond Metaphor: The Theory of Tropes in Anthropology.* Stanford, CA: Stanford University Press.

Fish, S. 1988. "*Interpreting the* Valorium," in D. Lodge (ed.), *Modern Criticism and Theory—A Reader.* London: Longman, 311–29.

Giddens, A. 1991. *Modernity and Self-Identity: Self and Society in the Late Modern Age.* Stanford, CA: Stanford University Press.

Gourevitch, P. 1993. "Behold Now Behemoth." *Harpers Magazine* (July): 55–62.

———. 1998. *We Wish to Inform You That Tomorrow We Will Be Killed with Our Families.* New York: Picador.

Huggan, G. 2009. *Extreme Pursuits: Travel/Writing in an Age of Globalization.* Ann Arbor: University of Michigan Press.

Jackson, M. 1998. *Minima Ethnographica: Intersubjectivity and the Anthropological Project.* Chicago: University of Chicago Press.

———. 2002. *The Politics of Storytelling: Violence, Transgression and Intersubjectivity.* Copenhagen: Museum Tusculanum Press.

———. 2008. *Existential Anthropology: Events, Exigencies and Effects.* Oxford: Berghahn Books.

Jacobson, D. 1994. *The Electronic Elephant: A South African Journey.* London: Penguin.

James, A., J. Hockey, and A. Dawson. 1997. "Introduction: The Road from Santa Fe," in A. James, J. Hockey, and A. Dawson (eds.), *After Writing Culture: Epistemology and Praxis in Contemporary Anthropology.* London: Routledge, 1–15.

Jameson, F. 1972. *The Prison-House of Language: A Critical Account of Structuralism and Russian Formalism.* Princeton, NJ: Princeton University Press.

Klopper, D. 2005. "Travel and Transgression: Dan Jacobson's *Southern African Journey.*" *Third World Quarterly* 26(3): 461–69.

Krakauer, J. 1997. *Into the Wild.* New York: Anchor Books.

Lennon, J., and M. Foley. [2000] 2004. *Dark Tourism: The Attraction of Death and Disaster.* Padstow, UK: Thomson Learning.

Lyng, S. 1990. "Edgework: A Social Psychological Analysis of Voluntary Risk Taking." *American Journal of Sociology* 95: 851–86.

Marcus, G., and M. Fischer. 1986. *Anthropology as Cultural Critique: An Experimental Moment in the Human Sciences.* Chicago: University of Chicago Press.

Mestrovic, S. 1996. *Post-Emotional Society.* London: Sage Publications.

Miles, W. 2002. "Auschwitz: Museum Interpretation and Darker Tourism." *Annals of Tourism Research* 29(4): 1175–78.

Miller, R. 1994. "Yad Vashem Foes Kitsch." *Australian Jewish News,* 22 July.

Mol, A. 2002. *The Body Multiple: Ontology in Medical Practice.* London: Duke University Press.

Murphy, D. 1998. *Visiting Rwanda.* Dublin: Lilliput Press.

Musgrove, B. 1999. "Travel and Unsettlement: Freud on Vacation," in S. Clark (ed.), *Travel Writing & Empire: Postcolonial Theory in Transit.* London: Zed Books, 31–44.

Muzaini, H., P. Teo, and B. Yeoh. 2007. "Intimations of Postmodernity in Dark Tourism: The Fate of History at Fort Siloso, Singapore." *Journal of Tourism and Cultural Change* 5: 28–45.

O'Rourke, P. J. 2002. *Holidays in Hell.* London: Picador.

Pattullo, P. 2000. *Fire from the Mountain: The Tragedy of Montserrat and the Betrayal of Its People.* London: Ian Randle.

Pelton, R., C. Aral, and W. Dulles. 1998. *The World's Most Dangerous Places.* Redondo Beach, CA: Fielding Worldwide.

Phipps, P. 1999. "Tourists, Terrorists, Death and Value," in R. Kaur and J. Hutnyk (eds.), *Travel Worlds: Journeys in Contemporary Cultural Politics.* London: Zed Books, 74–93.

Porter, D. 1991. *Haunted Journeys: Desire and Transgression in European Travel Writing.* Princeton, NJ: Princeton University Press.

Rapport, N. 1994. *The Prose and the Passion: Anthropology, Literature and the Writing of E.M. Forster.* Manchester, UK: Manchester University Press.

———. 2008a. "Afterword: Progress." *Journeys: The International Journal of Travel and Travel Writing* 9(2): 161–71.

———. 2008b. *Of Orderlies and Men: Hospital Porters Achieving Wellness at Work.* Charleston, NC: Carolina Academic Press.

———. 2008c. "Walking Auschwitz, Walking Without Arriving," *Journeys: The International Journal of Travel and Travel Writing* 9(2): 32–54.

Rojek, C. 1993. *Ways of Escape.* Basingstoke, UK: Macmillan.

———. C. 1999. "Fatal Attractions," in D. Boswell and J. Evans (eds.), *Representing the Nation: A Reader—Histories, Heritage and Museums.* London: Routledge, 185–207.

Rosenfeld, A. 1980. *A Double Dying: Reflections on Holocaust Literature.* Bloomington: Indiana University Press.

Seaton, T. 1996. "Guided by the Dark: From Thanatopsis to Thanatourism." *International Journal of Heritage Studies* 2(4): 234–44.

———. 2009. "Thanatourism and Its Discontents: An Appraisal of a Decade's Work with Some Future Issues and Directions," in M. Robinson and T. Jamal (eds.), *The SAGE Handbook of Tourism Studies.* London: Sage Publications, 521–42.

Sebald, W. G. 1998. *The Rings of Saturn.* London: Harvill Press.

Sharpley, R. 2005. "Travels to the Edge of Darkness: Towards a Typology of Dark Tourism," in C. Ryan, S. Page, and M. Aicken (eds.), *Taking Tourism to the Limit: Issues, Concepts and Managerial Perspective.* London: Elsevier, 215–26.

———. 2009 "Shedding Light on Dark Tourism: An Introduction," in R. Sharpley and P. Stone (eds.), *The Darker Side of Travel: The Theory and Practice of Dark Tourism.* Bristol, UK: Channel View Publications, 3–22.

Sharpley, R., and P. Stone. 2009a. "Life, Death and Dark Tourism: Future Research Directions and Concluding Comments," in R. Sharpley and P. Stone (eds.), *The Darker Side of Travel: The Theory and Practice of Dark Tourism.* Bristol, UK: Channel View Publications, 247–51.

——— (eds.) 2009b. *The Darker Side of Travel: The Theory and Practice of Dark Tourism.* Bristol, UK: Channel View Publications.

Skinner, J. 2000. "The Eruption of Chances Peak, Montserrat, and the Narrative Containment of Risk," in P. Caplan (ed.), *Risk Revisited.* London: Pluto Press, 156–83.

———. 2003. "Montserrat Place and Mons'rat Neaga: An Example of Impressionistic Autoethnography." *Online Qualitative Report* 8(3): 513–29.

———. 2004. *Before the Volcano: Reverberations of Identity on Montserrat.* Kingston, Jamaica: Arawak.

———. 2008a. "Ghosts in the Head and Ghost Towns in the Field: Ethnography and the Experience of Presence and Absence." *Journeys: International Journal of Travel and Travel Writing* 9(2): 10–31.

———. 2008b. "Glimpses into the Unmentionable: Montserrat, Tourism and Anthropological Readings of 'Subordinate Exotic' and 'Comic Exotic' Travel Writing." *Studies in Travel Writing* 12(3): 167–91.

Slade, P. 2003. "Gallipoli Thanatourism: The Meaning of ANZAC." *Annals of Tourism Research* 30: 779–94.

Spurr, D. 1994. *The Rhetoric of Empire: Colonial Discourse in Journalism, Travel Writing and Imperial Administration*. London: Duke University Press.

Stagl, J., and C. Pinney. 1996. "Introduction: From Travel Writing to Ethnography." *History and Anthropology* 9(2/3): 121–24.

Steiner, G. 1967. *Language and Silence: Essays in Language, Literature and the Inhuman*. New York: Athenaeum.

———. 1971. *In Bluebeard's Castle: Some Notes towards the Redefinition of Culture*. New Haven, CT: Yale University Press.

Stoller, P. 1989. *The Taste of Ethnographic Things: The Senses in Anthropology*. Philadelphia: University of Pennsylvania Press.

———. 1997. *Sensuous Scholarship*. Philadelphia: University of Pennsylvania Press.

Stolorow, R. 1999. "The Phenomenology of Trauma and the Absolutisms of Everyday Life: A Personal Journey." *Psychoanalytic Psychology* 16(3): 464–68.

Stone, P. 2006. "A Dark Tourism Spectrum: Towards a Typology of Death and Macabre Related Tourist Sites, Attractions and Exhibitions." *Tourism: An Interdisciplinary International Journal* 54(2): 145–60.

———. 2009. "'It's a Bloody Guide': Fun, Fear and a Lighter Side of Dark Tourism at The Dungeon Visitor Attractions, UK," in R. Sharpley and P. Stone (eds.), *The Darker Side of Travel: The Theory and Practice of Dark Tourism*. Bristol, UK: Channel View Publications, 167–85.

Stone, P., and R. Sharpley. 2008. "Consuming Dark Tourism: A Thanatological Perspective." *Annals of Tourism Research* 35(2): 574–95.

Strange, C., and M. Kempa. 2003. "Shades of Dark Tourism: Alcatraz and Robben Island." *Annals of Tourism Research* 30(2): 386–405.

Talil, K. 2010. *Worlds of Hurt: Reading the Literatures of Trauma*. Retrieved 16 March 2010 from http://www.kalital.com/Text/Worlds/Chap6.html.

Taussig, M. 1986. *Shamanism, Colonialism, and the Wild Man: A Study in Terror and Healing*. Chicago: Chicago University Press.

———. 2006. *Walter Benjamin's Grave*. Chicago: University of Chicago Press.

Taylor, J. 1998. *Paper Tangos*. London: Duke University Press.

Tyler, S. 1986. "Post-Modern Ethnography: From Document of the Occult to Occult Document," in G. Marcus and J. Clifford (eds.), *Writing Culture: The Poetics and Politics of Ethnography*. Berkeley: University of California Press, 122–40.

Urry, J. 2004. "Death in Venice," in M. Sheller and J. Urry (eds.), *Tourism Mobilities: Places to Play, Places in Play*. London: Routledge, 205–15.

Uzell, D. 1992. "The Hot Interpretation of War and Conflict," in D. Uzell (ed.), *Heritage Interpretation, Vol. 1: The Natural and Built Environment*. London: Bellhaven, 33–47.

Walter, T. 2009. "Dark Tourism: Mediating Between the Dead and the Living," in R. Sharpley and P. Stone (eds.), *The Darker Side of Travel: The Theory and Practice of Dark Tourism*. Bristol, UK: Channel View Publications, 39–55.

Wheeler, V. 1986. "Travellers' Tales: Observations on the Travel Book and Ethnography." *Anthropological Quarterly* 59(2): 52–63.

Wideman, D. 1998. "The Door of No Return? A Journey through the Legacy of the African Slave Forts: An Excerpt." *Callaloo* 21(1): 1–11.

Wiesel, E. 1960. *Night*. New York: Avon Books.

————. 1990. *From the Kingdom of Memory: Reminiscences.* New York: Schocken Books.

Wilmsen, E. 1999. *Journeys with Flies.* London: University of Chicago Press.

Young, A. 1995. *The Harmony of Illusions: Inventing Post-Traumatic Stress Disorder.* Princeton, NJ: University of Princeton Press.

CHAPTER 1

Between Trauma and Healing

Tourism and Neoliberal Peace Building in Divided Societies

JOHN NAGLE

There is an apocryphal story that during a visit by Catherine the Great to view her newly acquired lands in the Crimea, she was delighted to see beautiful villages nestled along the banks of the river Dnieper. Little did she know, the vision was a hollow façade built by her minister Potemkin to obscure the desolate tundra. Trite as the comparison seems, it is tempting to suggest that tourists visiting the modern-day Belfast city center are endowed with a variation of the "Potemkin Village" (see Nagle 2009b).

Certainly tourists see little signs of the violent legacy of the civil conflict in the city center today; it is here where the conflict seems to have been successfully ameliorated through inward investment, the arrival of "cathedrals of consumption," and inner-city regeneration. In a 2004 speech, US special envoy to Northern Ireland Mitchell Reiss (2004) welcomed the appearance of a "new peace" in Belfast, noting that "in a sure sign of the region's up-and-coming status, Starbucks coffee has already opened two shops and has plans for four more." As part of attempts to "normalize" Belfast, visitors are encouraged by the local tourist board to experience the cathedral, Laganside, and the Titanic Quarters—areas the authorities call "character zones" that they hope will facilitate "cultural reanimation" and the "local economy" (Belfast City Council 2004). Plans for the Titanic Quarter, an 185-acre site located on deindustrialized shipyards, feature over 180,000 square meters of leisure space, including a heritage center. Such portioning of selected parts of Belfast into cultural quarters is reminiscent of "urban cloning" seen in other cities across Europe, an almost identikit regeneration scheme that draws on a sanitized version of local identity for tourists.

Yet it is to peek behind the façade of the Potemkin Village of the city center that many tourists come to Belfast. Whether they venture alone, in packs, or they are carried along in small black taxis, tourists flock to see the working-class districts of Belfast, areas that bore the brunt of violent conflict. It is here that tourists can witness the signs of ethno-national division and conflict that make Belfast an archetypal example of "dark tourism" (Lennon and Foley 2000; Lisle 2006). These include paramilitary murals painted on the gable ends of houses or walls, flags tied to lampposts, memorial plaques bearing votives to the dead, and the euphemistically called "peace lines," Berlin Wall-style barriers segregating Irish nationalist and UK unionist districts.

Although Belfast City Council has promoted "a strong brand for Belfast, representing the city, will find it easier to attract … visitors," in order to "reposition the city as a neutral, modernising place that has left its parochial sectarianism behind" (Murtagh 2008: 3), a different reality exists behind the Potemkin Village. Despite the end of sustained violent conflict, Belfast remains a highly polarized city. When the peace agreement was signed in 1998, there were about twenty-five peace lines in Belfast. Recently some researchers have claimed to have counted over eighty peace lines stretching thirteen miles across the city. Rather than declining in number, ethnonational representations of space that festoon parts of Belfast have proliferated with over one hundred permanent murals, plaques, and memorials constituted in Belfast alone since 1998 (Nagle 2009c; Viggiani 2006). The fate of Belfast, thus, "lies somewhere between the uniformity of corporate globalization and the continual balkanizing of social and cultural life" (Shirlow 2006: 100).

Within this milieu an intense debate has emerged about how the city should be packaged and presented to tourists. There are those, on the one hand, who largely work within or represent the tourist industry, as well as some UK unionist politicians, who believe it is best to market Belfast as a normal European city suitable for short weekend cultural breaks and for stag- and hen-party excursions. In this branding exercise little reference is made to the fact that Belfast hosted, prior to the 1990s, the most violent post–World War II ethnic conflict in Europe. On the other hand, there are those who represent the groups in the segregated districts, especially Irish nationalists, who believe it is their duty to show the "real" Belfast to tourists, replete with murals, peace lines, and memorials. The point of this act of revelation is to export lessons to the world about how not only conflict emerged in this corner of northwest Europe, but the slow and problematic narrative concerning how a violent conflict that was once seemingly impervious to any solution has been replaced with an uneasy peace. Underwriting both perspectives is a consensus that tourism is vital to peace building in the region: the income generated by tourists can help contribute toward economic prosperity and even dissolve the material bases that putatively drive ethnic division and violence.

Despite the wide disjuncture concerning Belfast's branding, I argue that these competing narratives are unsatisfactory nostrums to help engender sustainable peace building in this divided region. They provide a spectrum containing a predilection toward social amnesia at one point and a surfeit of memory at the opposite end. By either trying to obliterate the memory and presence of conflict or by retaining the antagonistic markers of ethnonational division and conflict, competing approaches to tourism in Belfast provide an either/or representation of the city that lay in the interstices between trauma and unhealthy melancholia. This chapter examines why and how these contending representations of tourist Belfast have developed, the major problems with their approaches, and how tourism, as a generator of income to the region's economy, has come to be viewed as a major part of neoliberal solutions to ethnic conflict.

Trauma, Melancholia, and Tourism

It is common to read that societies that have undergone sustained violence possess collective psyches that are traumatized and that a process of catharsis, closure, and restoration should be instigated to engender societal healing. Such an analysis of ethnic conflict leads to it being categorized as a type of extreme medical condition. According to David Lake (1995: 3): "to use a pessimistic but apt metaphor, ethnic conflict may be less like a common cold and more like AIDS—difficult to catch, but devastating once infected." In this sense, ethnic conflict is a disease that requires some form of therapy and treatment.

War has thus increasingly become seen as something that is inherently traumatic, and some commentators are apt to speak of a war-torn society being collectively traumatized, showing signs of posttraumatic stress disorder (PTSD) and suffering from a state of unhealthy melancholia, which continues to ensure that unhealthy relations between the groups are maintained (e.g., Volkan 1997). The Freudian notion of unhealthy melancholia and healthy mourning is transposed from bereaved individuals to whole societies and groups. For Freud (1922), healthy mourning for an individual experiencing grief is outlined as a teleological process. Though the individual "goes through mourning," it is a fixed journey that reaches a definite conclusion. When completed, the individual can begin to move on. The mourning concludes when the libido has yielded its attachment to the lost object, leaving the individual free to form new attachments. "Healthy mourning" is framed as a passage, although often difficult, from point A (attachment to the lost object) to point B (attachment to the new object).

The dire consequence of failing to remember and mourn healthily through commemorative practice has been made exchangeable with collective processes. The Mitscherlichs (1975), two German psychoanalysts, applied Freud's distinction between "mourning" and "melancholia" to the collective inability of Germany to mourn through confronting the nation's Nazi past. The ability to recall whole segments of the national past faded away, leaving destructive blank spaces in individual autobiographies and creating patterns of intergenerational complicity and conflict that contributed to a culture of alienation from not only the past but to anything that entailed collective responsibility. Similarly, Volkan (1997: 35), examining ethnic conflict in places like Bosnia, Rwanda, and the Middle East, has written about the inability of the ethnonational group to accept, through processes of healthy mourning, the "loss of people, land, prestige" and the "feelings of fear, helplessness, and humiliation" that accrued from their loss.

The failure of a society to deal with traumatic memories has been framed as resulting in locking "societies into a pernicious cycle of violence, as it is assumed that the 'abused' will later become the 'abuser'" (Clancy and Hamber 2009: 12). By encouraging societies to deal with their trauma and psychological dysfunctionalism, it is hoped that this can pave the way for peace and prosperity by preparing populations for self-governance (Pupavac 2004: 151–52). Writing against the tendency to elide individual and societal process when speaking of trauma, Hamber and Wilson (2002: 7) explore the relationship between trauma and violence by showing how they denude "individual cognitive assumptions about the self and the world." At its most severe, trauma smashes the individual's capacity to view oneself positively and that the "world is a meaningful and comprehensible place" (2002: 7). The experience of extreme violence leaves the individual shorn of any ontological security, and their identity may even be eroded. Ethnic violence can be traumatic to the individual because it may contain elements of the uncanny: phenomena that are both strange and familiar, and the sense of unease that flows from this dual recognition (Freud 1922). Examples of the uncanny in ethnic violence include the abrupt degeneration of neighbor relations during interethnic violence; how the delineation between civilian and combatant becomes blurred during conflict; and how sites of "normality" are turned into places of horror (e.g., the massacre at Nyarubuye Church during the Rwandan genocide; Clancy and Hamber 2009: 16; see also Walker, this volume).

Nevertheless, when trauma is made indivisible with wider societal processes, there is a tendency to prescribe actions that either seek to normalize society by trying to restore its pretraumatized state or by working through the consequences of trauma to bring about healing, catharsis, and eventual closure. Heuristically speaking, the former etiology may promote amnesia to allow society to rebuild from new by forgetting historical grievances while the latter promotes the usage of memory, remembering, truth commissions, and commemoration.

The conceit that societies and places that have undergone conflict are shaped by trauma can lead to them becoming key tourist attractions. Many global tourist locations are actively branded as sites of trauma where people can go to experience the putative healing processes the society is undergoing. People visit these sites where they can make symbolic exchanges, votive deposits, and gift giving to and with the dead. Maya Lin's Vietnam Veterans Wall in Washington, DC, for example, allows the individual to see and even touch the names of the dead as well as to leave secret messages. Such symbolic exchange has almost become the defining feature of contemporary commemorative practices, many of which seem to spring up in spontaneous fashion overnight in what Santino (2001: 1) has termed "spontaneous shrines and the public memorialization of death." The tourist pilgrimage, in this context, becomes almost a literal embodiment of the journey from unhealthy melancholia to healthy mourning.

However, Doss observes that the "spontaneous and, often impermanent, and distinctly unofficial nature of many … grassroots memorials … seem less concerned with producing a critique of historical moments and tragic events than in catharsis and redemption" (2002: 60). Wholly fixating on the therapeutic, cathartic, and redemptive aspects of these sites can act to forget the messy and uncomfortable political causes that created the conflict in the first place. Assessing the memorials that sprung up in the aftermath of the Oklahoma City bombing in 1995, Doss notes that a

> superficial focus on psychic closure—on healing and closure—skirts the causal, historical dimensions of these visibly public deaths. It further fails to provide a shared set of rituals and commemorative forms that might allow citizens to consider critically how to change the conditions that contribute to the culture of violence in America. (2002: 71)

Specifically, looking at the memorial solutions offered to commemorate the Oklahoma bombing, Doss writes that the "Symbolic Memorial" contains "no references to why the bombing occurred and who was responsible, or to the nation's history of catastrophic violence" (2002: 74).

Rather than "opening a window" on traumatic events, thus expediting stages of mourning—from anger to closure, from mourning to acceptance—the memorials are "anaesthetic because the historical and political context of why these deaths occurred has been effaced" (2002: 78). The idea, then, that societies possess collective psyches is profoundly misleading. Indeed, "Nations do not have collective psyches which can be healed, nor do whole nations suffer post-traumatic stress disorder and to assert otherwise is to psychologize an abstract entity which exists primarily in the minds of nation-building politicians" (Hamber and Wilson 2002: 36).

Conflict, Social Amnesia, and Tourism

It is widely accepted now that the casus belli in Northern Ireland is the existence of competing ethnonational claims over the question of sovereignty, with unionists wishing for Northern Ireland to remain British while Irish nationalists desire the north to be unified with the Irish Republic (McGarry and O'Leary 1995). Similar to many divided societies, there is much shared between the two groups: they "look alike, wear the same sort of clothes, speak English in the same accents ... eat equally bad food, and often have trouble telling which side a person is from when meeting them for the first time" (Dryzek and Dunleavy 2009: 188). Despite this, Northern Ireland contains many of the key markers of difference characteristic of a divided society: most political parties mobilize along ethnonational lines; there are separate domains for socializing schooling, separate sporting affiliations; some examples of separate forms of employment and levels of residential segregation and endogamy are high (McGarry and O'Leary 1995).

Even though divisions are historically longstanding, they intensified during the phase of violent conflict, which broadly began in 1969, often euphemistically called the Troubles. Between 1969 and 1998, 3,500 people lost their lives as a result of the conflict and 40,000 were seriously injured (Morrissey and Smyth 2002: 3). Belfast, the capital of the region, hosted much of the violence. Around 1,700 people were killed in the city, 90 percent of whom died within 1,000 meters of a peace wall (Shirlow and Murtagh 2006). It is estimated that between August 1969 and February 1973 over 60,000 people in Belfast, 10 percent of the city's population, were forced to move due to violence (Nagle 2009a). Belfast city center—the nexus of the political, financial, and commercial quarters of the city—also hosted its fair share of violence. On one infamous occasion in 1972, the Irish Republican Army (IRA) detonated twenty-six bombs across the city, eleven in the city center, killing 9 and injuring 130 people.

Normalization and Forgetting

Due to the violence in the 1970s, tourist numbers for Northern Ireland were extremely low, and little effort was made to accommodate visitors. For instance, Northern Ireland attracted less than 10 percent of tourists that Cornwall expected per annum. Circumstances, however, began to change in the late 1980s. A strategic plan was formulated to regenerate Belfast city center, a corollary of which would be a Belfast attractive for visitors. The logic underlying this plan was articulated by Richard Needham, a British politician in Northern Ireland, an ostensibly consular figure appointed to help govern Northern Ireland in lieu of a regional legislature.

Reviewing the consequences of the IRA's bombing campaign against Belfast city center as part of its economic war against Britain, Needham (1998: 166, emphasis added) claimed that "by the early 1980s the city was in *trauma*." Under the aegis of Needham, a plan was engineered to commercially regenerate the city center. Needham (1998: 1) summed up this approach as the "the third arm of the British government's strategy to resolve the Northern Ireland conflict … the economic and social war against violence." The plan "was to isolate the terrorists by proving it was they … in Belfast who were the villains, delaying progress and strangling investment" (1998: 167). Under this rubric, the state encouraged the construction of private housing in the city center in a professed attempt to lure "yuppies" (1998: 167); they commercially redeveloped Belfast's riverfront, the Laganside, in a model borrowed from London's Docklands and Boston's Waterfront. It was through the creation of a commercially vibrant city center that the state believed it was facilitating "safe areas where both communities could mix and match" (1998: 168). By imagining the city center as a shared space of consumption, the state hoped to "build a shared sense of civic pride, security and enjoyment among people whose attitudes, shaped by separated experience, may well be mutually antagonistic … radiating a sense of citizenship outward to a divided population" (Hadaway 2001: 12).

As part of this counterinsurgency approach to regeneration, Needham tried to encourage greater levels of tourism in Belfast and Northern Ireland in general. During the "Belfast 1991" celebration, in which Needham could "show the world there was another side of Belfast," a Tall Ships festival was brought to the city that attracted 500,000 visitors. For the rest of Northern Ireland, a concerted effort was made to promote the region's outstanding natural and cultural beauty to lure in tourists. The Northern Ireland tourist board began to promote package tours, especially for US tourists, to stay in Northern Ireland. Within a few years of the early 1990s, tourist numbers began to grow from 930,000 to 1,436,000. Despite this, Needham (1998: 284) complained that "violence was denying tens of thousands of people employment in an industry that was as capable of offering as varied a holiday as anywhere in the world." It has been calculated, for example, that £1.5 billion of potential tourism revenue into Northern Ireland was lost between 1976 and 2005 (Deloitte and Touche 2007).

Notably, tourists were given little encouragement to visit the region's conflict hotspots, the peace walls, murals, and commemorative forms found in working-class nationalist districts. Instead, tourists were ushered into seemingly apolitical sites like the Giant's Causeway, a stretch of interlocking hexagonal basalt columns fused by volcanic activity that has been designated a UNESCO World Heritage Site; or the Anglo-Irish "big house," mansions once owned by the "Protestant ascendancy" and now cared for by the British National Trust.

As such, the official tourist strategy, as envisaged by Needham, could be described as one of deliberate social amnesia. It sought to purposely forget the traces and presence of violent conflict that continued to shape and scar the region. If Belfast, as Needham claimed, was in a state of "trauma," the palliative was to present an image of normality in the hope that its citizens would eventually subscribe to its image and act accordingly. Peace building would further be augmented by tourism that could advance prosperity and well-being, especially by creating employment in the tourist sector. By supporting indigenous free-market entrepreneurs to produce wealth through tourism, this would reduce the polarizing strategies of ethnonational leaders seeking to foment interethnic discord. By encouraging individualism and wealth creation facilitated by tourism, locals would no longer be encumbered by their affiliations to the respective ethnic "tribes."

Violence and Commemoration

Contrary to the image of normality conjured up by the state, an alternative representation was generated that illuminated the tangible material heritage of violence and ethnonational belonging that so characterizes Belfast. Tourists were increasingly encouraged to venture into the inner sanctums of Belfast's working-class "ghettoes" to witness the signs of war enmeshed in quotidian sites. As "dark tourism" increasingly became a profitable component of global tourism, working-class districts of Belfast attracted a new generation of mostly young tourists seeking to engorge themselves in the experience of the conflict. As early as 1992, the *Rough Guide* was writing that the murals were a significant attraction for tourists coming to Belfast. By 2007, the *Rough Guide* had labeled the murals of Belfast among the top twenty-five "must see" attractions in the whole of the UK (Lisle 2006), denoting that divided Belfast was as much a part of the mainstream tourist trail as sites protected by the National Trust.

As part of this nascent growth in "dark tourism," a small, local-based enterprise culture emerged in some working-class parts of Belfast as tourists were offered sightseeing visits to experience the murals and peace walls, often in small black taxis manned by former paramilitary prisoners. In Irish nationalist areas of Belfast, especially, where most of the tourists converged, the promotion of tourism served a purpose beyond bolstering the local economy: Irish nationalists were seeking to internationalize their political movement by forging links with global political movements. Some murals in nationalist districts of Belfast and Derry, for example, feature images of prominent nationalists next to international civil rights activists and indigenous campaigners like John Hume, Martin Luther King, Jr., and Che Guevara. Bringing in international visitors provided an opportunity for Irish nationalists to tell their story of the reasons that had promulgated violent conflict and how the peace process had emerged. Importantly, in a wider context, Northern Ireland was becoming framed by the media and politicians such as Tony Blair and Bill Clinton as a model for how intractable ethnonationalist disputes can be solved, and as such should be "studied" across the globe by those interested in securing peace in the world's hot spots. Tourism to Belfast was made almost synonymous with processes of collective memorialization and dealing with the past that seek to bring about healing and closure to a generation of violent conflict. Tourists are now even being asked to journey and work through the Troubles. In Derry, Northern Ireland's second largest city, where fourteen civil rights protestors were shot dead by the British army in 1972, a nationalist politician has called for the tourist board to create a Journey to Peace tourist trail that starts, predictably, at the beginning of the violent conflict and ends with the stabilization of peace in the region.

However, this portrayal of dark tourism as a process that links remembrance, pedagogy, conflict resolution, and closure is not so clear. In fact, some argue that the forms of memorialization, which continue to mark the landscape of working-class Belfast rather than bringing about societal healing through remembering, display unhealed scars borne by trauma, thus acting to keep alive ethnic antagonisms. For instance, Leersen argues that much of the commemorative practices and signs of war that tourists see in Belfast are contained within a "traumatic paradigm" (2001) that resembles Freud's concept of *unheimlich* (the uncanny). Murals and plaques, graffiti marking peace lines, commemorative parades, and paramilitary songs, notes Leersen, are "nightmarish recurrences characterized by their combination of repetitive familiarity and their disconcerting repulsion" (2001: 222). Here, Leersen draws our attention to representations that illuminate the violence that has been meted out to the group by their adversaries and the potential of the group to use violence in the name of self-defense. For instance, murals that depict hooded paramilitary gunmen underlined with a caption "Ready for War" illuminate a primordialist sense of identity in which never-ending conflict accrues from the clash of two opposing cultures: Catholics and Protestants. Other murals may depict historical events, such as Catholics indiscriminately killing Protestants in the sixteenth century, in order to show how history continues to dance to the same tune and cannot be altered under any circumstances. This process in which ethnonational groups use social memory for present political exigencies is not the sole preserve of Northern Ireland. Volkan has written of how competing ethnonational groups—ranging from the Middle East, the Balkans, and Rwanda (see Moffat, this volume)—commit what he calls a "time collapse": "the interpretations, fantasies and feelings about a past shared trauma co-mingle with those pertaining to a current situation. Under the influence of a time collapse, people may intellectually separate the past from the present one, but emotionally the two events are merged" (1997: 34–35). Equally harmful for the task of peace building are how public signs of paramilitary belonging make the establishment of democratic authority difficult. Goldstock suggested this in his report on paramilitarism and organized crime in Northern Ireland by noting that "[a]s long as groups have the de facto privilege to colour communal rights of way, paint or maintain aggressive or sectarian murals on walls, fly provocative flags over thoroughfares, [and] place symbols at the entrance to housing estates ... legitimate governmental power will be seen as secondary" (2004: 7).

The signs of war that tourists clamor to see when they visit working-class districts of Belfast are therefore not merely markers through which we come to understand and learn about conflict, assisting with societal healing after a generation of trauma. They are important signifiers through which atavistic expressions of intercommunal antipathy and mutually reinforcing victimhood conspire to keep groups on a permanent Cold War footing despite the encroachments of the peace process.

Contest, Consensus, and Neoliberalism

So far in this review of tourism in Northern Ireland two different and opposing representations are proffered for tourists. One image supplied, which has deeper roots in British state counterinsurgency strategies, purposely forgets the legacy of the violent conflict in Northern Ireland. It desires to infuse a sense of normality in an abnormal society. Such a benign image obscures and forgets that Belfast was riven by extreme violence and that it remains a deeply divided city. Tourism here ushers the visitor into Belfast city center or Heritage Ireland. The other image to attract tourists is one embodied in the markers of ethnonational belonging, "warts and all," thereby providing an "edutainment" experience of an authentic ethnic conflict. One model seeks to alleviate trauma by trying to negate its disruptive effects by instilling regularity; the other model seeks to work through trauma through processes of commemoration and remembrance.

The discrepancy regarding where tourists traveling to Northern Ireland should spend their time and money is also a major source of political debate between unionists and nationalists. Unionist politicians generally demand that Northern Ireland is represented in a way that ignores the horrors of the conflict by creating an alternative that emphasizes Belfast's industrial heritage—such as the shipyards where the Titanic was built—and the region's great cultural traditions and natural beauty. Many nationalist politicians, especially those representing working-class districts, call for an alternative that allows tourists to face the reality of the conflict. In debates, nationalist politicians claim there is a niche for "political tourism" because "more visitors would rather see attractions that relate to the Troubles than those that relate to the Titanic Quarter" (Maskey 2008). Alternatively, unionist politicians decry this "terror tourism" replete with imagery of "bombs blowing people to bits and destroying our towns and cities and of the numerous murders and shootings. ... Northern Ireland needs a positive image" (McCree 2008). Similarly, a fierce debate has surrounded the development of the Maze Prison (also known as the H-Blocks or Long Kesh) that had 25,000 paramilitary prisoners pass through its gates, including the republican hunger strikers like Bobby Sands who died there in 1981. As part of plans to regenerate the site, Irish nationalists have insisted that the site be turned into an International Centre for Conflict Transformation, "which may help others to learn some of the lessons of our Peace Process" (Sinn Féin 2006). For Sinn Féin (2006), the leading nationalist political party in Northern Ireland, the center would "provide us with a huge opportunity to bring about a major physical expression of the ongoing transformation from conflict to peace." Conversely, for unionists, these nationalist plans for an International Centre for Conflict Transformation represent little more than an attempt to create a "shrine to terror." Their proposal is for the British state to "Raze the Maze" (UUP 2008).

Despite the degree of conflict regarding how Northern Ireland should be represented to tourists, it is interesting to note there is a widespread consensus among political elites that tourist-generated revenue has a tremendous role to play in creating prosperity and sustaining reconciliation. Indeed, an article in *Spiegel Online* (Capell 2008) noted: "both sides [unionists and nationalists] seem to be willing to put aside their differences, at least in the business sphere." A major factor behind this is the emergence of the 1998 peace agreement and the political power-sharing government that underpins it. This form of power sharing involves Northern Ireland being granted a devolved regional assembly with the power of a legislature, although it is still subservient to the UK government in policies concerning defense, immigration, international relations, taxation, borrowing, and Europe. Although the power-sharing government has been fraught by a number of collapses, it is based on the idea that conflict resolution in divided societies is best achieved through the accommodation of the political elites representing the salient ethnic segments of society and institutionally anchored by inclusive coalitions, mutual vetoes, and proportionality in public appointments (Andeweg 2000: 512). In other words, power sharing in Northern Ireland is thus designed to guarantee that nationalists and unionists are accommodated in the legislature in proportion to their electoral support and that both groups possess the power of veto to ensure that no legislation can be passed that is perceived to be contrary to their community interests.

After a period of hiatus—from 2002 to 2007—the power-sharing government resumed following an election that witnessed the triumph of the so-called political extremes of unionism and nationalism: the Democratic Unionist Party and Sinn Féin. As the main forces in the power-sharing government, one of the first tasks they performed was outlining a program for government that was titled "Building a Better Future." The "business-friendly" emphasis of "Better Future" specified a plan of action for Northern Ireland: "Growing the economy is our top priority. This is vital if we are to provide the wealth and resources required to build the peaceful, prosperous, fair and healthy society we all want to see" (OFMDFM 2007: 2).

As part of its aim to create a wealthy and peaceful society, the Northern Ireland government has stated its desire to secure "inward investment commitments promising over 6,500 new jobs by 2011 ... 70% of new FDI [Foreign Direct Investment] projects secured to locate within 10 miles of an area of economic disadvantage" (OFMDFM 2007). The document also promises to increase "the number of tourists visiting each year from 1.98m to 2.5m by 2011 and increasing tourism revenue from £370m to £520m each year by the same date."

For some commentators "the economy is the one area where we can build true consensus" (Capell 2008), thus providing the raw material to ameliorate ethnic divisions and bring about sustainable reconciliation. The auspices of "Better Future" made it clear that economic growth precipitates the improvement of a divided society rather than the elimination of sectarianism and segregation as a prelude to prosperity and peace. Generating tourist footfall has thus become a central plank of "Better Future." Moreover, the emphasis on tourism can be seen as a fundamental part of an attempt to wed Northern Ireland's flagging economy, reliant on British state subvention and dominated by the public sector, to wider global neoliberal forces. The main thrust of this plan is to generate FDI into the region. The idea is to model Northern Ireland's economy on its neighbor, the Republic of Ireland and its Celtic Tiger. It has been estimated that in 2007 global foreign investment totaled $947 billion, of which Northern Ireland received almost $1 billion compared to the $27 billion received by the Republic of Ireland (Nagle 2009b).

The drive to increase FDI in Northern Ireland, as we have seen, is governed by the rationale that the production of wealth is a key counter to ethnic conflict. A recent report on the lessons of conflict resolution in Northern Ireland articulates this precise view:

> The importance of economics in conflict resolution is that it sets aside the question of motive, of grievance, of historical rights and wrongs, and focuses instead on the question of economic opportunity: what conditions—economic conditions in particular—have made the conflict possible? For if these conditions can be removed, progress to end the conflict might be made, just as surely as if the motives had been removed. (Portland Trust 2007: 5)

The idea that free-market neoliberal solutions, including tourist revenue, provide a model of lasting conflict resolution for deeply divided societies is currently a popular nostrum. Tourism has a central role to play in neoliberal-led attempts to bring about postwar or postdisaster reconstruction. For instance, because of the civil war in Sri Lanka, large parts of the region were "left uncolonized by go-go globalization" (Klein 2007: 392). The emerging peace process and the impact of the 2004 tsunami offered a chance to open up Sri Lanka's jungles, which once provided cover for Tamil insurgents, to ecotourists. To fully achieve this required the government to rescind barriers to private land ownership and create more flexible labor laws to help owners staff their resorts, and the modernization of infrastructure to host tourists. The government, unable to pay for such modernization, turned to the loans offered by the World Bank and the International Monetary Fund in exchange for opening up the country to public-private partnerships (Klein 2007: 393). Although many Sri Lankans resisted attempts to privatize the region, the apocalyptic tsunami, which had destroyed many coastal areas, provided the government an opportunity to push through emergency probusiness legislation allowing privatization, putatively to help with reconstruction efforts. Such plans, which included dispossessing thousands of people from the land and their villages to make way for new roads and re-sorts, did little to help stabilize the shock-induced temporary peace in the region. Although the government had supported the privatization legislation because it was seen as the best means to produce wealth and peace, barely anything was done to deal with the root causes of ethnic conflict, or even to rebuild the dispossessed villagers' schools and homes. In fact, in the rush to create a propitious environment for tourism to flourish, the government missed a rare opportunity to build on the trust and reconciliation that emerged out of the tsunami disaster. "The enor-mous outpouring of generosity after the tsunami had held out the rare possibility of a genuine peace dividend—the resources to imagine a more equitable country, to repair shattered communities in ways that would rebuild trust as well as buildings and roads" (Klein 2007: 404). Although it is too simplistic to state that the resumption of violence in December 2005 was due to the Sri Lankan government's neoliberal strategy, the failure to build on some of the goodwill that emerged after the tsunami struck was significant.

In trying to account for the success of what she calls "disaster capi-talism"—which uses desperation and fear to constitute privatization strategies and land grabs before the locals are able to effectively resist—Klein appropriates the discourse of trauma. Klein (2007: 8) states that when disaster strikes a particular region, venture capitalists are ready to pounce "using moments of collective trauma to engage in radical so-cial and economic engineering." In Klein's narrative, locals are simply too bewildered—"traumatized"—to resist. Klein likens this strategy to a "shock doctrine," which is analogous to electroshock therapy and sen-sory deprivation where patients are rendered blank templates on which any identity can be constituted. For the so-called neoliberal practitioners of the shock doctrine, the collective trauma wrought through disaster supposedly provides a vacancy that can be filled by free-market reforms to help build a new type of society. Although the harbingers of neoliberalism are handsomely rewarded for their venture capitalism, the local population, like the victims of electroshock therapy, is left irreparably damaged.

Yet the idea that war engenders collective trauma can be critiqued on a number of levels. As Clancy and Hamber (2009) note concerning Northern Ireland, there is no reliable evidence that the conflict had a negative impact on mental health. War cannot be simply seen as something that is inherently trauma inducing and peace as a positive space for societies to work through their trauma. War can have positive social aspects, including camaraderie and community bonding. Then there is the problem of using one culture's diagnostic categories to assume that phenomena have the same meaning across cultures. For instance, in Angolan society individuals have a range of terms for mental illness and distress, but none of these correspond to Western conceptualizations of PTSD, and such external categorizations can silence local people's understandings of distress (Wessells 2006).

Conclusion

The Potemkin Village analogy referred to at the beginning of this chapter to describe tourist Belfast appears ever more apposite. The commercial regeneration of the city center continues in a marketing exercise led by politicians who speak of Northern Ireland as "open for business and ready to meet the challenges ahead," but there appears little sign that Belfast's divisions are ameliorating. Depressingly, in 2006 the Northern Ireland Office constructed a twenty-five-foot-high peace wall in the grounds of an integrated primary school (a purposely nondenominational school for Catholics and Protestants) in north Belfast.

It is thus tempting to see Belfast as a city traumatized, and, as we have seen, the language of trauma has been used to justify divergent tourist strategies in the city. Yet we should be highly wary of viewing tourism as something that can help communities and divided cities deal with the legacy of political violence. We should be attuned to how the discourse of collective trauma is interpreted in different ways to suit competing ethnonational projects. These opposing definitions, in turn, support different etiologies to help deal with putative trauma. For the British state, as well as many unionists, the trauma engendered by IRA bombs created a void societal psyche. The citizens of Northern Ireland had been placed in an abnormal situation caused by ethnic conflict, and the job of the state was to try to restore normality. This allowed the British state to usher in privatization and FDI strategies, of which tourism was one of the central supporting planks. In trying to foster a picture of normalcy in the face of intense ethnic strife, tourism to Northern Ireland was packaged to reflect this benignity, creating a social amnesia to the scars of war. For many nationalists, they began to promote tourism for their war-torn areas, another method to deal with the trauma of violence. The murals, memorials, and peace lines that dominate working-class areas of Belfast were packaged as traumatized images where tourists, through their literal journey, could help work through trauma and, as such, help the world contribute to peace in the region as well as export lessons of the conflict abroad. Both tourist strategies provide nostrums that do little to contribute toward sustainable peace. One strategy—that of the British state—elides the "elephant in the corner," thus missing the central fact that the legacy of the war needs to be addressed to help facilitate societal reconciliation. The other strategy—the one largely led by Irish nationalists—suffers from an excess of memory, turning remembrance and division into a particularistic ethnonationalist project that maintains antagonistic expressions and paramilitary control over working-class districts.

The future may not be so terminally bleak regarding how Belfast should be represented for tourists. One particular project that has been quite successful in recent years is Belfast City Council's "Re-Imagining Communities" project. In this project "sectarian murals, emblems, flags and graffiti will be replaced by positive images which reflect the community's culture, as well as highlight and promote the social regeneration taking place in communities today" (Belfast City Council 2008). This project has successfully worked with local leaders and groups in working-class districts to have the murals painted over with new positive images. These new images depict more benign representations of the local "community" less rooted in antagonistic politics characterized by a perpetual binary relationship with the "other." The new images seek to portray the local district's proud industrial roots, its cultural heritage and famous characters. Rather than simply forgetting the legacy of conflict, the new images provide a more nuanced view of history, one which does not presuppose interminable ethnic conflict. The salient question, however, is whether these new images of Belfast will provide an attraction for tourists seeking the darker side of the city.

Notes

This is a revised and updated version of an article that appeared as "Between Trauma and Healing: Tourism and Neoliberal Peace–Building in Divided Societies" in J. Skinner, ed. (2010) *Journeys: The International Journal of Travel and Travel Writing*, Special Edition, *Writing the Dark Side of Travel* 11(1): 29–49.

Bibliography

Andeweg, R. 2000. "Consociational Democracy." *Annual Review of Political Science* 3: 509–36.

Belfast City Council. 2004. "Sharing Belfast's Public Space." *The Development Brief: Newsletter* 22: 1–4.

———. 2008. "Re-Imaging Communities Project." Retrieved 25 October 2009 from http://www.belfastcity.gov.uk/re-image/.

Capell, K. 2008. "The New Celtic Tiger: Belfast is Open for Business." *Spiegelonline*. Retrieved 25 November 25 from http://www.spiegel.de/international/business/0,1518,563841,00.html.

Clancy, M-A., and B. Hamber. 2009. "Trauma, Development, and Peacebuilding: Towards an Integrated Psychosocial Approach," *Incore*. Retrieved 25 November 2010 from http://www.incore.ulst.ac.uk/pdfs/IDRCconferencesummary.pdf.

Deloitte and Touche. 2007. *Research into the Financial Cost of the Northern Ireland Divide*. Belfast: Deloitte and Touche.

Doss, E. 2002. "Death, Art and Memory in the Public Sphere: The Visual and Material Culture of Grief in Contemporary America." *Mortality* 7(1): 63–82.

Dryzek, J., and P. Dunleavy. 2009. *Theories of the Democratic State*. Basingstoke, UK: Palgrave Macmillan.

Freud, S. 1922. "Mourning and Melancholia." *Journal of Nervous and Mental Disease* 56(5): 543–45.

Goldstock, R. 2004. *Organized Crime in Northern Ireland: A Report for the Secretary of State and Government Response*. Belfast: OFMDFM.

Hadaway, P. 2001. "Cohesion in Contested Spaces." *Architects Journal* (November): 38–40.

Hamber, B., and R. Wilson. 2002. "Symbolic Closure Through Memory, Reparation and Revenge in Post-Conflict Societies." *Journal of Human Rights* 1(1): 35–53.

Klein, N. 2007. *The Shock Doctrine*. London: Penguin.

Lake, D. 1995. "Ethnic Conflict and International Intervention." Institute on Global Conflict and Cooperation Policy Brief no. 3. La Jolla: University of California.

Leersen, J. 2001. "Monument and Trauma: Varieties of Remembrance," in I. McBride (ed.), *History and Memory in Modern Ireland*. Cambridge: Cambridge University Press, 204–22.

Lennon, J., and M. Foley. 2000. *Dark Tourism: The Attraction of Death and Disaster*. London: Continuum.

Lisle, D. 2006. "Local Symbols, Global Networks: Re-Reading the Murals in Belfast." *Alternatives: Global, Local, Political* 31(1): 27–52.

Maskey, P. 2008. "Private Members Business: Tourism." *Northern Ireland Assembly*, 19 February.

McCree, L. 2008. "Private Members Business: Tourism." *Northern Ireland Assembly*, 19 February.

McGarry, J., and B. O'Leary. 1995. *Explaining Northern Ireland: Broken Images*. London: Wiley-Blackwell.

Mitscherlich, A., and M. Mitscherlich. 1975. *The Inability to Mourn: Principles of Collective Behaviour*. New York: Grove Press.

Morrissey, M., and M. Smyth. 2002 *Northern Ireland and the Good Friday Agreement: Victims, Grievance and Blame*. London: Pluto.

Murtagh, B. 2008. "New Spaces and Old in "Post-conflict" Belfast." *Divided Cities/ Contested States*, Belfast: Queen's University of Belfast.

Nagle, J. 2009a. "Belfast City Centre: From Ethnocracy to Liberal Multiculturalism?" *Political Geography* 28(2): 132–41.

———. 2009b. "Potemkin Village: Neoliberalism and Peacebuilding in Northern Ireland." *Ethnopolitics* 8(2): 173–90.

———. 2009c. "Sites of Social Centrality and Segregation: Lefebvre in Belfast, a 'Divided City'." *Antipode* 41(2): 326–47.

Needham, R. 1998. *Battling for Peace*. Belfast: Blackstaff Press.

OFMDFM. 2007. *Building a Better Future: Draft Programme for Government 2008–2011*. Belfast: OFMDFM.

Portland Trust. 2007. *Economics in Peacemaking: Lessons from Northern Ireland*. London: Portland Trust.

Pupavac, V. 2004. "War on the Couch: The Emotionology of the New International Security Paradigm." *European Journal of Social Theory* 7(2): 149–70.

Reiss, M. 2004. "Northern Ireland: American Principles and the Peace Process." Speech delivered to the National Committee on American Foreign Policy, 30 September. Retrieved 2 November 2005 from http://www.state.gov/s/p/rem/36749.htm.

Santino, J. 2001. *Signs of War and Peace: Social Conflict and the Use of Public Symbols in Northern Ireland*. Basingstoke, UK: Palgrave Macmillan.

Shirlow, P. 2006. "Belfast: The 'Post-Conflict' City." *Space and Polity* 10(2): 99–107.

Shirlow, P., and B. Murtagh. 2006. *Belfast: Segregation, Violence and the City*. London: Pluto Press.

Sinn Féin. 2006. "Sinn Féin to Respond to Launch of Long Kesh Proposals." Retrieved 8 December 2009 from http://www.sinnfein.ie/contents/6759.

UUP. 2008. "Raze the Maze—Armstrong." Retrieved 8 December 2009 from http://www.uup.org/news/general/general-news-archive/raze-the-maze-armstrong.php.

Viggiani, E. 2006. "Public Forms of Memorialisation to the Victims of the Northern Irish 'Troubles' in the City of Belfast." Retrieved 25 October 2009 from http://cain.ulst.ac.uk/viggiani/introduction.htm.

Volkan, V. 1997. *Blood Lines: From Ethnic Pride to Ethnic Terrorism*. New York: Farrar, Straus and Giroux.

Wessells, M. 2006. *Child Soldiers: From Violence to Protection*. Cambridge, MA: Harvard University Press.

CHAPTER 2

Sebald's Ghosts

Traveling among the Dead in The Rings of Saturn

SIMON COOKE

In a recent tribute to W. G. Sebald, the artist Jeremy Millar traveled to the exact spot by the side of the A146 in Framingham Pigot where the celebrated German émigré author died in a car crash on 14 December 2001, not far from his adopted home of some twenty years near Norwich, England. After setting off a firework at the side of this minor road, Millar then took a series of photographs of the smoky apparitions that were left behind, "in memory—and celebration" of Sebald's life and work (Millar 2007: 592). Commenting on the piece, the writer Robert MacFarlane—himself currently engaged in producing an "unconventional biography" of Sebald by following in his footsteps to re-create the routes described in his books—has noted with some astonishment that, in one of these photographs, he could just make out the "spectral image of Sebald's own distinctive, moustached face" (2007: 82).

The distinctly thanatouristic dimensions involved in seeking out Sebald's "ghosts" in such commemorative gestures and re-creations are clear enough. Millar's tribute is a strikingly literal transformation of Sebald's place of death into an example of what Chris Rojek (1993: 136) calls "Black Spots," akin to the annual vigils at the site of James Dean's fatal car accident. But whatever view we take of the ethical questions raised by such acts of homage, there is little doubt that they are very much informed by the practices and fabric of Sebald's own books, or at least an interpretation of them. Indeed, Sebald might well be regarded as the literary dark traveler par excellence. Born in the German village of Wertach in the Allgau in the Bavarian Alps in 1944, he figured his own biography as lying under the shadow of World War II. All of his work is written with a view of history as "but a long account of calamities" ([1998] 2002: 295). And, in the photographic and pictorial elements of the books, as well as in the text, the narrator returns with an insistent steadfastness to scenes of atrocity, death, and destruction including—not exclusively, but perhaps most controversially—the Holocaust. Numerous reviewers and commentators have responded to the haunted, haunting quality of Sebald's work by suggesting he writes "like a ghost" (e.g., Iyer 2000; McCrum 1999).[1]

All of Sebald's books would be worthy of study in the context of questions of writings on the dark side of travel, then, but *The Rings of Saturn* has its own special resonance with the theme. As the most recognizable travelogue among Sebald's works, *The Rings of Saturn*—first published in German as *Die Ringe des Saturn* in 1995—lends itself to exploring the links between thanatourism and travel writing as a genre. And it is in no small part through its engagement with the issues of dark travel that *The Rings of Saturn* is, in the German publisher's phrase, "ein Reisebericht besonderer Art" (a travel report of a special kind). The narrator, a semifictional version of W. G. Sebald, recounts a walking tour of Suffolk—not high on the thanatouristic itinerary—after completing a "long stint of work" ([1998] 2002: 3). The narrator records having become "preoccupied not only with the unaccustomed sense of freedom but also with the paralyzing horror that had come over me at various times when confronted with the traces of destruction, reaching far back into the past, that were evident even in that remote place" ([1998] 2002: 3). Indeed, through the course of the walking tour, the narrator encounters all but one of the five degrees of thanatourism delineated in the article in which Tony Seaton (1996) coined the term. The narrator visits sites where actual deaths have occurred; numerous graves and monuments; battle reenactments and representations of violent death, notably Waterloo ([1998] 2002: 124–25); and a museum described as a "Chamber of Horrors" ([1998] 2002: 10). Only "travel to watch death" (Seaton 1996: 240) is entirely absent. As Sebald's evocation of the words of the seventeenth-century doctor and writer Thomas Browne has it, "one might, in following the setting sun, see on our globe nothing but prone bodies, row upon row, as if levelled by the scythe of Saturn—an endless graveyard for a humanity struck by falling sickness" ([1998] 2002: 79). Darkness is thus so pervasive in *The Rings of Saturn* that it is difficult to know where one might begin or end.

I approach this pervasive and varied darkness here with a widening thematic focus. Initially, attention is on the traveler-narrator's sense of his own mortality in Sebald's engagement with the intimate relations between travel, writing, and death. The focus then opens out into an assessment of the ethical questions posed by writing the spectacle of the suffering and deaths of others: here the concern is with the tension between ethical duty and fascination, between redress and appropriation, and Sebald's response to the association of death and suffering with "darkness." Finally, we turn to Sebald's response to a sense of those sufferings that are not directly witnessed but hover on the peripheries of consciousness in memory or imagination: dark sites at a distance. Cumulatively, the argument is that Sebald's text persistently resists the idea of a discrete darkness in which suffering, death, and disaster can be contained, working instead toward an integration of this darkness into experience and history and life. The darkness is everywhere, so to speak. And it is in the insistence on its pervasiveness that darkness is most powerfully resisted.

Travels in the Undiscovered Country

In delineating forms of thanatouristic or dark travel and travel writings with reference to specific sites associated with death and disaster, it is worth noting that both the journey and writing have a long, perhaps fundamental, association with death—fearing it, facing it, and escaping it, as well as seeking out encounters with it. The refrain of *The Epic of Gilgamesh*, by broad consensus one of the oldest surviving written texts, is a case in point. Motivated by a quest for immortal fame, Gilgamesh is overtaken by "the doom of mortals" after the death of his companion, Enkidu, resolving into a causal logic between morbid fear and wandering: "[I grew] fearful of death, [and so wander] the wild" (Anon. 1999: Tablet X, 239). If the anonymous poet of *Gilgamesh* sees in questing and wandering a relation to immortal ambitions and mortal fears, so too can the "travel narrative, published or recounted" be seen as "a record of survival," as Gillian Beer writes, in that "the narrator is here to tell it in retrospect even as the reader sets out on the journey" (Anon. 1999: 55). The travel narrative, as a record of survival, is thus often imbued in its basic form with an idea of the risk of death. As Joseph Jacobs writes in his notes to *The Book of Wonder Voyages*, in most such journeys and their narratives "there are traces of the influence of the last voyage of man. ... They are connected with the hopes and fears of man's last moments" ([1896] 2008: 216). And, as Sebald himself observes, "Psychoanalyse verzeichnet Reise und Wanderschaft als Symbole des Todes (Psychoanalysis registers travel and wandering as symbols of death)" ([1985] 2003: 78).

The Rings of Saturn brings such perennial links among travel, writing, and death to the fore. The shape of the journey itself has thanatological implications. The route involves traveling south along the east coast toward Orfordness before moving inland again—and, as in Dante's descent into Hell, to travel south is, symbolically, to travel toward death (Hulme 2002: 227). Similarly, the time of year in which the journey is taken is rendered significant, taking place "under the sign of the Dog Star" ([1998] 2002: 3)—suggesting a general fatalism (or engagement with fatalism). In their study of the cultural history of the association of Saturn with melancholy, Kilbansky, Panofsky, and Saxl cite the *Schönspergerscher Kalender* (Schönspergerscher's Calender) of 1495 as stating that Saturn is "hostile to our nature in every way and stands over to the east" (1964: 195). That a substantial portion of the journey takes place along the coast also has liminal—even apocalyptic—undercurrents. The devastation of the now submerged coastal town of Dunwich, "dissolved into water, sand, and thin air" ([1998] 2002: 159), for example, is a striking realization of what Robert Pogue Harrison has identified as a key feature of the eschatological imagination in which "the sea, in its hostility to architecturally or textually imprinted memory, often figures as the imaginary agent of ultimate obliteration" (2003: 4). In its most basic geography and atmosphere, then, *The Rings of Saturn* thus presents itself as a landscape haunted by death.

If there is a sense in which *The Rings of Saturn* is spatially and temporally structured around a thanatalogical principle, there are a number of times in which there is an implication that the story is that of a traveler who has himself ventured into the "undiscovered country from whose bourn no traveler returns" (Sebald alludes to Hamlet's famous cartography of death once more in characterizing Schiphol Airport as an antechamber to death [(1998) 2002: 89]). Throughout the book, there are hints that we are reading the account of a kind of ghost. When the traveler visits the poet and translator Michael Hamburger, he records that "the quite outlandish thought crossed my mind that these things, the kindling, the jiffy bags, the fruit preserves, the seashells and the sounds of the sea within them had outlasted me, and that Michael was taking me round a house which I myself had lived in a long time ago" ([1998] 2002: 185). When Mrs. Ashbury (a significant word-compound in itself) answers the door to the traveler at the bed and breakfast in Clarahill, "she gazed at me wide-eyed, or rather, she looked right through me" ([1998] 2002: 210). Among the papers held at the Deutsches Literaturarchiv in Marbach is a letter from Sebald to his publisher on his work in progress in which the implicit identification of the narrator with the Vicomte de Chateaubriand in his *Mémoires d'outre-tombe* (*Memoirs from Beyond the Grave*) is given an almost literal slant:

> gerade wie der exilierte französische Graf, so macht auch der Erzähler dieses Buchs seine Aufzeichnungen an einem Ort, der schon zu seinen Lebzeiten ein stückweit jenseits liegt des eigenen Grabs [just like the exiled French Vicomte (de Chateaubriand), so the narrator of this book makes his notes on a place that, already in his own lifetime, lies some way beyond his own grave]. (N. Sebald 1995: 3)

The most subtle yet concrete suggestion that *The Rings of Saturn* can be read as memoirs from beyond the grave is made elliptically. In the opening chapter, the narrator tells us that "several times during the day I felt a desire to assure myself of a reality that I feared had vanished forever by looking out of that hospital window, which, for some strange reason, was draped with black netting" ([1998] 2002: 4). A photograph depicting such a window is inserted into the narrative. This image is echoed in the closing passage of the book that retrospectively invests that opening scene with a symbolic supplement to the "strange reason" for the black netting draped over the hospital window. The narrative draws again on Thomas Browne, who

> remarks in a passage of the *Pseudodoxia Epidemica* that I can no longer find that in the Holland of his time it was customary, in a home where there had been a death, to drape black mourning ribbons over all the mirrors and all canvasses depicting landscapes or people of the fruits of the field, so that the soul, as it left the body, would not be distracted on its final journey, either by a reflection of itself or by a last glimpse of the land now being lost forever. ([1998] 2002: 296)

The black netting on the hospital window thus becomes, symbolically and retrospectively, a portent of death.[2] Sebald's book is so carefully composed that this must be more than coincidence, and it is perhaps significant that the observation of the black netting across the hospital window does not appear in the first draft of the chapter and was added after the completion of the full draft.[3] The opening chapter then takes on something like the quality of a figurative, autobiographical death scene: his nurses are described as "ministering angels" ([1998] 2002: 18) and, looking out of this window, the narrator sees an airplane trail in the sky. Though he "at first took this as a happy sign," in retrospect, Sebald's narrator fears it "marked the beginning of a fissure that has since riven my life" ([1998] 2002: 18). Although a crass literalism would clearly be reductive here, there is a sense that we are reading the account of one in a kind of limbo. *The Rings of Saturn* is presented—or rather, remembered in closing—as the account of a "soul ... distracted on its final journey" ([1998] 2002: 296).

Within the logic of the account, Sebald's travel narrative can be read as the performance of the record of a ghost. It draws on and dramatizes the thanatological dimensions implicit in travel writing generally, but also marks the book's innovation as one deeply linked with issues in dark travel in its subtle but fundamental subversion of the generic contract of travel writing as a tale of survival. That *The Rings of Saturn* can be read as the record of a traveler in the undiscovered country is, in a sense, its most quietly audacious underlying fiction. That we can read the narrative as Sebald's imagining of this narrative situation is one of the most fragile yet tenacious ways in which the text lives, documenting the investment of death with life, as well as life with death. *The Rings of Saturn* is thus written from a perspective in which writings on the dark side of travel cannot strictly be limited to a consideration of sites publicly associated with death and disaster: the thanatological is invested in travel and writing more widely. One might also suggest that Sebald's approach to such sites of death and suffering is filtered through his own foregrounded sense of mortality: he sides with the dead, so to speak. Yet the substance of *The Rings of Saturn* is also an account of a "soul ... *distracted* on its final journey" ([1998] 2002: 296, emphasis added). These distractions are to a large degree the sufferings of others, and it is to the spectacle of other people's misfortune that we now turn.

"Other People's Misfortune": Writing the Spectacle of Suffering

In *Kafka's Other Trial*, Elias Canetti writes that "in the face of life's horror—luckily most people notice it only on occasion, but a few whom inner forces appoint to bear witness are always conscious of it—there is only one comfort: its alignment with the horror experienced by previous witnesses" (1974: 4). This ethically unsettling idea—that the horror experienced by others provides the only comfort for those "whom inner forces appoint to bear witness"—points towards the moral tensions involved in attending to the spectacle of suffering. It is a psychological mechanism echoed closely in Sebald's writing from early on. In his first major nonacademic publication, *Nach der Natur: Ein Elementargedicht* (1988), translated by Michael Hamburger and published in 2002 as *After Nature,* the narrator reflects that if life is like a "Nordic chess tragedy," and an "arduous enterprise," then "For comfort there remains nothing but other people's / misfortune" (2002: 92–93). The ethical commitment to memory is thus accompanied by the open admission of the comforts of other people's sufferings. And if there is a kind of comfort that accompanies concern, there is also a danger of something more like a pornography of suffering. Sebald suggests this most overtly in the postscript to *The Natural History of Destruction* in describing an interest in the bombing of Dresden:

> To this day, any concern with the real scenes of horror during the catastrophe still has an aura of the forbidden about it, even of voyeurism, something these notes of mine have not entirely been able to avoid. I was not surprised when a teacher in Detmold told me, a little while ago, that as a boy in the immediate post-war years he quite often saw photographs of the corpses lying in the streets after the firestorm brought out from under the counter of a Hamburg second-hand bookshop, to be fingered and examined in a way usually reserved for pornography. ([1999] 2003: 98–99)

The question thrown up by the consolations and even the titillations of the spectacle of sufferings experienced by others is further compounded in the case of writers who occupy a special place in the taxonomy of the dark tourism spectrum. The act of writing may imply critical distance and a certain ethical authority, rendering the traveler an observer, rather than a participant, in the practices described. But, as Patrick Holland and Graham Huggan imply in the title of *Tourists with Typewriters* (1998), the writer is no less a tourist and consumer through writing than any other voluntary traveler. Moreover, there is an additional ethical dilemma in that the writer utilizes the experience more directly than others. For dark tourists with typewriters, to slightly modify the title, misery is material as well as spectacle. The writer approaches sites and experiences of suffering to consume and utilize. This too is an issue Sebald has been acutely sensitive to. As he once remarked in an interview with Christopher Bigsby:

> Writing is by definition a morally dubious occupation … because one appropriates and manipulates the lives of others for certain ends. When it is a question of the lives of those who survived persecution the process of appropriation can be very invasive. … A writer's attitude is utilitarian. I think Graham Greene said somewhere that most writers have a splinter of ice in their heart. This seems to me a very perceptive remark because writers have to look upon things in a certain way. There is this horrible moment when you discover, almost with a sense of glee, something that, although in itself horrid, will fit exactly with your scheme of things. (Bigsby 2001: 153)

How does Sebald's approach to the suffering of others fit into this nexus of problems? More precisely, how does Sebald's writing—his means of presentation and engagement in terms of his aesthetics—engage with these complex relations?

Sebald's self-reflexivity is the most immediately significant factor here. As the quotations above indicate, Sebald is not simply conscious of these issues in his work; his work is written out of these very concerns. At another level, the reader is frequently given the opportunity to see Sebald's traveler through the eyes of those he encounters. When, in the first chapter of *The Rings of Saturn*, Sebald recounts setting out in search of Thomas Browne's skull at the Norfolk & Norwich Hospital, not only do the "ladies and gentlemen" of the administrative staff "stare ... in utter incomprehension," but he "even had the impression" that some of those he spoke to regarded him as "an eccentric crank" ([1998] 2002: 10). It registers, often, more subtly still as ironic self-awareness that is less overtly expressed than implied through narrative organization and sequencing. Sebald continues this passage as follows:

> Curiously enough, Browne himself, in his famous part-metaphysical treatise, *Urn Burial,* offers the most fitting commentary on the subsequent odyssey of his own skull when he writes that to be gnaw'd out of our graves is a tragical abomination. But, he adds, who is to know the fate of his own bones, or how often he is to be buried? ([1998] 2002: 11)

This passage is followed immediately in the text by an image: a painting reprinted in black and white of what is presumably Thomas Browne's skull resting on a pile of books. In the original German, the name "Thomas Browne" appears underneath it on a separate line, like a title ([1995] 2004: 21). The irony of Sebald's attempt to exhume Browne's skull while also exhuming his views against this is left open for the reader to draw his/her own conclusions. Nevertheless, the organization of the narrative presents this irony for inspection and provides the reader with the same choice. Sebald's desire to unearth the skull is also part of a desire to recover the physical bodies, the individual lives, from the obfuscations of representational or schematic organization. According to Sebald's reading of Rembrandt's *Autopsy of Aris Kindt,* "it is debatable whether anyone ever really saw that body, since the art of anatomy, then in its infancy, was not least a way of making the reprobate body invisible" ([1998] 2002: 13–17). He continues by noting that the eyes of the medical students are not on the body but on the "open anatomical atlas in which the appalling physical facts are reduced to a diagram, a schematic plan of the human being" ([1998] 2002: 13). Recalling standing before the much-cited dark site, the war memorials at Waterloo, the narrator's line of thought goes against the grain of the memorial function, inquiring after the bodies: "Are they buried underneath the memorial? Are we standing on a mountain of death?" ([1998] 2002: 125). Sebald's work is thus culturally reflexive as well as self-reflexive and works to undo the commodification of sites of suffering in the process.

Such skeptical scrutiny of self and cultural form is a mark of the conscientiousness that attends to Sebald's journeying among the dead; but this in itself might suggest only that Sebald be seen as a more conscientious dark tourist. Yet there is a sense in which Sebald's approach to sites of death and destruction runs directly counter to the thanatouristic. If we follow Anthony Seaton's suggestion that the "more differentiated and comprehensive the traveller's knowledge of the dead, the weaker … the purely thanatouristic element" (1996: 240), then Sebald is the opposite of the dark tourist. Or perhaps: the thanatouristic element is self-defeating in his writing, always transforming itself into an interest in life, but an interest in life that acknowledges the mortality that makes that life possible. What it resists is not our interest in death so much as the assumption that an interest in death is any more specific than an interest in life: it resists the separation of the interest in *death* from an interest in the *dead*.

It also harasses us out of the assumption that concern with *death* is self-evidently and unquestionably associable with the *macabre,* as is sometimes implied (Stone 2006; Stone and Sharpley 2008). The macabre is the grim, ghastly, theatrical, and artificial. The association of death and the macabre has a long history going back to the Middle Ages,[4] but the macabre is not, for all this, synonymous with death. It is rather a way of responding to death. It is a vestige of psychology, anthropology, and cultural history that this association among death, suffering, and the macabre is so automatic. But might it be that this association is the most pervasive way in which death is sequestered in many contemporary societies? The journey taken by Thomas Browne's skull in *The Rings of Saturn* enacts a movement toward and then away from the thanatouristic. The placement of Thomas Browne's skull in a "Chamber of Horrors" is macabre; as, perhaps, is the narrator's interest in tracking it down at the beginning of the narrative ([1998] 2002: 9). But Sebald's desire to see the skull is first self-reflexively satirized as such ([1998] 2002: 11), and then later manifestly becomes elegiac. In the process, object becomes subject: Sebald's traveler may go in search of Browne's skull at the outset, but it is Thomas Browne who is given the last word in the book.

Darkness and Distance: Atrocity and the Everyday

One of the most influential arguments that has been put forward as to why dark tourism became so prominent (if not new) in the late twentieth century is that of Lennon and Foley (2007). Their understanding of dark tourism is that it is an "intimation of postmodernity" brought about in part by global communication technologies opening up the "territory between the global and the local, thereby introducing a collapse of space and time" (2007: 11). Visiting dark sites is an attempt to make real that which we encounter in mediated form, that which we are aware of but in which we are not directly involved.

One of the formative experiences behind Sebald's work is closely aligned with this. Sebald spoke of the "sense that while I grew up in what was, after all, quite an idyllic environment, at the same time the most horrendous things happened in other parts of Europe," and continued as follows:

> While I was sitting in my pushchair and being wheeled through the flowering meadows by my mother, the Jews of Corfu were being deported on a four-week trek to Poland. It is the simultaneity of a blissful childhood and these horrific events that now strikes me as quite incomprehensible. I know that these things cast a very long shadow over my life. (Bigsby 2001: 144)

What Sebald here presents as the awareness of an "incomprehensible simultaneity" of bliss and horror is perhaps one of modernity's most exemplary ethical problems.[5] In terms of dark tourism, the issue is that the dark experience does not begin and end on site. The dark sites of the contemporary world are not only experienced in situ, but in extended consciousness, in prospect, and in memory. This is not to forget that imprisonment and the lack of freedom defines the experience of those whose sufferings mark dark sites—or that the most tragic extension of the experience of suffering is the trauma that pursues the survivors of atrocity. It is only to insist that these sufferings, whether at the hand of persecution or conflict or natural disaster, have no discrete place. Voltaire's "Poem on the Lisbon Disaster" neatly encapsulates the sense of ethical paradox arising from an awareness of sufferings elsewhere:

> Earth Lisbon swallows; the light sons of France
> Protract the feast, or lead the sprightly dance. ([1756] 2000: 100)

One of the features of Sebald's work is that it develops a narrative form appropriate to this moral paradox. We see this in Sebald's frequent narration of lists of events that share a particular day as an anniversary. The day on which the narrator brings *The Rings of Saturn* to completion is 13 April 1995:

> It is Maundy Thursday, the feast day on which Christ's washing of the disciples' feet is remembered, and also the feast day of Saints Agathon,

Carpus, Papylus and Hermengild. On this very day three hundred and ninety-seven years ago, Henry IV promulgated the Edict of Nantes. ([1998] 2002: 294–95)

But as the list continues, increasingly incommensurable events are linked together: the anniversary of the first performance of Handel's *Messiah* coincides with the day on which the Anti-Semitic League was founded. And, finally, Maundy Thursday was also the day on which the narrator's wife's father died. As far as is known in the public domain, Sebald never went to the most iconic dark site, Auschwitz-Monowitz, though his work records journeys made in his own life to Breendonk in *Austerlitz* (Sebald [2001] 2002: 33). Sebald strenuously resisted having his work categorized as Holocaust literature, condemning it as "a dreadful idea that you can have a sub-genre and make a speciality out of it; it's grotesque" (Jaggi 2001: unpaginated). His sense of sites of atrocity similarly resists the impulse to subcategorize or compartmentalize.

One of the most remarkable "visits" to such a scene in *The Rings of Saturn* occurs in chapter 3, which accounts for the stretch of the walking tour as it moves south from Lowestoft along the coast toward Southwold. The listings in the table of contents— "Fishermen on the beach—The natural history of the herring—George Wyndham le Strange—A great herd of swine—The reduplication of man—Orbis Tertius"—indicate already that a degree of departure from the base level of the walk is involved in the narrative. There is no mention, however, of the most harrowing site—an image of the Nazi death camp at Bergen Belsen. Its emplotment proceeds as follows: reflections on the fishermen who sit on the beach—who "themselves are dying out"—lead into a history of the herring in which the narrator discusses their eerie luminosity after death and challenges the "assumption that the peculiar physiology of the fish left them free of the fear and pains that rack the bodies and souls of higher animals in their death throes" ([1998] 2002: 53, 57). As the cumulus clouds brew up and cast their shadows over the earth, the narrator switches course:

> Perhaps it was that darkening that called to mind an article I had clipped from the *Eastern Daily Press* several months before, on the death of Major George Wyndham Le Strange, whose great stone manor house in Henstead stood beyond the lake. During the last War, the report read, Le Strange served in the anti-tank regiment that liberated the camp at Bergen Belsen on the 14th of April, … but immediately after VE-Day returned home from Germany to manage his great uncle's estates in Suffolk, a task he had fulfilled in exemplary manner, at least until the mid-Fifties, as I knew from other sources. ([1998] 2002: 59–62)

The ellipsis in the passage stands in for an image of a photograph of what the reader is invited to assume must be connected to the camp of Bergen Belsen. Human corpses cover the forest floor of what might, at first glance, have appeared to be a pastoral composition. The image receives no direct commentary; and Bergen Belsen appears as a site with its photographic counterpart embedded in the story of Le Strange's eccentric relationship with his housekeeper to whom, according to the *Eastern Daily Express* article that the narrator paraphrases (and of which a photograph is also provided), the major left his entire fortune ([1998] 2002: 62). Inasmuch as Bergen Belsen is a site of death in *The Rings of Saturn,* it appears without warning as an element of another story alongside more extended reflections on other subjects, such as the suffering experienced by the herring. It is this passage that is noted by Mark McCulloh when, summarizing the controversy that such juxtaposition arouses, he asks: "Is it tasteful to lump such qualitatively different data together?" (2003: 65). What is clear is that the technique is so intrinsic to Sebald's approach that in an assessment of the ethics of his aesthetic we cannot view such juxtapositions as anomalies. It is as endemic to his approach to sites of atrocity as the longer, part-fictionalized biographical engagements with human beings who have suffered them. What is the effect? And is this an ethically viable aesthetic?

The initial impact of the image as it appears derives precisely from its incommensurability and from its interruption of the narrative: the lack of explication or emplotment registers, irreducibly, this silence. The image is important in part in that it *is* part of the story of Le Strange that cannot be worded into his story: the narrative is literally broken. And we can begin to see Sebald's insertion of the photograph as a kind of psychoanalytic enlargement on that detail of Le Strange's story, volunteering it as a cause implicated in his subsequent silent relationship with his maid. As we move beyond the story of Le Strange—it is a narrative that is constantly departing—the image becomes part of a wider canvas, again echoing through the narrator's own account as well as Le Strange's. We might also note that the image echoes the photograph a few pages earlier of a haul of herring ([1998] 2002: 54). It is here that the patterning is most controversial. Since the German "historians' dispute" of the 1980s in particular, the question of the relativization of historical events, the comparison of the Holocaust with other genocides, has been a highly charged public debate. The effect can be compared to that of a montage film such as Resnais's *Night and Fog* (1955). As Andrew Hebard has argued, the scandal surrounding the film may have "resulted not so much from the images themselves" but from the "use of archival material juxtaposed with present day footage" and the sense of "moral contamination" this involved (1997: 89). Sebald's prose, like Resnais's film, frequently allows leakage between the horrific and the everyday, providing no framework for the logical connections between the different forms of data. The sense of contamination is especially subversive in that, in the absence of discursive comparison in the text itself, the reader is implicated in seemingly incommensurable experiences, images, and events.

Whether this is compositional manipulation, or the expression of a mind in motion resisting the censorship of questionable proximities, it represents an insistence on the implicatedness of such harrowing histories in the rest of human experience. Sebald quotes the philosopher Emil Cioran: living is only possible "par les deficiences de notre imagination et de notre mémoire" (through the deficiencies in our imaginations and our memories) (quoted in Sebald [1999] 2003: 147–71). As a narrative, *The Rings of Saturn* performs the effort to live in imagination and memory. Except in the brutal sense that persecution is in itself an act of imprisonment, it is thus centrally formed around the principle that dark sites are never self-contained, and that, if one is alive to the world, no darkness is discrete.

Conclusion

Sebald's work is both exemplary of, and divergent from, the dark tourism paradigm. *The Rings of Saturn* does contribute to what Philip Stone and Richard Sharpley have suggested to be dark tourism's potential to "offer a revival of death within the public domain, thereby de-sequestering mortality and ensuring absent death is made present, transforming (private) death into public discourse and a communal commodity upon which to gaze" (2008: 588). As we have seen, he foregrounds the sense of mortality in his own traveler, he pays constant attention to the sufferings of the living and the dead, and he insists that dark sites are implicated in one another. But Sebald's approach is very different to that which arrives at classifications such as "Dark Camps of Genocide" (Stone 2006)—as if "dark" were sufficient, or there were another kind of death camp. *The Rings of Saturn*, for all that it confronts us with many shades of darkness, goes against the argument that the "confrontation of death and contemplation of mortality, within a socially acceptable dark tourism environment, may potentially bracket out some of the sense of dread death inevitably brings, by insulating the individual with information and potential understanding and meaning" (Stone and Sharpley 2008: 588). *The Rings of Saturn* shows that death is part of all our journeys. It insists that the dead are not a separate category of being from the living, and that our mortality cannot be isolated from life. It approaches sites of suffering not as a solution to the tourist's dread of death but as a challenge to the security of insulating the individual against this knowledge. It is the potentially deadening effect of such insulation—either of the dead from the living, or of the dead from their lives—that Sebald so persistently circumnavigates.

Notes

This is a revised and updated version of an article that appeared as "Sebald's Ghosts: Traveling among the Dead in *The Rings of Saturn*" in J. Skinner, ed., *Journeys: The International Journal of Travel and Travel Writing*, Special Edition, *Writing the Dark Side of Travel* 11, no. 1 (2010): 50–68.

1. This chapter takes its place in a long line of academic responses to Sebald's work that emphasize the reference to ghosts, specters, and hauntings in their titles. See, for example, Diedrich (2007), Barzilai (2006) and Cueppens (2006).
2. John Beck has also noted this detail of the text's beginning and ending, suggesting that the narrative may thus be understood as "the record of a final passage from this world to another" (2006: 77). Beck's interpretation differs slightly, however, in arguing that the narrator "has journeyed toward death, perhaps, to return with a message from the other side" (2006.: 77). Although this is literally the case, my reading pursues the possibility that the book is haunted by a sense that the narrator, strictly within the logic of the narrative, has not returned from the other side.
3. See Folders 7–9 of the Sebald Nachlass that contain handwritten drafts of the work in progress.
4. See Seaton (1996: 236) quoting Huizinga ([1924] 1968): "At the close of the Middle Ages the whole vision of death may be summed up in the word macabre, in its modern meaning. ... [The] sentiment it embodies, of something gruesome and dismal, is precisely the conception of death which arose during the last centuries of the Middle Ages."
5. This has been called the "meanwhile problem" (Buzard 1998: passim) and has been linked to the way in which the Diaspora in the wake of the French Revolution led to a "dramatic reorganization of modern time and space, so that contemporaries felt themselves *contemporaries*, as occupants of a common time zone" (Fritzsche 2004: 9–10; emphasis in original). Stephen Kern, similarly, links the inception of World Standard Time and the rapid development of telecommunications "worked to create the vast extended present of simultaneity" (1983: 318). Susan Sontag has written that to be "a traveller—and novelists are often travellers—is to be constantly reminded of the simultaneity of what is going on in the world, your world and the very different world you have visited and from which you have returned 'home'" (2007: 228).

Bibliography

Anon. 1999. *The Epic of Gilgamesh.* Trans. Andrew George. London: Penguin.

Barzilai, M. 2006. "Facing the Past and the Female Spectre in W. G. Sebald's *The Emigrants,*" in J. J. Long and A. Whitehead (eds.), *W. G. Sebald: A Critical Companion.* Edinburgh: Edinburgh University Press, 203–16.

Beck, J. 2006. "Reading Room: Erosion and Sedimentation in Sebald's Suffolk," in J. J. Long and Anne Whitehead (eds.), *W. G. Sebald: A Critical Companion.* Edinburgh: Edinburgh University Press, 75–88.

Beer, G. 1999. *Open Fields: Science in Cultural Encounter.* Oxford: Oxford University Press.

Bigsby, C. 2001. *Writers in Conversation,* vol. 2. Norwich: EAS Publishing in conjunction with Pen & Inc Press, for the UEA Arthur Miller Centre for American Studies.

Buzard, J. 1998. *The Beaten Track: European Tourism, Literature and the Ways to 'Culture' 1800–1918.* Oxford: Clarendon Press.

Canetti, E. 1974. *Kafka's Other Trial: The Letters to Felice.* Trans. Christopher Middleton. New York: Schocken Books.

Cueppens, J. 2006. "Seeing Things: Spectres and Angels in W. G. Sebald's Prose Fiction," in J. J. Long and A. Whitehead (eds.), *W. G. Sebald: A Critical Companion.* Edinburgh: Edinburgh University Press, 190–202.

Diedrich, L. 2007. "Gathering Evidence of Ghosts: W. G. Sebald's Practices of Witnessing," in L. Patt (ed.), *Searching for Sebald: Photography after W. G. Sebald.* Los Angeles: Institute of Cultural Inquiry, 256–79.

Fritzsche, P. 2004. *Stranded in the Present: Modern Time and the Melancholy of History.* Cambridge, MA: Harvard University Press.

Harrison, R. 2003. *The Dominion of the Dead.* Chicago and London: University of Chicago Press.

Hebard, A. 1997. "Disruptive Histories: Toward a Radical Politics of Remembrance in Alain Resnais's *Night and Fog.*" *New German Critique* 71 (Spring–Summer): 87–113.

Holland, P., and G. Huggan. 1998. *Tourists with Typewriters: Critical Reflections on Contemporary Travel Writing.* Ann Arbor: University of Michigan Press.

Huizinga, H. [1924] 1968. *The Waning of the Middle Ages.* Harmondsworth, UK: Penguin.

Hulme, P. 2002. "Patagonian Cases: Travel Writing, Fiction, History," in J. Borm (ed.), *Seuils & Traverses: Enjeux de l'écriture du voyage,* vol. 2. Brest: Centre de Recherche Bretonne et Celtique, 223–37.

Iyer, P. 2000. "The Strange, Haunted World of W.G. Sebald." *Harper's Magazine* (October): 86–90. Jacobs, J. [1896] 2008. *The Book of Wonder Voyages.* London: Adams Press.

Jaggi, Maya. 2001. "*The Guardian* Profile: W.G. Sebald. Recovered Memories." The Guardian, 22 September. http://www.guardian.co.uk/books/2001/sep/22/artsand humanities.highereducation (accessed 9 October 2011).

Kern, S. 1983. *The Culture of Time and Space 1880–1918.* Cambridge: Harvard University Press.

Kilbansky, R., E. Panofsky, and F. Saxl. 1964. *Saturn and Melancholy: Studies in the History of Natural Philosophy, Religion and Art*. London: Thomas Nelson and Sons.

Lennon, J. and M. Foley. 2007. *Dark Tourism: The Attraction of Death and Disaster*. London: Thomson.

McCrum, R. 1999. "Ghost Writer." *The Observer*, 12 December. http://www.guardian .co.uk/books/1999/dec/12/2 (accessed 9 October 2011).

McCulloh, M. 2003. *Understanding W.G. Sebald*. South Carolina: University of South Carolina Press.

Millar, J. 2007. "A Firework for W. G. Sebald (2005–6)," in L. Patt (ed.), *Searching for Sebald: Photography after Sebald*. Los Angeles: Institute of Cultural Inquiry, 550–11.

Resnais, A. V. 1955. *Nuit et Brouillard*. France: Argos Films.

Rojek, C. 1993. *Ways of Escape*. Basingstoke: Macmillan.

Seaton, A. 1996. "Guided by the Dark: From Thanatopsis to Thanatourism," *International Journal of Heritage Studies* 2(4): 234–244.

Sebald, W. G. [1995] 2004. Deutsches Literaturarchiv Marbach, Marbach am Neckar. "Die Ringe des Saturn—Handschrift." Fols. 1–9.

———. [1985] 2003. "Das unentdeckte Land: Zur Motivstruktur in Kafkas *Schloß*," in W. G. Sebald, *Die Beschreibung des Unglücks: Zur österrischen Literatur von Stifter bis Handke*. Frankfurt am Main: Fischer Verlag GmbH, 78–92.

———. [1995] 2004. *Die Ringe des Saturn: eine Englische Wallfahrt*. Frankfurt am Main: Fischer Verlag GmbH.

———. [1998] 2002. *The Rings of Saturn*. Trans. Michael Hulse. London: Vintage.

———. [1999] 2003. *The Natural History of Destruction*. Trans. Anthea Bell. London: Hamish Hamilton.

———. [2001] 2002. *Austerlitz*. Trans. Anthea Bell. London: Penguin.

———. 2002. *After Nature*. Trans. Michael Hamburger. New York: Random House.

Sontag, S. 2007. *At the Same Time: Essays and Speeches*. London: Hamish Hamilton.

Stone, P. 2006. "A Dark Tourism Spectrum: Towards a Typology of Death and Macabre Related Tourist Sites, Attractions and Exhibitions." *Tourism* 54(2): 145–60.

Stone, P. and R. Sharpley. 2008. "Consuming Dark Tourism: A Thanatological Perspective." *Annals of Tourism Research* 35(2): 574–95.

Voltaire F. [1756] 2000. "Poem on the Lisbon Disaster," in F. Voltaire, *Candide and Related Texts*. Trans. David Wootton. Indianapolis: Hackett, 99–107.

CHAPTER 3

Graphic Wounds
The Comics Journalism of Joe Sacco

TRISTRAM WALKER

Over the past twenty years a new hybrid has emerged within bookshops: the travel comic or graphic travelogue, combining two forms that have often individually provoked suspicion and denigration. Comics artists have journeyed across the globe reporting on their travels in increasing numbers. Josh Neufeld has taken readers with him and his wife into the caves of Thailand, to a funeral in Bali, and onto the set of a Singaporean soap opera in *A Few Perfect Hours* (2004). K. Thor Jensen, in the wake of losing his job and girlfriend, and the terrorist attack on the World Trade Center, leaves New York to travel across America on Greyhound buses, living outside mainstream society as an "internet hobo" in *Red Eye, Black Eye* (2007). Craig Thompson's sketchbook journal *Carnet de Voyage* (2006) follows his trip to Europe and Morocco as he researches for his graphic novel *Habibi* (2011). Traveling comics artists could be seen to be carrying on the tradition of wandering artists such as Eugene Delacroix or Lester Hornby. They represent a new breed of travel writers combining the traditions of visual and literary arts.

This chapter provides a background to the emergence of the graphic travelogue before examining the work of one of its more noteworthy practitioners, Joe Sacco. It discusses his works on Bosnia and Palestine and how they may relate to a wound culture that demands fresh images to sustain its appetite, and how the portrayal of trauma operates through his pages as a constitutive force moving towards a shared human experience. It explores how Sacco represents trauma and considers whether these representations are more than a voyeuristic exploitation of human suffering.

Comix

Comics historian and critic Roger Sabin considers the modern comic to be an invention of Victorian Britain "designed as cheap and cheerful entertainment for the working classes" (1993: 13). They were throwaway items, popular travel accessories for the nineteenth-century commuter, and became known as "railway literature" (Sabin 2001: 18). The first of these comics was *Ally Sloper's Half Holiday* published by Gilbert Dalziel in 1884. However, it was in the twentieth century that interest in comics surged and caught the attention of a wider public, sometimes to the detriment of the medium.

Comics were deemed to have a stifling effect on literacy (Versaci 2007: 7–8). They could, argued the detractors, be found to be at the root of most juvenile delinquency (Coard 1955). They were even, in the words of John Mason Brown, "the marijuana of the nursery" (Cavanagh 1949: 28). Crime, war, and horror comics were especially targeted, but even the superheroes did not escape criticism. One of the most well-known and influential anticomics campaigners was Fredric Wertham. Wertham was the author of *Seduction of the Innocent* (1953), a study that pushed the link between a young life of crime and the reading of comics. He had a particular obsession with what he saw as deviant sexuality; to him Wonder Woman was obviously a lesbian, and Batman and Robin were gay. As supporting evidence, he used testimony from one gay man who stated "that he would have been willing to trade places with either of the dynamic duo" (Daniels 1971: 87). It is tempting to look upon the moral panic of just over half a century ago with little more than a wry smile, but the campaigners were effective and met many of their goals. In the United States, the bulk of the comics industry was compelled to sign up to the Comics Code Authority, a body that prohibited the printing of references to sex, excessive violence, or challenges to authority. Noncompliance would mean no approved cover stamp and no distribution (Sabin 2001). In Britain, the Children and Young Persons (Harmful Publications) Act 1955 was passed to "prevent the dissemination of certain pictorial publications harmful to children and young persons." The act is still in force, yet many of the books that would have once been banned are widely available in anthologies and academic texts exploring the history and censorship of material such as Martin Barker's *A Haunt of Fears: The Strange History of the British Horror Comics Campaign* (1984). This, perhaps, represents a shift in the focus of moral outrage to new media territory such as computer games and the Internet: the minds of children may no longer be considered to be at risk from comics.

Sex, drugs, violence, and yet more sex were to become staples of a new kind of comic book in the late 1960s, one that did not even attempt to get through the Comics Code Authority. Underground comics, or comix with an "x" to emphasize their x-rated nature and distinguish them from their code-approved counterparts, sprung from counterculture America (Sabin 1993). The underground comix played with irony and dismantled taboos, tackling issues that would antagonize the moral establishment. It became a competitive underworld among some of the artists: as comics critic and historian Paul Gravett has remarked, "Robert Crumb, S. Clay Wilson and others all tried to out do each other in breaking all taboos" (Gravett 2005: 22). One of the consequences of this competition was a number of court cases in the United States and abroad that were brought against the comix creators on charges of obscenity (Sabin 2001). The fourth issue of *Zap,* a comic edited by Crumb and featuring his own work, and that of other underground artists including S. Clay Wilson and Spain Rodriguez, was released in 1969 and became the subject of an obscenity trial in New York.

The story that seemed to occupy most of the prosecutor's attention was "Joe Blow," Crumb's explicit but satirical depiction of incest within American suburbia (Estren 1993). The prosecutor was determined to focus the judge's attention on the sexual content of the comix and to ignore the satire contained in its strips. The judge's limited view caused him to find no value or idea in the comic that would stem his moral indignation (Estren 1993). Michael Barrier, founding editor of the comics and animation journal *Funnyworld,* suggests that Crumb's true crime in the eyes of the court was, not that he depicted incest but, that he did not coat it with the same layer of indignation that informed the judge's decision. Crumb refused "to feign shock" without adding the "frosting of morality" that accompanies other depictions of incest (Barrier cited in Estren 1993: 237). Crumb and other comix artists were prepared to take their readers inside dark places without a moral comfort blanket. S. Clay Wilson's strips relied on the shock of extreme, often sexual, violence to explore free expression. It was an exploration that was not appreciated by everyone, including feminists "who pointed out that the majority of the violence was directed against women" (Sabin 2001: 103). Spain Rodriguez used comics to promote a radical political agenda of opposition to the Vietnam War with the character Trashman, the trigger-happy superpowered anarchist hero of a future fascist dystopia, becoming a symbol for protestors, and opposition to police brutality in stories of a police detective using his status to cover up his own murderous sadism (Sabin 2001). This willingness to explore the limits of frank expression was developed further in the 1970s and applied to the artists' personal lives with the beginning of what Robert Crumb's wife, the artist Aline Kominsky-Crumb (2007: 136), refers to as the "autobiographical 'let it all hang out' genre [of] comics."

The first to realize the potential of autobiography in comix was Justin Green. In 1972 he created *Binky Brown Meets the Holy Virgin Mary* (1972), a frank, uncensored confessional comic that inspired Kominsky-Crumb and her husband Robert, Art Spiegelman, and countless others to attempt their own autobiographical works (Gravett 2005). The underground and later alternative comics scene has moved from threat-to-status-quo-to-acceptance as an important part of the cultural arena. Indeed, in 2005, an exhibition of Robert Crumb's work was held at the Whitechapel Gallery in London. It marked his "strange reversal: from the hero of underground comics to establishment grandee" (Cumming 2005). It is from this underground autobiographical tradition that much of today's travel comics seem to emerge. Joe Sacco, a journalism graduate of the University of Oregon, draws himself as an almost Crumb-like figure declaring his genius as a comics artist while living on the breadline and following a rock band on their European tour later collected in *Notes from a Defeatist* (2003a). This collection also includes an account of the Italian occupation of Malta during World War II, as remembered by Sacco's mother Carmen, and a satirical exploration of what it is to be glued to the television set, obsessing over every movement of the Gulf War in 1991, as the title of that strip states—a "War Junkie." Sacco moved from the safety of being an armchair observer to travel into zones of conflict and see the trauma for himself. His accounts of war and life under occupation have punctured the mainstream with appearances in newspapers and exhibitions across the globe, making his name synonymous with comics journalism.

Sacco is certainly not the first traveler to take both notes and sketches, and though his style and politics owe much to the underground and alternative comics scenes, he follows the path of previous artist travelers into zones of conflict and political maneuvering. The French Orientalist artist Eugene Delacroix accompanied the Comte de Mornay on a diplomatic mission to Morocco in 1832. His journal recorded illustrations and comments on what he saw as a world unchanged since ancient times (Nochlin 1989). The American illustrator Lester Hornby took his sketchbook behind the lines of World War I, having been given a pass by General Pershing in 1917 to travel with American forces in France (Johnson 1980). Hornby arrived in Yugoslavia in the early twentieth century to produce *Balkan Sketches: An Artist's Wanderings in the Kingdom of the Serbs* (1926) roughly seven decades before Sacco traveled with his own notebook to Bosnia. Yugoslavia, a kingdom with fourteen acknowledged languages and various competing claims for dominance within the state, had formed from the wreckage that the first quarter of the twentieth century had wrought (Almond 1994). *Balkan Sketches* contains a mix of illustration and prose. Hornby intersperses his prose travelogue with the occasional sketch of landscapes or individual characters.

Hornby expresses his admiration for a controlling power that can keep the West safe from the consequences of multiethnic conflict and addresses his acknowledgement to the king and queen "of the romantic kingdom 'where East meets West'," praising the political and military strength of Serbia, seeing its power among the Balkan states as fortunate for the Western world (Hornby 1926: v). Hornby's travelogue, and occasional paean to Serbian might, is not presented as sequential art, and his politics appear to be wildly different to those of Sacco. However, segregated as the two forms may be in Hornby's text, it does show illustration being used to reinforce prose observation of the Balkans. The comic book by definition is a hybrid medium using both image and text to convey narrative. Sacco's work takes this mixed form and adds to it further, including the unflinching explicit depictions of uncomfortable imagery that marked much of the underground's output and the wandering curiosity of the traveling artists that began to beat the path to conflict zones so many years ago.

Shock and Draw

Joe Sacco is perhaps best known for his work on Bosnia and Palestine. In 1996, he received the American Book Award for his 1993 nine-issue comic book series, *Palestine*. Edward Said introduced the collected edition. It was released in 2003, and in it Said described the liberating, subversive qualities of comic books and his double shock of recognition upon first reading Sacco's Palestine series: "I was plunged directly back into the world of the first great Intifada (1987–92) and, with even greater effect, back into the animated enlivening world of comics I had read so long ago" (2003b: iii).

Sacco had become disillusioned by what he saw as the misrepresentation of Israel and the Palestinians in the American media. He has stated that one effect of this skewed portrayal was that he "grew up thinking of Palestinians as terrorists" (Khalifa 2008). He began to read more of what he describes as "the right things" and realized that the situation was more complicated than the portrayal offered by the American media (Khalifa 2008). He went to Palestine to see things for himself and spent two months in the Occupied Territories during the winter of 1991/1992 as the first Intifada began "to run out of steam" (Sacco 2003b: vi).

Sacco first went to Bosnia in 1995, joining the army of journalists recording the events of Yugoslavia's collapse and the wars that followed. Many of the journalists had used the Holiday Inn at Sarajevo as a base throughout the wars (Sells 1996). However, Sacco moved from its relative safety to stay with the Bosnian Muslim people of Gorazde, a UN-designated "safe area" on the banks of the river Drina. The creation of safe areas came as part of what Noel Malcolm describes as the signing of Bosnia's "final death warrant" in May 1993 (2002: 250). Bosnia's remaining Muslims would be concentrated in the safe areas where there was no guarantee of safety and no protection from the UN should Serb forces attack them. The UN mandate allowed only for fire to be returned if the UN forces themselves were attacked. The most infamous of the safe areas was perhaps Srebrenica that fell to Serb forces on 11 July 1995 (Malcolm 2002).

Following *Safe Area Gorazde* were *The Fixer: A Story from Sarajevo* (Sacco 2004) and *War's End: Profiles from Bosnia, 1995–96* (Sacco 2005), the last collection featuring the stories "Soba" and "Christmas with Karadzic." These stories concentrate on two very different characters from opposing sides of the war. Soba is an artist from Sarajevo who stays behind during the war to fight and defend his home. Sacco interviews him in between stints on the front line and joins him for parties in the besieged city. At the end of the war, Sacco is there for Soba's brief chat with the U2 singer Bono and the start of a postwar career as a rock star. Radovan Karadzic was a Bosnian Serb leader and former psychiatrist and poet. Years before the war his lines—"Take no pity let's go / kill that scum down in the city"—had made clear his feelings for Sarajevo and Bosnian Muslims (Hukanovic 1998: 56). "Christmas with Karadzic" chronicles Sacco's attempts to track Karadzic down during the Orthodox Christmas of January 1996 along with two radio journalists. It shows the excitement of the chase and the triumph of journalists getting access to an elusive quarry. It also highlights the distinction between Karadzic as the symbol (of massacres, death camps, snipers, and hatred for Bosnian Muslims), and Karadzic as the man (of whom Sacco felt nothing in his presence, nothing more than embarrassment to be seen near him by the television cameras). These two stories are good examples of Sacco's portrayal of the human face of conflict, whether of those the world would consider as victims or of those it would be more convenient to describe as demons.

Sacco is never far from the panels of his own work. His cartoon—Crumb-like double with blank, all-seeing spectacles; Mick Jagger lips;

and fingerless gloved hands—features throughout the books, is at the fore asking questions, making notes, and tucking into the food his hosts provide. He also draws himself into the background as a near-constant figure whose presence dismantles the conceit of detached journalistic objectivity. His graphic representation of himself shows his interaction with his new environment and becomes our connection to worlds shaped by war and occupation and distorted by the rapid frames of twenty-four-hour rolling news. The blank spectacles made up of solid white disks call to mind Art Spiegelman's comments about the heads of his anthropomorphic mice in *Maus* (1986), comparing their eyes to those of the 1920s comic strip character Little Orphan Annie whose eyeballs are "a white screen the reader can project on" (1994b: 46). Spiegelman's blank mouse heads were an entry for the reader into the horror of Auschwitz. Sacco's spectacles are supplements to our own gaze, allowing entry for the price of a comic book into dark places far from the tourist track and perhaps more familiar through the lens of a news bulletin than our own experiences. The spectacles represent a tool for witnessing for Sacco and the reader. They are a "white screen" upon which trauma can be projected and reconstituted through a process of what comics artist and theorist Scott McCloud refers to as "closure" (1993: 63).

McCloud uses "closure" to describe the process of gap filling that occurs when the mind completes pictures from limited information, such as by observing the corner of a bank note and knowing from experience what denomination it is, or seeing the side of a soda bottle and being able to describe its brand (1993: 63). The gaps are filled based on experience, a process exploited by comics artists to connect individual panels. McCloud suggests that by filling in those gaps between panels, the reader becomes complicit in the construction of narrative imagery. The space between panels, otherwise known as "the gutter," blurs the line between witness and accessory. As McCloud states, "panels fracture both time and space, offering a jagged, staccato rhythm of unconnected moments" (1993: 67). "Closure" occurs when the reader connects these moments to "mentally construct a continuous, unified reality" (1993: 67). Sacco's work requires the reader to mentally construct the reality of trauma. The "white screen" of the spectacles and the gutter may allow for our own interpretation and imagination, but ultimately we are guided in deciding the degree of brutality between frames by the images and written narration provided by Sacco. His work is not short of harrowing scenes reconstructed through witness testimony for the reader to navigate.

In *Safe Area Gorazde*, one eyewitness describes to Sacco seeing two hundred to three hundred people killed over a period of three days and

"Sometimes they shot them, but they preferred to cut their throats."

Illustration 3.1. Eyewitness testimony informs Sacco's representation of mass killing on a bridge over the Drina in Visegrad in 1992. *Safe Area Gorazde,* 110. Courtesy of Fantagraphics Books. Copyright Joe Sacco.

nights on the bridge over the river Drina in Visegrad in May 1992 (2000: 109–19). Sacco surrounds the frames of the representation of this testimony in solid black. He uses this technique to distinguish between events of the past in which he was not involved and the clear-bordered panels of events for which he was present. Throughout the eleven pages and eighty-seven panels of testimony, all but seven panels are accompanied by either the eyewitness's narration in text boxes or speech in word balloons, and in some cases both. One panel on the bridge is left without comment, but it seems far from silent (2000: 110). The violence on display has been described to Sacco, the listener, by an eyewitness, and then rendered by the artist in deliberately explicit detail, leaving room for the reader to connect and process the slaughter guided by Sacco's interpretation. In this panel our eyes are drawn to an open-mouthed screaming child being dragged to the wall of the bridge. Near him is a man, held at knifepoint with his hands tied behind him. In the next panel we see the knife just as it has cut the man's throat, his blood sprays from his neck to join that of the other victims all over the bridge. The fate of the child is left for us to imagine with little doubt as we put together the horrific pieces that Sacco has provided.

The horror of the massacre of Bosnian Muslims on the bridge, with its slaughter of all regardless of sex or age, is shocking and fits into the American Psychiatric Association's definition of traumatic events as being "outside the range of usual human experience" (Herman 1994: 33). For most of Sacco's readers, mass slaughter will not enter their range of experience and will remain unusual. However, for some people, including those in the collapsing Yugoslav states during the 1990s, cruelty and murder can become part of the fabric of their everyday existence. The scene on the bridge fits into a sadly more commonplace larger pattern of killing in Bosnia, answering Karadzic's call to "take no pity" (Hukanovic 1998: 56). Yet the reoccurrence of atrocities throughout the war does not diminish their standing as extraordinary events. Judith Herman states: "Traumatic events are extraordinary, not because they occur rarely, but rather because they overwhelm the ordinary adaptations to life" (1994: 33). Before the war broke out in Bosnia in April 1992, ordinary life in Gorazde saw Serbian and Muslim neighbors living as friends, sharing coffee, and celebrating weddings and Orthodox Christmas together (Sacco 2000: 77). Sacco interviews residents who recall the first Serb attack on Gorazde and how they recognized their neighbors as part of the assault force (79). One remembers being told that a former Serb neighbor, an old friend with whom he used to play football or just spend time together, had burned down his house during the attack (87). The shock of being attacked by one's neighbors or friends brought with it a need for rapid mental readjustment. This sudden plunge into a living nightmare is an experience for which, in spite of propaganda and memories of World War II, there could be no preparation or a sense of, to use Freud's term, *Angstbereitschaft* (the readiness to feel anxiety) (LaCapra 2001: 90). The break or shock can, if the subject survives, manifest itself throughout their life leaking into the everyday, often in a manner that plays out or remembers the original event(s). These are often deeply personal traumatic events that are played out and represented through panels in Sacco's graphic travelogues.

The representation of trauma within Sacco's work could be seen as belonging to what Mark Seltzer describes as a "*wound culture*—the public fascination with torn and open bodies and torn and opened persons, a collective gathering around shock, trauma and the wound" (1998: 1). He provides plenty of imagery that would fascinate those searching for gore. In the aftermath of the first attack on Gorazde, we are shown half a body sitting against a wall. All that remains of him are his legs, his lower torso and part of his spine jutting upwards (Sacco 2000: 90). Sacco then shows scenes from a year later when a mass grave from the first attack is discovered containing seven bodies (92). Two of the rotting bodies are shown in close-up (93). Sacco achieves the detail of the bodies through discussion with his friend Edin from Gorazde, a recurring character throughout the book who was there for the exhumation and reburial. During production of the book, he e-mailed Edin for greater description of the mutilated and decaying bodies and also spoke with someone who worked in forensics (Groth 2001: 62). However, this visual detail is also accompanied by biographical captions, in Edin's voice, describing the men as his best friends. The personal detail makes them more than just bodies displayed for our fascination, and at the bottom of the page a silent panel with no captions shows more of Sacco's attention to detail. He remembered Edin describing to him how the men had prayed over the bodies. He asked for more description of how they prayed and was able to portray the scene as accurately as he could (Groth 2001: 62). Edin and the other men gather around the bodies and pray. Their collective action is not out of fascination for trauma but out of grief for their fallen friends. The presentation of this in a comic risks being seen as an artifact of a wound culture, but Sacco's determination to depict both decomposition and prayer with accuracy ensures that, overall, those who have suffered are treated by him with dignity and respect. It is not gore merely for the sake of it, but the horror is shown to reinforce the idea of the impact it has had on the Bosnian community.

The representation of trauma can also be used to bolster ideologies. Trauma is exploited by the reiteration of the legend of Serbian defeat in Kosovo by Ottoman invaders in 1389 that creates a focus point for a fervent nationalism and sense of victimhood, fueled further by the living memory of Nazi occupation and the collaboration of Croatian Ustasha (LeBor 2003). In *Palestine*, in particular, Sacco shows how wounds can be used to foment a sense of belonging and national pride, especially among a people who have lost so much.

In Sacco's *Palestine*, a congregation gathers around a public parade of wounds for the benefit of the visiting foreign journalist. At the beginning of chapter two, "Public & Private Wounds (Nablus)," we move swiftly from Sacco being quizzed about his nationality and religion, and being offered a bag of milk, to a brief showcase of past wounds suffered by members of the crowd around him. The man offering Sacco milk takes a teenage boy from the audience and declares: "He is shot five times!" (29). The present tense of the Palestinian's broken English, as condensed into a word balloon by Sacco, implies that the injuries are not just confined to the past, but that the boy *is* shot, now in the present and, as the occupation continues, in the future. Another member of the crowd lifts his fringe to reveal a scar left by a plastic bullet. In the next panel, another rolls up his sleeve to show a scar created by "*Live* ammo" (30; author's emphasis). "Wounds!!" declares an excited caption. It is the voice of Joe Sacco as narrator, and audience as voyeur, eager to clamor around the spectacle of torn bodies. Excitement is provoked by the offer of proof and the opportunity to satisfy a morbid lust for visual evidence apparent in the physical extremes suffered by a people under occupation. Sacco is offered the chance to see more, to "flesh out" the statistics from the appendices of books on the Intifada. The promise of more displayed wounds removes the injured from a list of the statistics and figures and assigns a face to the abstracted ideas of pain indexed in human rights reports. Trauma becomes grounded in a reality in which "seeing is believing." A Volkswagen camper serves as a trauma tour bus delivering him to his next stop: the hospital (30). The young Palestinians are shown to stride forcefully into the hospital. Sacco draws his own legs as long as theirs but awkward and swept along with the force of their determination to show him the wounded. The Palestinians' feet are ahead of Sacco's, disappearing into another panel in their eagerness to expose as much as possible.

The cascading captions are composed of short phrases. The placement on the page draws the reader's eyes across the irregular panels depicting the hospital ward. We are swept along almost as fast as Sacco. The final panel is a reproduction of a photograph. Sacco states that he takes many photographs of people and his surroundings to act as references for the final product. He makes few sketches (Groth 2001: 61). The "sticky taped" corners of this panel give the impression that it has been stuck into a scrapbook or photograph album of Sacco's trauma tourism. Unlike the previous patient, whose cast we are shown, we are not told why this man is in the hospital. However: "He wraps on a keffiyeh! ... For Palestine!" (31). The keffiyeh is passed from patient to patient, dressing their wounds in pride and giving their presence in hospital a nationalist purpose. In the middle of the keffiyeh passing and excitement about a foreign journalist's presence in the ward, we are shown a patient in real pain, his face locked in a grimace: "Dry blood on his pillow case. ... Small intestine and liver shot up." Joe asks if he can take a photo. The patient manages "'La!' 'No' in Arabic ... Say no more. ... A private wound" (32). Yet, despite not being able to take a photograph, his wound enters the public sphere via a drawing in a comic. His pain activates the switch from private life to public, his refusal arousing more curiosity. This shift into the public sphere is demonstrated by his prominence on the page. His full length, angled slightly, takes up the center. Sacco's commentary covers his body in narrative boxes and describes his injuries at the same time as drawing his pain and bringing his trauma into our public view. It could be considered that the needs of a wound culture are satisfied as the trauma is brought into the open, but the moment of voyeurism is mixed with the realization that, for now, the victim does not wish to be seen by us. This panel slows Sacco's tour through the hospital for a moment and also stops the flow of the keffiyeh and the link of wounds with national pride. It disturbs the fascination of the wound for voyeurism and nationalism and, though we know nothing of the man, it forces a consideration of his wishes as an individual.

Later, in *Palestine,* in a section titled "Moderate Pressure Part 2," Sacco begins a black-bordered journey into a vision of torturous imprisonment with the assertion that certain realities exist concurrently:

> Make no mistake, everywhere you go, not just in Marvel Comics, there's parallel universes. ... Here? On the surface streets: traffic, couples in love, falafel-to-go, tourists in jogging suits licking stamps for postcards. ... And over the wall behind closed doors: other things—people strapped to chairs, sleep deprivation, the smell of piss ... (102)

Sacco's reference to Marvel Comics, publisher of titles including *Uncanny X-Men, The Amazing Spider-Man,* and *Incredible Hulk,* draws attention to the retail space that his work shares with superhero comics either by being under the same roof in a specialist comic book store or by being placed in the same "graphic novels" section of a bookstore or public library. His work exists in parallel to the fantastic world of Marvel but, unlike Marvel, there are no costumed heroes to save the day, no deus ex machina to restore truth and justice. In Sacco's *Palestine* there is just the journalist investigating a wounded people and attempting to show the world their trauma. In Ghassan he finds what he is searching for: "He shows me his back and wrists, he's still got the marks ... he's a fresh case all right ... right off the rack" (102). Ghassan holds up his shirt and Joe inspects the fresh wounds, peering into them before we are taken below their surface, uncovering the invisible psychic trauma beneath. Ghassan's narrative is not unique. Sacco notes its conventional beginning: "And sleep is where Ghassan's story starts ... where stories like this always start ... when people are asleep" (102).

Dori Laub states that "the listener to trauma comes to be a participant and a co-owner of the traumatic event: through his very listening, he comes to partially experience trauma in himself" (1992: 57). Sacco's work becomes a conduit for the traumatic experience, a coauthorial artifact giving itself over to become, like Joe's spectacles, a blank screen for its projection. His own narrative voice seems to disappear, subsumed by that of the victim. The moment of trauma overwhelms in its retelling as we see both outside of Ghassan, with him as subject of the frame, and inside of his mind as hallucinations manifest themselves within individual uniform panels.

The uniformity of panel size and shape in this sequence is unusual for *Palestine*, suggesting the enforced order of imprisonment. The black border offers no escape, panels do not overlap or bleed into one another as with elsewhere in the text, and thus we are confined to the same boundaries as Ghassan. The only freedom is that it is left to us to fill in the gap of the dark, empty gutter with the terror of the unknown with which the hooded prisoner must cope. The panel size decreases as we reach Ghassan's fourth day in solitary confinement, which sees the beginning of his hallucinations. The sense of claustrophobia heightens further with available space filled by new, constantly shifting realities projected through the sack hood and into the tiny cell. The hallucinations are drawn into being by Sacco and accompanied by Ghassan's statements: "My daughter is dead" (Sacco 2003b: 109). During the traumatized state Ghassan's hallucinations are rendered by Sacco's pen as real, existing within the physical space of the cell. Herman describes "the salient characteristic of the traumatic event [as] its power to inspire helplessness and terror" (1994: 34). The imprisoned Ghassan is no longer in a position to offer paternal protection; his fears fill the cell, mixing the reality of his physical situation with the realities imagined through his hallucinations. Ghassan is kept in prison for over two weeks, without evidence or charge before being released. He climbs into a car and is taken home. As the car drives away, our view is obscured by people on the street—walking, laughing, kissing, and enjoying life. We no longer see Ghassan's parallel universe of torture and hallucination. On the surface, the wound is again covered, waiting for us to look closely and carefully enough to see what lies beneath the façade.

On the Ground

Near the beginning of *Safe Area Gorazde*, Sacco is in a classroom with other journalists (2000: 13). Edin, his guide and friend, is giving the class and says that Joe and his colleagues can ask any question. Instead, they ask the class if they have any questions for them. A girl asks, "Why did you come to Gorazde?" (2000: 13). His reply hovers in caption boxes stretching over a double page spread, undivided by separate panels. "Why? Because you are still here ... not raped and scattered, not entangled in the limbs of thousands of others at the bottom of a pit. Because Gorazde had lived, and—how?" (2000: 14–15). Gorazde had made it

Illustration 3.2. Sacco's reasons for visiting Gorazde hover as captions over a panorama of life in the war-ravaged "Safe Area." *Safe Area Gorazde*, 14–15. Courtesy of Fantagraphics Books. Copyright Joe Sacco.

this far, and Sacco sets out to investigate how they had survived and how they live in the present. He avoids stating that Gorazde has lived, perhaps because that would imply a stable state of survival. Gorazde at this point is still surrounded by Serb guns, and there is still a danger that what had happened in Srebrenica could happen to them. Tense becomes a precarious matter, and the only time that can afford any certainty is the past.

Time in comic books is divided—along with narrative—by panels or frames. The artist controls the flow of action, guiding the reader from moment to moment and containing all that they want us to see. With the splash page above, the boundaries of the panel are those of the book itself. It is a "non-frame." Will Eisner, in *Comics and Sequential Art*, describes how "the non-frame speaks to unlimited space. It has the effect of encompassing unseen but acknowledged background" (2006: 45). Gorazde, indeed Bosnia and the rest of the former Yugoslavia, continues beyond the edges of the page to be completed by our own knowledge and preconceptions. The fate of Srebrenica, another safe area, may form part of that background and inform our reading of the actual image on the page. Each person captured on that page is representative of the potential horror of the war but also of the potential to escape and, as Sacco states, survive.

Sacco appears to have captured on the splash page a cross-section of life in Gorazde. It is a life thrown back decades by war: cars are shown as useless wrecks rusting in the background among the shelled buildings; a three-legged dog watches as children play football; people chop wood, some walk and chat, engrossed in their own world, one into which Sacco aims to bring us. Sacco has stated that he uses the fragmented captions to "emphasize a scattered feeling, that all sorts of things are going on at once" (Groth 2001: 63). They mimic the scattering of refugees and families broken up by conflict, and prompt the viewer to consider the questions posed by Sacco and, along with the non-frame as a whole, the wider context of the image. The captions take our eyes across the page, pulling us deeper into the text and the conflict until we are, to use a military phrase co-opted by journalists, "on the ground" with Sacco in Gorazde asking that great question along with the final caption of the spread: "How?" (2000:15).

In *Palestine* we are asked to look beyond the surface to see the often hidden trauma of a people under occupation. Sacco's Bosnian work features a conflict displayed in full color on the television news of the early 1990s. The roots of the conflict may be obscured by propaganda and misunderstanding, but the violent terror of the wars was readily accessible by audiences across the world. Sacco asks us to see beyond the wounds and to see people instead, to see the families and communities affected by war. Each of the scenes depicting the genocide in *Safe Area Gorazde* are contextualized and interrupted by more personal—and sometimes lighter—moments. The people whom Sacco befriends in Gorazde, including Edin and Riki, amuse themselves with the latest English idioms that they have learned; they ask for news on Hollywood movies and basketball and sing American pop songs such as "Born in the USA." In an interview with the *Comics Journal*, Sacco described how he wanted to avoid the individual stories and moments of trauma blending into one in order to show that "each horror is its own horror" (Groth 2001: 60). A consequence of this approach is the idea that each person is his/her own person. Even crowd scenes are filled with individually drawn faces in order, as Sacco states later in the interview, "to show that this is not a mass of humanity. These are individuals that make up this mass of humanity" (62).

Without Sacco's humanizing endeavor, his work would have been closer to one of the amateur videos of atrocity footage doing the rounds in Gorazde at the time of his visit. In the section of *Safe Area Gorazde* titled "Total War," he is urged to watch, along with his Turkish colleague Serif, one such trauma compilation tape: "You must look! You must look! She was a Serb!" (2000: 120). The reader is required to gauge the level of atrocity through the reactions of Sacco and Serif. They are being shown the video not for political or particular ideological reasons, but for money. Serif believes she can use the footage for Turkish television and asks for a price. Their host compels them to sit through a further hour and a half "while the video procession of dead children and shrieking parents went on and on" (2000: 121) until outside in the cold air away from the roaring stove, he finally names his price. It is, a caption informs us, "a figure so outrageous that it seemed to disgust Serif as much as all those full-colour images of the dismembered and the disemboweled" (2000: 121). Serif's objections to showing her audience the tape stems from both disgust at the images and the amount of money she would have to pay for it. Sacco does not have to pay to share it with his audience. His objection to showing the images from the video at that point seems to be that it lacks context and respectful commentary. He refuses to reproduce the tape if it is accompanied only by the cries of "Look!"

In the second part of "Total War," Sacco interviews the director of Gorazde's hospital, Dr. Alija Begovic. They sit in his office and watch the same video. This time the shouts of "You must look!" are replaced by Dr Begovic's professional commentary. We are shown the images only under the doctor's guidance as he recalls performing the operations that they are watching. Sacco allows himself to share the horror of war and its consequences for civilians but does so only within a context that respects people and their suffering. Throughout Sacco's war reporting we find an affirmation of life, even hope amid the gaping wounds, and there is a sense that though this may be happening far from the comfort of your sitting room, as you catch up with the latest from CNN, it matters to you as an individual making up the mass of humanity.

Sacco and the comic book have traveled a long way since the underground comix of the 1960s. He retains their energy and sense of political frustration and uses it to question the status quo. He presents uncomfortable ideas and situations and does not hide his hand as an artist to appear detached and objective. His personal approach owes much to the autobiographical tradition of the underground and alternative scene, but he does not fall into solipsism. Rather, he uses this form to engage with the people he meets and bring out their personalities as well as his own.

The images that he presents are often horrific. However, he shifts his work away from that of the shock artist feeding the fascination of a wound culture. He contextualizes the horrors within their own political and historical frames but, more importantly, he looks deeper than the grand sweep of history and finds the people affected by the trauma. It is by bringing attention to their individuality that we can begin to identify with them as people and not just canvasses for wounds for our fascination.

Finally, in a wordless spread from *The Fixer* (2004), Sacco trudges towards the Holiday Inn in Sarajevo. To his left lie two towers battered and scarred by the war. The imagery of a globalized American corporation standing near two buildings echoing New York's late landmark disturbs the reader with their familiarity (Sacco 2004: 12–13). These could be our streets. These could be our neighbors. It could even be ourselves pictured here. Based on *Palestine*, after *Safe Area Gorazde*, and Sacco's other war reportage, we can form through witnessing and sharing trauma an affirmation of another identity, not just that we are all perhaps "Palestinian, Muslim, or Bosnian now" but that we are all human, connected by something more fundamental than national boundaries.

Notes

This is a revised and updated version of an article that appeared as "Graphic Wounds: The Comics Journalism of Joe Sacco" in J. Skinner, ed., *Journeys: The International Journal of Travel and Travel Writing*, Special Edition, *Writing the Dark Side of Travel* 11, no. 1 (2010): 69–88.

Bibliography

Almond, M. 1994. *Europe's Backyard War: The War in the Balkans*. London: Mandarin.

Barker, M. 1984. *A Haunt of Fears: The Strange History of the British Horror Comics Campaign*. London: Pluto Press.

Cavanagh, J. R. 1949. "The Comics War." *Journal of Criminal Law and Criminology* 40(1): 18–22.

Children and Young Persons (Harmful Publications) Act. 1955. London: The Stationery Office.

Coard, R. L. 1955. "The Comic Book in Perspective." *Peabody Journal of Education* 33(1): 25–35.

Cumming, L. 2005. "The Artist Who Ain't Brougil," *Observer*, 3 April. Retrieved 17 May 2010 from http://www.guardian.co.uk/artanddesign/2005/apr/03/art.robertcrumb.

Daniels, L. 1971. *Comix: A History of Comic Books in America*. New York: Outerbridge & Dienstfrey.

Eisner, W. 2006. *Comics and Sequential Art*. Tamarac, FL: Poorhouse Press.

Estren, M. J. 1993. *A History of Underground Comics*. Berkeley, CA: Ronin.

Gravett, P. 2005. *Graphic Novels: Stories to Change Your Life*. London: Aurum.

Groth, G. 2001. *The Comics Journal Special Edition*, vol. 1, *Cartoonists on Cartooning*. Seattle, WA: Fantagraphics.

Herman, J. L. 1994. *Trauma and Recovery: From Domestic Abuse to Political Terror*. New York: Basic Books.

Hornby, L. G. 1926. *Balkan Sketches: An Artist's Wanderings in the Kingdom of the Serbs*. Boston: Little, Brown.

Hukanovic, R. 1998. *The Tenth Circle of Hell: A Memoir of Life in the Death Camps of Bosnia*. Trans. C. London and M. Ridjanovic. London: Abacus.

Jensen, K.T. 2007. *Red Eye, Black Eye*. Gainesville, Florida: Alternative Comics

Johnson, U. E. 1980. *American Prints and Printmakers: A Chronicle of Over 400 Artists and Their Prints from 1900 to the Present*. Garden City, NY: Doubleday.

Khalifa, O. 2008. "Joe Sacco on Palestine," *Al Jazeera*. Retrieved 17 May 2010 from http://english.aljazeera.net/news/middleeast/2007/11/2008525185042679346.html.

Kominsky-Crumb, A. 2007. *Need More Love*. London: MQ.

LaCapra, D. 2001. *Writing History, Writing Trauma*. Baltimore, MD: Johns Hopkins University Press.

Laub, D. 1992. "Bearing Witness or the Vicissitudes of Listening," in S. Felman and D. Laub (eds.), *Testimony: Crises of Witnessing in Literature, Psychoanalysis, and History*. New York: Routledge, 57–74.

LeBor, A. 2003. *Milosevic: A Biography*. London: Bloomsbury.

Malcolm, N. 2002. *Bosnia: A Short History*. London: Pan.

McCloud, S. 1993. *Understanding Comics: The Invisible Art*. New York: Harper Perennial.

Neufeld, J. 2004. *A few perfect hours (and other stories from Southeast Asia & Central Europe)*. Gainesville, Florida: Alternative Comics.

Nochlin, L. 1989. *The Politics of Vision: Essays on Nineteenth-Century Art and Society.* New York: Harper & Row.

Sabin, R. 1993. *Adult Comics: An Introduction.* London and New York: Routledge.

———. 2001. *Comics, Comix & Graphic Novels: A History of Graphic Novels.* London: Phaidon Press.

Sacco, J. 2000. *Safe Area Gorazde.* Seattle, WA: Fantagraphics Books.

———. 2003a. *Notes from A Defeatist.* London: Jonathan Cape.

———. 2003b. *Palestine.* London: Jonathan Cape.

———. 2004. *The Fixer: A Story from Sarajevo.* London: Jonathan Cape.

———. 2005. *War's End: Profiles from Bosnia, 1995–96.* Montreal and New York: Drawn & Quarterly.

Sells, M. A. 1996. *The Bridge Betrayed: Religion and Genocide in Bosnia.* Berkeley and London: University of California Press.

Seltzer, M. 1998. *Serial Killers: Death and Life In America's Wound Culture.* New York, London: Routledge.

Spiegelman, A. 1994a. "Mightier than the Sorehead: Drawing Pens and Politics." *The Nation,* 17 January: 45–54.

Spiegelman, A. 1994b. "Little Orphan Annie's Eyeballs." *The Nation,* 17 January.

Thompson, C. 2006. *Carnet de voyage.* Marietta, Georgia: Top Shelf Productions.

———. 2011. *Habibi.* London: Faber.

Versaci, R. 2007. *This Book Contains Graphic Language: Comics as Literature.* London: Continuum.

CHAPTER 4

Visiting Rwanda

Accounts of Genocide in Travel Writing

RACHEL MOFFAT

> Leontius ... was coming up from the Peiraeus ... when he saw some
> dead bodies lying near the executioner, and he felt a desire to look at
> them, and at the same time felt disgust at the thought, and tried to turn
> aside. For some time he fought with himself and put his hand over his
> eyes, but in the end the desire got the better of him, and opening his
> eyes wide with his fingers he ran forward to the bodies, saying
> "There you are, curse you, have your fill of the lovely spectacle."
>
> — Plato (2010)

Issues of dark tourism are generally focused on established memorial
sites, be these war cemeteries, Auschwitz, the Cambodian Killing Fields,
Graceland, or the location of the sinking of the Titanic. John Lennon
and Malcolm Foley emphasize that it is the events of recent history that
carry the greatest poignancy and meaning for visitors, introducing "anxiety and doubt about ... modernity and its consequences" (2000: 12).
This chapter discusses memorials and encounters that elicit the same
reactions. It excludes the analysis of issues of commercial tourism in
Rwanda; the tourist industry in Rwanda has only recently begun to develop as Rwandans gradually rebuild their society in the aftermath of
the 1994 genocide. I will focus predominantly on the accounts of two
individual visitors, Philip Gourevitch and Dervla Murphy, whose narratives of investigation and travel through Rwanda were published in
1998, long before the tourist trade had begun to recover.

The genocide in Rwanda in 1994 and the events that led up to it
have been described and analyzed in numerous narratives. Of the many
narratives that offer a thorough investigation and analysis of the historical background to the tensions between Hutus and Tutsis, as well

as a detailed account of events during the conflict and its aftermath, Gourevitch's *We Wish to Inform You That Tomorrow We Will Be Killed with Our Families* (1998) is among the most well-known and widely acclaimed texts. Gourevitch traveled to Rwanda as an experienced journalist who had previously been on the staff of the Jewish-American newspaper, the *Forward,* before joining the *New York Times.* He has been widely involved with various concerns, chairing the International Committee of PEN American Center and serving on the Council on Foreign Relations.

Gourevitch traveled to Rwanda in 1995 in order to find out "how Rwandans understood what had happened in their country, and how they were getting on in the aftermath" (1998: 7). Like many armchair travelers, Gourevitch initially followed the news of genocide in Rwanda while at home and far removed from the scene of the conflict. The scale of the violence shocked him, and he felt that being at such a distance impeded his ability to understand the genocide. He was also puzzled by the manner in which the violence was reported. In an interview with Harry Kreisler (2000) he notes that:

> nobody really had explained it. ... It was described as anarchy and chaos, which struck me as implausible simply because in order to kill at that clip requires ... method, it requires mobilization. ... Mass destruction is not arbitrary. ... I felt the story was being told wrong ... and that in some basic way a great calamity had happened which we were quite content to be ignorant of.

Gourevitch spent three years conducting research, interviewing victims of the attacks and those alleged to have carried them out, or to have been indirectly responsible in some way. His aim is to represent the horror of genocide as fully as possible and make the West aware of its far-reaching consequences.

Dervla Murphy is a prominent figure in modern travel writing, with a prolific output. Since her first major journey, cycling from Ireland to India in 1963, Murphy has traveled extensively, most often in remote areas of African and Asian countries, regularly publishing accounts of her travels. *Visiting Rwanda* (1998), Murphy's account of travels in former Zaire and Rwanda, is less well-known than Gourevitch's narrative but brings a unique perspective to studies of Rwanda, at least compared to those written in the few years following the genocide. Few people chose to travel in or around Rwanda for leisure at this time and, in fact, Murphy's extended visit to Rwanda apparently occurred by chance: her original aim had been to spend some time trekking in Zaire. Having spent a successful family holiday in Bukavu in 1996, she is emboldened to return in 1997 "in order to trek through the mountains of Kivu province" (Murphy 1998: 73). Certainly, it is not uncommon for Murphy to choose journeys that are regarded as unusual or even obscure. She does not, however, habitually travel through areas where conflict is still ongoing, preferring remote areas through which she may cycle or trek unhindered.

Unlike Gourevitch, and other researchers at this time, Murphy did not travel to Rwanda with the intention of collecting eyewitness accounts of genocide. The outbreak of civil war prevents Murphy from flying into Zaire, and she plans to make her way back to Bukavu from Kigali "and perhaps trek on into those unforgettable mountains" in Kivu Province (1998: 73). But Rwanda is still unstable three years after the height of the Hutu-Tutsi conflict. Murphy successfully travels as far as Gisenyi, near the border of Zaire, but roadblocks prevent her from traveling south to get nearer to Bukavu (1998: 104). She is soon forced to return to Kigali, where a security bulletin issued to aid workers clarifies the situation: travel, other than commuting to and from Kigali, is discouraged due to more outbreaks of violence (1998: 126). She becomes the guest of aid workers in the region who take her to see how people are now living after the conflict (1998: 127).

This change of plan alters the nature of Murphy's narrative that is considerably different from her other publications: *Visiting Rwanda* becomes more journalistic, recording accounts of personal tragedies and giving background information to place individual histories in their wider context. Jeremy Gavron comments that *Visiting Rwanda* is

> barely a travel book. Murphy bravely tries to make it into one, but on a succession of sinister hillsides she is forced to turn back, and in the end the only travelling she does is in the relative safety of aid-agency Land Rovers, transmuted by danger and horror from a traveller into a journalist, a witness. (1998: 30)

Although Murphy's travel plans are proven to be impractical, the focus of her narrative is still ostensibly travel rather than investigation. Murphy wishes to make her audience aware of the scale of human suffering that she encounters but endeavors to maintain her role as a traveler rather than to accept a new role as reporter.

Both writers interrogate the practice of gathering highly sensitive information. The decision to look or not to look is determined by their different conceptions of their roles. George Steiner highlights the difficulty of investigating atrocity:

Not only is the relevant material vast and intractable: it exercises a subtle, corrupting fascination. Bending too fixedly over hideousness, one feels queerly drawn. ... I am not sure whether anyone, however scrupulous, who spends time and imaginative resources on these dark places, can, or indeed, ought to leave them personally intact. Yet the dark places are at the centre. Pass them by and there can be no serious discussion of the human potential. (1971: 32; see also Lennon and Foley 2000: 28)

As a journalist, Gourevitch forces himself to look; Murphy, the travel writer, may look away and choose not to ask questions. Both are cognizant of the impact that the knowledge of genocide has on them. Gourevitch explains his compulsion to look, the need to bend "too fixedly over hideousness" (1971: 32). Murphy may step back in her text if she feels overwhelmed by the knowledge of such atrocities.

The issue of looking at horror also raises questions about whether, by publishing their accounts, there is any way for writers such as Gourevitch and Murphy to avoid a kind of exploitation of horror. Is it possible for writers to give their audiences a greater awareness of crimes against humanity without, to some degree, benefiting themselves? To some extent, the development of official memorial centers in Rwanda perhaps sheds some light on this issue. In Rwanda's reemerging tourist industry there is a clear agenda not only to create specific sites where Rwandans may mourn or contemplate this period in their history but also to offer information to foreign visitors, promoting awareness of the events that have so radically impacted upon modern Rwandan society.

Gourevitch and Murphy in Rwanda

In the light of dark tourism, it is Murphy's experience that corresponds more closely to definitions suggested by Lennon and Foley, for whom "the basis of dark tourism" consists of "those who visit due to serendipity, the itinerary of tour companies or the merely curious who happen to be in the vicinity" (2000: 23). This description is realized more accurately, if unintentionally, in Murphy's chance visits to survivors than Gourevitch's three-year research program, although of course, neither Murphy's nor Gourevitch's travels are undertaken in the context of structured tourism.

Indeed, Murphy has made it clear on a number of occasions that she dislikes tourists and is anxious to distance herself from being described as such. As Patrick Holland and Graham Huggan point out: "Contemporary travel writers ... pride themselves on being individualists" and distance themselves, at times with irony, "from the vulgar herd" (Holland and Huggan 2000: viii). Murphy does not employ irony in her reaction to commercial tourism; she avoids it as far as possible and expresses her distaste when she encounters it. In South Africa, for example, she is outraged to hear of plans for the construction of a road through rural areas near Mafefe: "The sheer crassness of it ... to destroy a prosperous community while exposing such an ecologically precious corner to the physical and spiritual pollutions of motorized mass-tourism" (Murphy 1997: 47).

But her identity as a traveler is a little complicated: she travels as a professional writer in order to make a living, but each journey is also undertaken for pleasure and as something of a holiday, although a challenging one, which extends over a period of several months. She describes her trek from Kenya to Zimbabwe as "self-prescribed unwinding therapy" (Murphy 1993: 1). Murphy's journeys, therefore, fall within the definition of tourism, albeit in a general way, whereas Gourevitch is conducting research.

It is arguable that Murphy becomes a sort of dark tourist in Rwanda. She did not travel there with the intention of investigating the genocide, and in this respect she differs from tourists who plan to visit memorial sites. But, being unable to travel without the protection of aid agencies, Murphy's daily encounters with survivors results in a very dark tour indeed. Jeremy Gavron (1998: 30) calls Murphy a journalist and the last part of *Visiting Rwanda* does resemble reportage. As I have suggested, Murphy does not always behave as Gourevitch does: she does not enquire minutely into the details of the genocide as a reporter must. By contrast, Gourevitch's travels were undertaken from the start with a view towards investigating the development of the violence and the international reaction. From the beginning of his narrative, Gourevitch sets out to take his readers on a dark tour in an attempt to clarify what has occurred.

Because it is impossible to be in Rwanda without hearing and understanding something about the genocide, it is inevitable that there are similarities between the two narratives. In both, horrific personal accounts stand out more than summaries of historical background. Both include eyewitness accounts to enable a fuller understanding for readers who will not hear such accounts first-hand. Gourevitch recounts events at the Seventh Day Adventist mission in Mugonero, a complex that included medical and educational facilities as well as a church. Many Tutsis congregated there after fleeing their own homes, bringing accounts of the violence in their home towns or villages:

In Gishyita, the mayor had been so frantic in his impatience to kill Tutsis that thousands had been slaughtered, even as he herded them to the church, where the remainder were massacred. ... In Rwamatamu, more than ten thousand Tutsis had taken refuge in the town hall, and the mayor had brought in truckloads of policemen ... and militia with guns. ... Behind them he had arranged villagers with machetes in case anyone escaped when the shooting began—and, in fact, there had been very few escapees from Rwamatamu. (1998: 27)

In Mugonero, roughly two thousand refugees made their way to the mission complex. As a hiding place it was ineffectual: "Nobody could leave; militiamen and members of the Presidential Guard had cordoned off the complex" (1998: 27). Those taking shelter were relying on the intervention of those who ran the mission, but no one was forthcoming; the refugees were informed that they would be attacked on 16 April and that they "must be eliminated" (1998: 28). An eyewitness, Samuel, recalls this terrible instruction:

> There were many attackers. ... They killed the people at the chapel and the school and then the hospital. ... The local citizenry also helped. Those who had no guns, only machetes. ... In the evening ... they began firing tear gas. People who were still alive cried. That way the attackers knew where people were, and they could kill them directly. (1998: 29)

Such accounts are typical of the reports that Gourevitch receives from survivors, and most chapters include eyewitness accounts that give greater depth to the historical overview.

The stories that Murphy hears are gathered as she travels with aid workers and meets fragmented groups of survivors who have lost their friends and family but must now try to continue with their lives. One of the most striking reports is her encounter with a woman whose experience illustrates the impossibility for many to return to anything resembling a normal life: "An elderly barefooted woman ... suddenly rushed towards me. When I extended a hand she seized my forearms, stared intently into my eyes ... then hugged me with manic strength. ... Her face was anguished, her speech a hysterical babbling" (1998: 177).

Murphy learns from an unnamed source that this woman's name is Alphonsine. She was a Hutu who had married a Tutsi and saw "her own brothers ... hacking her husband to death" (1998: 177). Members of the *interahamwe* (those who stand together), "always including her brothers," visited Alphonsine's house "three times within a month" to search for her eight children, who were killed (177). Alphonsine "successfully smuggled two grandchildren ... to a distant friend's [house]" (177–78).

She returned to collect them when a doctor who had been involved in organizing the violence in that area

> called a public meeting and announced that order had been restored, the *interahamwe* disbanded and everyone could come out of hiding. Next day, when Alphonsine fetched her grandchildren from their refuge, they were murdered at a roadblock—as were all the other Tutsi who had believed the doctor. She tried to hang herself but failed. Then she went mad. (178)

Murphy offers no further comment on this account; her narrative moves on to other events. This abrupt transferal leaves the shocking account to speak for itself, and yet it is not clear whether Murphy felt unable to add her own observations, or whether the sudden change of subject was deliberately brutal so that the stark contrast would add greater pathos to the account.

Reporting Horror

Both writers understand the problematic nature of being an observer of human suffering and, for Murphy, this sometimes results in her decision not to ask for more details. Gourevitch, who chooses to reveal horror as bluntly as possible, discusses the ethical problems of making such a close investigation of horrific and emotionally sensitive events, using Plato's account of Leontius to present the dilemma of wishing to know but feeling disgust at one's curiosity. As a parallel to Leontius's experience, Gourevitch describes the sight of bodies in a church in Nyarabuye where many Tutsis had been killed in 1994 and uses this explicitly graphic account to discuss the issue of the morality of such close scrutiny: "They had been killed thirteen months earlier, and they hadn't been moved. Skin stuck here and there over the bones. ... The more complete figures looked a lot like people, which they were once" (1998: 15). Gourevitch is careful to point out that the grotesque and vivid details interest him "only insofar as a precise memory of the offense is necessary to understand its legacy." But he admits an uneasiness when addressing his readers: "I presume you are reading this because you desire a closer look, and that you, too, are properly disturbed by your curiosity" (1998: 19).

Gourevitch admits his personal disquiet and, at the same time, assumes that his readers experience a similar dilemma, indicating the moral ambivalence of the act of reading as well as the act of writing. Gourevitch's dilemma is whether his scrutiny involves an inappropriate desire to look on appalling sights and to hear horrific and graphic accounts of murder, violence, and rape. The reader's dilemma is whether or not choosing to read such an account suggests an equally morbid curiosity. Gourevitch's answer is that "the best reason I have come up with for looking closely into Rwanda's stories is that ignoring them makes me even more uncomfortable about existence and my place in it" (1998: 19). He relies on his overall purpose to soften his unabashed gaze: "Those dead Rwandans will be with me forever, I expect ... I had felt compelled to come to Nyarubuye: to be stuck ... with the experience of looking at them" (1998: 16).

Murphy expresses a similar sentiment: "Deeply disturbing as are the minute details of the genocide, we do need to confront them, to remember them" (1998: 118). It is also important to note that Murphy, although aware of the importance of understanding the extent of genocide's brutality, cannot always bring herself to inquire as minutely as Gourevitch. She hears many tragic accounts, and these become the most memorable details of her text, but she does not make gathering information her priority because she does not like inquiring into people's tragedies unless they choose to tell her. Murphy has shown this reluctance in an earlier text, *The Ukimwi Road* (1993). In Uganda in 1992, locals suggest that she interview AIDS patients: "See those people? They're waiting for the AIDS clinic to open. Go and talk to them, they'll give you something real to write about" (1993: 55), implying that any other material Murphy had gathered is in some way unreal or insignificant compared with the accounts of those who were suffering. Murphy eventually agrees to talk to the AIDS patients but reluctantly, as she is very sensitive about approaching them: "I'm not a journalist looking for a story, I'd prefer not to intrude" (1993: 55).

Similarly, in Rwanda, Murphy turns away at times. While visiting a health center near Kigali she notes: "a long, red-brick, two-storey seminary" adjacent to the center (1998: 147). The seminary was "now derelict, all its windows broken, its doors removed, every fitting looted, the floors and walls still darkly stained. I didn't ask 'What's the story?' I don't want to hear any more of those stories" (1998: 147). Murphy, who has not traveled to Rwanda to investigate the killings, finds it necessary to turn away when she feels overwhelmed. She is not obliged to look or listen in the same way that Gourevitch must, and she need not ask questions if she does not want to. By contrast, because Gourevitch has a deliberate purpose in Rwanda, he forces himself to look: "I had never been among the dead before. What to do? Look? Yes. I wanted to see them, I suppose; I had come to see them ... and there they were so intimately exposed" (1998: 15–16).

Both narratives remain problematic. The sensational nature of the accounts complicates the fact that both writers gain material benefit from writing about their experience. It is true that both express the wish to bring greater awareness to a wider audience. Both writers can claim to have increased the awareness of their readers, but their self-promotion is intrinsically involved in the popularity of their narratives. It is important to ask, then, to what extent the writers may be perceived to have exploited tragedy in order to market their work.

The Question of Exploitation

Published in 1998, Gourevitch's account was highly acclaimed, winning a number of awards including the National Book Critics Circle award and the Guardian First Book award. It was subsequently translated into ten languages. As far as promoting awareness of the conflict in Rwanda and its consequences, *We Wish to Inform You* has been a significant success. Gourevitch's career and his five years as the editor of the *Paris Review* do not rest solely on the success of one book, but its popularity was a significant factor in the subsequent development of his career. *Visiting Rwanda* has made little such impact, and Murphy does not appear to have benefited far beyond her usual aspirations to maintain her living and traveling costs. But this is the pattern of Murphy's life: since 1965, the publication of her work has allowed her to maintain what many would consider a privileged standard of living. Overall, however, the modest success of *Visiting Rwanda* might ironically be perceived as morally less problematic, despite the fact that Gourevitch's popularity has enabled him to inform a far wider audience.

Gourevitch's reputation as a journalist depends on discerning what information most successfully attracts public attention. A more mercenary motive may exist alongside the desire to bring awareness, but this is necessary for professional writers. It is difficult to attach genuinely innocent motives to such writers; the success of Gourevitch's goal depends on a wide readership, and with this comes inevitable recognition for the writer. It is not likely, however, that he could have anticipated the extent of his narrative's success and the consequent acclaim. A degree of self-promotion is inevitable in the travel writing industry, but Gourevitch's primary motivation is humanitarian: he wants to raise awareness of the conflict in Rwanda, particularly in light of the response of the international community.

The explicit details in both narratives probably horrify their readers, but the texts create different overall impressions. Murphy's narrative is

less focused than Gourevitch's, as reports of genocide compete with earlier accounts of her visit to Zaire. The first section of her narrative contains pleasant and amusing accounts of her holiday in Bukavu in 1996
that are dominated by anecdotes about her first grandchild. Murphy
returns to Africa in 1997, and the narrative follows her unsuccessful attempts to trek in Zaire and Rwanda. Unable to progress alone, Murphy
must accept the hospitality of aid workers, which at least enables her to
travel to areas around Kigali in relative safety.

It is at this point that genocide becomes the central focus of the narrative. Murphy's prologue gives a brief overview of the 1994 events, and
she has made some reference to the historical background of the tensions
between Hutus and Tutsis (1998: 88–89), but, up to this point, Murphy
has dwelt in much greater detail on the events of her own journeys.
Arguably, this attempt to make her text a travel narrative risks trivial-
izing genocide by giving equal prominence in her narrative to more light-
hearted travel stories.

Murphy's title, *Visiting Rwanda,* implies that the text deals with the
subject of genocide but Gourevitch's title, which invokes the plea made
by Tutsi victims at Mugonero to a pastor and the mayor (1998: 28, 42),
immediately demands an emotional response from the reader. Gourevitch later tells the story in some detail, from the perspective of survivors
and alleged perpetrators (1998: 25–31, 40–43), using this poignant and
ultimately hopeless plea to illustrate the desperation that characterizes
all reports of genocide. Having created this general impression in his
title, Gourevitch then reinforces the sense of intense desperation in his
first chapter, revealing something of the extremity of horror in Rwanda
by describing the carnage at Nyarabuye. But it is important to note that
this was not one of the first places he visited. Rather than documenting
his research chronologically, he arranges details to achieve the greatest
emotional impact.

Both narratives are deliberately shocking for the reader, and Gourevitch, in particular, augments the horror of what he sees and hears by
relating potentially controversial details of his experience as an observer.
He describes an incident at Nyarabuye where he hears "a crunch" and
realizes that the Canadian Colonel accompanying him has stepped "on
a skull and broken it." Gourevitch feels "a small but keen anger at this
man." Then he hears "another crunch" and feels "a vibration underfoot.
I had stepped on one too" (1998: 20). The shock value of this incident
is based on the carelessness of the Colonel and Gourevitch. It certainly
implies that there were so many skulls on the ground that it was hard to
avoid treading on them, but, even so, their mistake seems disrespectful.
Gourevitch narrates the incident as though he does not realize what will

happen, and his admission acts as a punchline intensifying the disturbing impact of the story. Although it does not reflect well on himself, Gourevitch appears to have maximized the shock value of this account in order to increase its potential impact on his readership.

Neither Gourevitch nor Murphy write simply to appall their readers: both want to stimulate a more definite reaction. The narratives are deliberately constructed to elicit a specific response from the audience. Murphy's narrative urges her readers "to put pressure on the 'international community' to fund the Rwandan government's effort to punish, proportionately, the organizers and perpetrators" (1998: 202). Her reaction to what she has encountered is to focus on an appropriate form of justice, and her idea of proportionate punishment includes the execution of those who have organized the massacres. She admits that "all my life I have passionately opposed capital punishment," but her experience forces her to revise this position: "Now I see the execution by the state of the organizers of the genocide as necessary. ... I am convinced that the creation of an atmosphere in which reconciliation will be possible requires the judicial killing of the organizers" (1998: 202).

Murphy acknowledges that the Rwandans who are rebuilding their country and their communities must forget the past to some extent if the future is to be peaceful, but she feels that there can be no sense of security or reconciliation if the threat of organized genocide is not removed entirely. The trials are still ongoing and have progressed only slowly. The death penalty was part of the Rwandan justice system at the time, the last execution being in 1998. But the government was not intent on executing everyone who had carried out genocide or even those who had organized it (BBC 2007).

Gourevitch indicates that President Paul Kagame is also willing to implement the more radical policy of forgiveness: "You can't give up on ... such a person ... some people can ... benefit from being forgiven" (1998: 312–13). Kagame is asking for a more complete sort of forgetfulness, one that allows the guilty to live and be assimilated into their culture again in order to avoid "another round of mass butchery," this time of the guilty (1998: 311). Kagame believed that Rwanda had "no alternative," although Gourevitch notes that, of course, "many survivors ... [do] not share Kagame's view" (1998: 312–13).

Gourevitch does not specifically exhort his readers to a particular action as Murphy does, but his arguments reveal that he is appalled by the failure of the international community to uphold the Genocide Convention of 1946 and intervene on behalf of the Tutsis. He argues that Western integrity is called into question when historical atrocities such as the Jewish Holocaust are deprecated but equivalent atrocities occurring in the present day are effectively ignored. He draws attention to the fact that in 1946 the General Assembly of the United Nations drew up the Convention on the Prevention and Punishment of the Crime of Genocide that obliged the signatories to "undertake to prevent and to punish … acts committed with intent to destroy … a national, ethnical, racial or religious group" (1998: 149). Gourevitch comments that "denouncing evil is a far cry from doing good" and that "it's pretty easy to take the right position on the Holocaust" after the event (Kreisler 2000), but faced with evidence of similar aggression in Rwanda, the international community did not respond at any point. Gourevitch concludes: "The fundamental lesson of Rwanda is that we are not serious about genocide prevention. … Rwanda was the test, and … [there was no intervention because] there was no strategic interest. There was no economic interest. The only claim that Rwanda laid on us was fellow humanity, and that's not enough" (Kreisler 2000).

Gourevitch's response shows as much outrage as Murphy's, but his anger is directed primarily at the international community and the United Nations. Instead of discussing methods of punishment, Gourevitch argues that the international community is too apt to forget the horrors of genocide. He is concerned that the memory of Rwanda may not result in intervention of future genocides any more than the memory of the Jewish Holocaust provoked intervention on behalf of the Tutsis. TV journalist John Simpson expressed the same concern in 2005 in reference to the conflict in Darfur, stating, "We haven't yet managed to persuade those who think they can slaughter people as a matter of policy that they will inevitably pay a price for doing so." There has since been a response to conflict in Darfur, although it took five years for the United Nations to mobilize troops for the protection of civilians. The international community does intervene at times, but not with much consistency.

Both writers, therefore, acknowledge the need to grieve and respond to the impact of such widespread violence in Rwanda and the destruction of social and cultural stability. But part of this response involves forgetting the past and moving on, even from the horror of atrocities that arose from tensions within Rwandan communities and families. It is significant that Gourevitch is Jewish and Murphy is Irish; both carry the awareness of tragic grievances in the history of their cultures, most recently figured in the Holocaust and the Troubles. Although Murphy does not refer to it, she understands the national fragmentation and disruption that occurs when communities deliberately remember grievances that were inflicted many years ago, as indicated in her analysis of life in Northern Ireland, *A Place Apart* (1978). As Gourevitch observes, the deliberate remembering of past war crimes is only useful if it results in preventive measures being taken to protect other ethnic groups from the same suffering. Toni Morrison recognizes the twin need to memorialize and to forget in her *Beloved* (1987): its last chapter is punctuated by three reminders that the story the novel tells is "not a story to pass on." That is to say, it is not a story to pass on to others in order to keep grievances alive, but neither is it a story to pass on or to forget (1987: 274–75). This paradox informs the work of both Gourevitch and Murphy. Like the horrors of slavery, Rwanda's genocide requires the near-impossible conjunction of remembering and forgetting.

Memorials in Rwandan Tourism

There are over two hundred sites in Rwanda that mark the violence that was carried out during the genocide. The most prominent of these is the international memorial centre at Kigali that has sponsored the development of memorials at seven other sites at places such as Nyarabuye, Murambi, and Ntarama. These places offer Rwandans fixed points around which to focus their mourning, and, like similar sites around the world, they starkly reveal the nature of human atrocity to visitors, deliberately prompting the interrogation of modernity and its values as articulated by Lennon and Foley (2000). These sites were not tourist destinations in 1998, although they have since become so, and neither Gourevitch nor Murphy suggest that readers need to visit Rwanda. They do not discuss the idea of people traveling to look at the memorial sites, and this suggests that they consider it neither necessary or appropriate. Their purpose, as they perceive it, is to bridge the gap between Rwanda and their readers—not to encourage sightseeing—so that people will put pressure on the international community to intervene on behalf of Rwanda's justice system and, in the long term, on behalf of other communities who are subjected to genocide.

It is also important to note the fact that memorial sites are now tourist destinations and that they are deliberately promoted as such by Rwandans who do not want the world to forget the impact of genocide or the particular circumstances of Rwanda's conflict. Memorial sites, such as Nyarabuye where skulls originally lay underfoot, have since been organized more formally, corresponding to a number of other sites around the world. Lennon and Foley observe, for example, that artifacts at Auschwitz I include "mounds of spectacles, shoes or artificial limbs" and that "[e]xhibits such as these have become images to be replicated the world over in the interpretation of such sites" (2000: 24, 25). At Choeng Ek, the most notorious of the Cambodian Killing Fields, skulls are displayed in order to convey to visitors some idea of the scale of the atrocity. Images of prisoners at Tuol Sleng Prison in Phnom Penh highlight the poignancy of so many individual tragedies. Memorials in Rwanda follow the same pattern: bones and skulls are arranged on tables, clothes and shoes are displayed separately. In some places, such as Murambi, bodies preserved in lye are put on display (Sharp 2007).

The Kigali Memorial Centre has been "designed to engage and challenge an international visitor base" (Kigali Memorial Centre 2009). The personal, national, and international consequences of genocide are represented to provoke a response from visitors. The center is adjacent to eight mass graves; part of its function is as "a place in which the bereaved could bury their families and friends" (Kigali Memorial Centre 2009). The permanent exhibition presents the history of the genocide and its aftermath; clothes and photographs emphasize the personal impact of the violence. Outside is a Wall of Names, to which names are still being added, and a world map that invokes reflections on genocide in its historical and international context. Furthermore, as Sally Emerson (2009: 6) observes, "All tourists are encouraged to go to the museum" in order to gain some insight into the scale of the violence, the debilitation and gradual renewal of Rwandan society, and the continued impact of such a conflict on day-to-day life in the years that have followed.

The number of genocide memorial centers in Rwanda indicates the emphasis that is placed on remembrance and promoting awareness. The construction of these centers has revealed problematic aspects in the issues of remembrance: at Murambi many locals "were suspicious of the memorial. ... It was widely believed that the memorial was being designed to stir up hatred against the Hutus" (Murambi Memorial Exhibit: 2009). The center has attempted to address this issue, and this has presented further complications. The attempt to create a balanced representation by finding Hutus who had protected Tutsis revealed that some of these rescuers had also killed other Tutsis, leading to more problematic conclusions about their roles as rescuers. A survivor, Emmanuel Mugenzira, whose family was killed, observes that such complications pose a challenge to reconciliation and rehabilitation in Rwanda: "There are people who committed genocide and are involved in *Gacaca* [community justice], so I don't know how they'll conclude some of the cases. I think they might cover up some things because these people might be accused as well" (Murambi Memorial Exhibit 2009).

Conclusion

The narratives this chapter discusses prefigure the reemergence of tourism in Rwanda since 1994. Both Gourevitch and Murphy publicize the facts of genocide in Rwanda by taking their readers on a dark tour of memorial sites augmented by the stories of survivors. Although not tourists themselves, at least in a commercial sense, the travel writers are both still outsiders, the observers of horror who are faced with the decision to look or to turn away. They must also engage with the moral issue of whether their behavior reflects a morbid curiosity or a more compassionate desire to acknowledge the intensity of such atrocity.

Both writers make it clear that their decision to publish is connected to their conviction that the knowledge they have gained—in particular the individual accounts of suffering—must be communicated both to promote awareness of the scale of human tragedy in Rwanda and to memorialize those who were killed. The decision to publish does raise questions of the possible exploitation of horror, but it could be said that Gourevitch and Murphy do no more than the Rwandans themselves. Of course, there is profit both in publishing narratives about genocide and incorporating memorial sites into the nation's tourist trade, but it seems a necessary promotion. What exists of ghoulish curiosity in this dark tourism is challenged by the need to know, to understand, and to remember the impact of genocide.

Notes

This is a revised and updated version of an article that appeared as "Visiting Rwanda: Accounts of Genocide in Travel Writing" in J. Skinner, ed. (2010) *Journeys: The International Journal of Travel and Travel Writing*, Special Edition, *Writing the Dark Side of Travel* 11, no. 1 (2010): 89–106.

Bibliography

BBC News. 2007. "Rwanda Scraps the Death Penalty." Retrieved 2 December 2010 from http://news.bbc.co.uk/1/hi/world/africa/6735435.stm.

Emerson, S. 2009. "Welcome Back to Rwanda." *Sunday Times*, 8 November, 6.

Gavron, J. 1998. "Journey among the Ghosts." *Times Literary Supplement*, 11 December. Retrieved 2 December 2010 from http://www.timesonline.co.uk.

Gourevitch, P. 1998. *We Wish to Inform You That Tomorrow We Will Be Killed with Our Families: Stories from Rwanda*. New York: Farrar, Straus and Giroux.

Holland, P. and G. Huggan. 2000. *Tourists with Typewriters: Critical Reflections on Contemporary Travel Writing*. Ann Arbor: University of Michigan Press.

Kigali Memorial Centre. 2009. "Kigali Memorial Centre." Retrieved 2 December 2010 from http://www.kigalimemorialcentre.org/old/centre/index.html.

Kreisler, H. 2000. "Conversations with History: Reporting the Story of a Genocide." Retrieved 2 December 2010 from http://globetrotter.berkeley.edu/people/Gourevitch/gourevitch-con0.html.

Lennon, J. and M. Foley. 2000. *Dark Tourism: The Attraction of Death and Disaster.* London and New York: Continuum.

Morrison, T. 1987. *Beloved.* London: Chatto & Windus.

Murambi Memorial Exhibit. 2009. "Murambi Memorial Exhibit." Retrieved 2 December 2010 from http://www.cnlg.gov.rw/sites/murambi/pages/murambi-2.htm.

Murphy, D. 1978. *A Place Apart.* London: John Murray.

———. 1993. *The Ukimwi Road: From Kenya to Zimbabwe.* London: John Murray.

———. 1997. *South from the Limpopo: Travels through South Africa.* London: John Murray.

———. 1998. *Visiting Rwanda.* Dublin: Lilliput Press.

Plato. 2010. *The Republic IV.* Retrieved 12 December 2010 from http://www.bostonleadershipbuilders.com/plato/republic/book4.htm.

Sharp, J. 2007. "Rwanda Genocide Memorial." Retrieved 2 December 2010 from http://www.pri.org/theworld/?q=node/7997.

Simpson, J. 2005. "War Crimes—Have We Learned Anything?" Retrieved 2 December 2010 from http://news.bbc.co.uk/1/hi/world/europe/4456043.stm.

Steiner, G. 1971. *In Bluebeard's Castle: Some Notes towards the Re-Definition of Culture.* London: Faber and Faber.

CHAPTER 5

Walking Back to Happiness?

Modern Pilgrimage and the Expression of Suffering on Spain's Camino de Santiago

KEITH EGAN

> Where does it start? Muscles tense. One leg a pillar, holding the
> body upright between the earth and the sky. The other a pendulum,
> swinging from behind. Heel touches down, the whole weight of the
> body rolls forward onto the ball of the foot. The big toe pushes off,
> and the delicately balanced weight of the body shifts again ... the
> most obvious and the most obscure thing in the world, this walking
> that wanders so readily into religion, philosophy, landscape, urban
> policy, anatomy, allegory and heartbreak.
>
> (Solnit 2002: 3)

Rebecca Solnit's walk through the history and philosophy of pedestrianism sketches a pastoral idyll of slow bipedal progression that stands
opposed to the encroachment of modernity. For her, walking involves
a space and a practice that can remain transcendent in its mundane-
ness, generating "the time inbetween" (Solnit 2002: xiii) for a productive wastefulness conducive to self-becoming. It is this experience of
movement, walking as empowerment, that resonates with contemporary
pilgrims to the Camino de Santiago. The Camino, a medieval pilgrimage route across Europe to Santiago de Compostela in Galicia, northern
Spain, where the bones of Saint James are reputedly interred, takes up
to one month to finish and annually draws hundreds of thousands of
pilgrims from around the world. The pilgrimage's allure among non-
Spanish walkers (and cyclists) is often not particularly religious, though
the increasing popularity of the route can be seen as a response to the
pressures of modern life by engaging nostalgically with nature and the

past in a manner characteristic of post-industrial Western societies (Reader 2007: 9).[1] Enthusiastic pilgrims engage with ideas of authentic travel on the pilgrimage as a type of spiritual tourism where the term *spiritual* acts to mediate between the secular traditions from which the pilgrims arrive on the pilgrimage and the institutional religious formation of what is for most a cultural pilgrimage into a religious activity.[2]

To talk of a culture of the Camino can be to invoke a too-rigid notion of what culture actually can be on a month-long pilgrimage stretched nearly a thousand kilometers; the utopian goal of *communitas* cannot be an enduring reality. It is also a mistake to believe that tropes shaping our habitual being are more real than actual people. Writing in the foreword to Nigel Rapport's *I Am Dynamite*, Michael Jackson (2003: xii) states unequivocally that the symbols that hold our attention are empty ciphers; it is our creative capacity for connection and communication that fills them: "Social and cultural macrocosms have no reality except through the energy, creativity and will that individuals impart to them." Daniel (1987: 288) too, argues against an overemphasis on symbols and the systematicity of culture, both of which denigrate the value of indices and icons in the analysis of cultural contact.

My research brought me to the Camino de Santiago on foot, following pilgrims along the Camino for four weeks at a time, teasing out their complex motivations. Why did they remove themselves for such long periods from their lives in order to trek along the pilgrimage route? The overlapping, ambiguous, and powerful motivations seemed to suggest the prevalence of existential pilgrims, people not reliant on religious affiliation or spiritual inclination as primary motivators. Many pilgrims had reached a point of stagnation or depression at home. They had become desperate for a means to overcome disorientation and stasis by absenting themselves, casting off certain aspects of their identity and obligations in order to rediscover a sense of purpose, direction, and momentum (Rapport 2003). The people in this chapter are reconfiguring relationships and delaying meanings. Through three core vignettes I highlight the centrality of intersubjective moments in the pilgrimage's successful outcome. The pilgrimage itself provides a context for meetings between strangers in ad hoc communities of interpretation during the day's fluctuating rhythms. New experiences emerge in the struggle, and people use them to narrate their lives and thus exercise some control. In three key relationships—between John and his deceased sister; between Michael and me, his confidant; and between Thomas and Helene, an elderly Norwegian couple revisiting the pilgrimage decades later—I explore how each of these meetings lies at the limits of meaning between selves in motion and the intricate intersubjective encounters that shape the contours of the pilgrimage experience for all of us.

The paradox of the *communitas* being robustly ephemeral allows people to do their work on the Camino by temporarily suspending other problems in order to answer the deeper existential call of lives searching for purpose, direction, poetry, and, that most fragile of human qualities, hope. It is the fragility of the *communitas* that is celebrated, through drinking and laughter, philosophies espoused, and life-stories revealed in the heat of the moment and forgotten the following day. The many opportunities to come together at liturgical celebrations, the shared meals at refuges, the performance of a *quiemada* (traditional drink and drinking), and the pilgrim mass at the cathedral in Santiago are nodal points of contact and interaction. Pilgrims, however, spend much more time in the flux of the pilgrimage, moving between groups and towns on the trails in search of what has eluded them at home. As a result, many pilgrims move with Matsuo Bashō's much-quoted words "Every day is a journey and the journey itself is home" (Bashō 1998: 3) echoing in their steps.

Reclaiming time from a period of unsatisfying employment and family duties to recharge, embarking on an adventure, and escaping into therapeutic experience are common themes among pilgrims.[3] The trip also attracts pilgrims in their late teens enjoying the opportunity to travel Europe on foot. Yet the protracted temporality of walking and immersing oneself in Spain—through its food, beds, peoples, language, heat, and nature—brings about a much more profound experience the longer one travels. For most Camino pilgrims, walking becomes a convincing alternative to what Solnit calls modern "Sisyphean" gyms—arenas that remove space as a coordinate of exertion—where muscles, "like tans ... are an aesthetic of the obsolete" (2002: 261). In these terms, walking can also be a reaction to the privatization of public space that transforms city wanderers into potential loiterers and a defense against the "suburbanisation of the modern psyche" (Solnit 2002: 249). She offers the slow, meaningful amble through main streets and rustic byways as a curative and a corrective for the maladies of modernity—a more authentic pedestrianism to counteract the existential inertia of contemporary civilization. Those who adopt this modern calisthenic spirituality brave the difficult trek with stories that have refused to bleed: stories often too difficult, too personal to talk of directly. These stories are instead taken on a journey where they can be traced out on a landscape and shared in new and exciting ways among fellow travelers who hold little else in common but the road ahead.

Stories are itineraries that engage pilgrims bodily through the extended ritual activity of walking (Tweed 2006). These stories help to invent coping strategies by enlisting bodies to work out and walk out a response to personal difficulties and crises. Journeys, de Botton (2002: 57) commented, can become "midwives for thought." They can help an abstract cognitive process become "a physical rhythmic act" (Solnit 2002: 13) where the body can think itself through the landscape of the mind. The Camino thus embodies an emergent "avenue of objectification"—of taking inner experience and bringing it out of "the inarticulate pre-language of 'cries and whispers' into the realm of shared objectification, where it could be recognized, shared and acknowledged" (Scarry cited in Orsi 1996: 135). In this new terrain a more critical experience implicates sexuality and spirituality in what anthropologist Michael Jackson calls our shared "struggle for being," where these stories are not narrative fictions; rather they are existential strategies for coping with the fact that being is "both scarce and unequally distributed" (Jackson 2005: 182, 186). They are spatial practices rather than constrained, implicit, or elaborated textualities: "Walking affirms, suspects, tries out, transgresses, respects, etc., the trajectories it "speaks"" (de Certeau 1977: 99). Pilgrims, especially, compose these "walking rhetorics" (de Certeau 1977: 100). Walking is thus, as Solnit (2002: 250) puts it, "a cultural activity ... an ancient and profound relationship between body, world and imagination." There is an isomorphism, then, between metaphors of visceral bodies and social bodies as paths and roads, durable tropes of intersubjectivity that capture the fluctuations of ontological insecurity "driv[ing] people relentlessly to recover and sustain their sense of Being in the face of forces that threaten to reduce them to nothingness" (Jackson 1998: 192).

The interconnectedness between existential and spatial orientation is a valuable resource when pain resides in the body (Glucklich 2001: 47ff) but even more so when tragedies become accessible in the body, when, as Kleinman writes, suffering acts as "political performance and moral commentary" (1997: 96). At such a time, we require stories, quests, other places, and other people to follow and map out our difficulties in order to feel in control of them, even if mastery is not possible. Jackson argues that what matters most are the "truth effects of telling stories, the empathy they generate, the exchange of experience they enable, and the social bonds they mediate" (1998: 180). Intersubjective experience of distraught lifeworlds is more important than preserving coherence (Jackson 1998: 201), and bloody stories endure in particular as ambiguous artifacts of painful experience. As Jackson notes, lived experience—in order to move from privately held, potentially meaningful situations, into publicly shared forms—must be told by selecting the relevant aspects of situations to signify it, an event, "an occasion, a happening, where something vital is at play and at risk ... quickly blur[s] into and become[s] stories ... a social hermeneutics" (2005: xxix, 11). In retelling experiences together, different interests, capacities, and values can be explored and tested, stories reworked, and fresh relationships realized as one comes into being on pilgrimage (Coleman and Elsner 2003: 5). As much as one is drawn along by the availability of a network of refuges that houses hundreds of thousands of weary pilgrims each night, the "narrative hospitality" shelters almost as many pilgrims in the long days (Ricoeur cited in Rapport and Overing 2000: 290). Stories travel between the peripatetic pilgrims, calling on imagination and sympathy to reach across to another's world with our own stories that are also on the move, calling up a sense of mutual ownership and herding of these narrative fragments between pilgrims.

For both Michael and John, my key informants here, the stories they had come to tell strangers took time to evolve as they found their feet on the Camino. John refused to speak to me about his reasons for days, and Michael took weeks to choose me as his confidante. In fact John only began to talk after having broken down at a roadside memorial for a pilgrim who had died while on pilgrimage. Having come face-to-face with the situation that had brought him to Spain, he began to weave his grief and his pilgrimage together into a story that eventually spread across the Camino, helping to frame others' searches for contact with reality or religiosity while on pilgrimage. Neither Michael nor John were religious pilgrims, exhibiting more *curiositas* in their wandering than the more traditional *peregrinatio* of proper pilgrimage (Coleman and Elsner 2003: 12), which has its subscribers on the Camino too, but both moved between the religious structures and the more richly textured experiential dimensions of a more immediate engagement with the Camino and other pilgrims.

Intersubjectivity, following Jackson, does not reduce the experience of betweenness to a "synonym for shared experience, empathic understanding or fellow feeling," treating it rather as a dialectic or an interplay, "a site for constructive, destructive and reconstructive interaction" (1998: 4, 8). Pilgrims attempted to meet others on the journey to give each other their attention in a way that recalls how Csordas characterizes attention as a "somatic mode ... a turning toward ... a more bodily and multisensory engagement" (2002: 244). It extends beyond meetings between people, as for John trying to reach out to the physical and emotional traces of the sister he had lost to cancer while she walked the Camino the previous year. In this self-reorientation, people came to acknowledge one another bodily, walking, resting, eating, drinking together, and often massaging each other's broken feet, and in doing so achieved some shared experience of pain, of healing or accommodation of suffering in their lives.

Peregrino, ¿Quién te llama? [Pilgrim, who calls you?]
(written on a wall outside Najerá)

Although the Camino presents modern pilgrims with a leisurely walk—through a vigorous experience of European history via an escape into exotic Spanish culture—it is also a singular opportunity to explicitly evaluate the distance between a pilgrim's life and his plans. Camino stories testify to this unfolding critical experience. Some begin to acknowledge the wandering spirit within them, to give room for the "undeveloped self" to grow (Rupp 2005: 19). Others encounter reasons to keep walking long after their initial aspirations have become routine; for the anthropologist Nancy Frey, the Camino became a catalyst for her divorce. "I discovered when I returned home that I was no longer able to pass through the doors of my past. ... I realized that what I had unleashed within myself while walking could no longer be contained [in her marriage]" (Frey 1998: 195). At the same time, as some relationships are ending, young Spanish couples use the Camino to walk before they commit to marriage, seeing the time together as a test of their relationship.

For others still, motivations remain obscure until they take to the road. Kerry Egan (2004) only gradually realized that she walked in part to mourn her father's death. Having spent an afternoon laughing in the company of other pilgrims, Egan became aware that she had been numb for months since her father's passing. "I began to understand just how odd and off I had been living" (2004: 47). The ritual Camino, in the swinging of the giant *botafumeiro* (incense burner) at the pilgrim mass in Santiago, which takes seven men to keep moving, stood in stark contrast to her father's passing in hospital without a priest. This feeling of *communitas* is powerful for every pilgrim at the Mass, as it is the last time they are together as Camino pilgrims. For Egan the experience diverged from her mother's double sense of loss: of her husband, and of some ritual to give his passing meaning in that moment, "something small to do because we cannot comprehend the big right then" (2004: 221).

Walking with his daughter Maria, and publishing the letters they wrote to each other, Donald Schell only knew he had to "walk out of a depression" (Schell and Schell 2001: 1). For many the pain and difficulty that forms the basis of the Camino's draw is real and literal: Nicolas

Luard (1998) walked parts of the road over a number of years as a way to cope with the loss of his daughter to AIDS. Feeling enriched and able to encounter some sense of God along the way, Luard nevertheless felt that faith had not helped him "one whittle or tittle, scrap or jot" (1998: 175). Still, he found himself lighting candles, praying, and crying anyway in that penumbral region between grief and acceptance in Léon cathedral, asking for the intercession of the "carpenter" to take his deceased daughter (1998: 193). The echoes of Housman's *Epitaph on an Army of Mercenaries* were more suited to his grief than any prayer: "When God abandoned / they defended / and saved the sum of things for pay" (cited in Luard 1998: 224).

In my own experience, too, the attraction of the Camino allowed me to embody the convergence of my developing fascination with an anthropological sensibility as a means to explain the world to myself, and my waning identity as a Roman Catholic. As I walked with others in similarly fluctuating relationships with the institutional Church, I became aware of a welcome loss of objectivity; I was moving from participant observer to becoming what Michalowski and Dubisch call an "observant participant" (2001: 20). Objectivity in such close quarters is rarely desirable anyway; Haraway argues that others discern it as hostility rather than neutrality (2007: 24). Studying witchcraft practices in France, for instance, Jeanne Faavret-Saada could not remain neutral during her fieldwork and felt forced to adopt a position that would allow her to be placed in her fieldsite in the French Bocage. Witchcraft, as spoken words, is power, "not knowledge or information ... and there is no neutral position with words: in witchcraft, words wage war" (Favret-Saada 2007: 469). Even though Favret-Saada worked there as an ethnographer, she nevertheless became identified by locals as a "bewitcher"; people asked for her assistance: "They had identified me as the unwitcher who could get them out of their troubles" (2007: 471). She also began to think of herself as "bewitched," and entered therapy with a local ritual healer (called an *unwitcher*) to become "uncaught" by supposed spells cast on her (2007: 471).

Similarly, on the Camino there are no innocent questions one can ask. To engage with someone for information is to reveal more than a scholarly interest in the ways of the world and one's fellow pilgrims. It is to accede to the rules of the road and to share what we have according to what is needed. When I spoke to Michael, it was because he had certain expectations that, as I was asking so many questions, I had some answers. Telling me the awful story of living a difficult life lived out of place was not so that I could have more data but that I could recognize that something was at stake for both of us. With such an ethos of mutual responsibility orienting the walk, few pilgrims, myself included, just walk to travel through the wilds of the Spanish Camino.

In today's world, truly wild places can even be difficult to imagine. For many contemporary European and American pilgrims, the Spanish Camino is both wild and tamed, a Catholic wilderness that ambivalently evokes a feral innocence and a history of civilizing Catholicism from the Crusades to Franco's Republican Spain. Pilgrims view this religious landscape as free, or wild, but also replete with an abstract history. It draws those with impoverished narratives, people walking slowly in search of suffering bodies and stories within which their struggles may dwell. These people edge bit by bit toward the penumbra, "a piece of Africa loosely welded to Europe," in Auden's memorable phrase. The pilgrimage thus remains betwixt and between religious and secular configurations of modernity—some pilgrims seek out communion with the saints or God, others search for something else that they can call reality. Both are versions of the blood in the tale—bodies, suffering, history, stories, and a sense of freedom when they mingle.

Walking towards Happiness: Thomas and Helene

For many who travel it, the Camino is an example of what Jackson calls the "ambiguous borderlands," marked out between the real and the religious, "disorienting moments when we feel compelled to speak but words fail us, and though desperate for understanding, find ourselves lost for words" (2009: 51). The pilgrimage both induces crisis in its extended physical challenge and represents it so that the experience of the crisis can be modified, away from reified notions of institutional religion. Language is not the primary goal, to codify the crisis ("*la meta no es Santiago, la meta es el Camino*" ["the goal is the way itself, not to reach the relics of St. James"] is a common aphorism). Most pilgrims seek first to enter into the borderlands of experience, outside the immediacy of their lifeworlds, to inhabit their struggles, to mark them as real. It is, I suggest, insufficient to declare that some people only attempt such a large undertaking as the Camino pilgrimage for fun, simply for a vacation. It is a fiction of will and denies the unfolding circumstances wherein motives are uncovered or created while on pilgrimage.

For Thomas and Helene, an elderly Norwegian couple I walked with from the town of Los Arcos for several days, the Camino was a gradual drunken revelry toward old age and their eventual passing, a journey of months on the route punctuated with litres of beer starting at noon each day. They spoke openly and with equanimity about this, their third and final Camino, and the reality that they would not be able to walk it again. Growing old with grace together, they brought great joy to those who shared their Camino, their stories and their beers. The Camino was thus an existential coda; it was a way of comparing eras in their lives by facing the changes that time had wrought (Rapport and Overing 2000: 287). Moreover, the normal rules of the Camino defining the normative authentic pilgrimage did not apply to people like Thomas and Helene who drank heavily and stayed up after the strict curfew. Although normally frowned upon by refuge workers tasked with evoking the better possibilities of the pilgrimage as a sincere endeavour, the rules did not impinge on these two old pilgrims. The transgression however, reminded the rest of us, as we went meekly to our beds, of the license for rebellion that the Camino could promise (Gluckman 1970: 130).

Thomas and Helene reconciled themselves to the notion that none of us are in control of our lives, that we are subject to forces beyond either control or comprehension. At the same time, though, they did not subscribe to any self-description that would paint them as completely at the will of the fates. It is in how we strive, imperfectly, to rise to the boundaries of our lives, felt so intimately in frustration, loss, pain, or death, that we are forced to contemplate the course of our lives where thoughts are, as Arendt observed, always afterthoughts, subsequent reflections on matters or events overtaking us (cited in Jackson 2009: 203). "Because our actions follow from a *need* to act before they follow from any conception of *how* to act, all action is to some extent magical ... action implies an element of faith or absurdity" (Jackson 2007: 152). It is in these sometimes awful situations that we are *forced* to recover some deliberate sense of our shared humanity. It is in the small things, the ways of relating, the gestures and choices that populate our days that we are "redeemed as thinkers and renewed as persons" (Jackson 2009: 202).[4]

The pilgrimage thus stands between the immediate lifeworld where pilgrims try to be actors in their lives, and the non-immediate distant world where they sense how the world happens to them; where, in the chaos of a loss of life, livelihood, or lifeworld, "we are simply acted upon;" where we are "most alive to the real and the religious" (Jackson 2009: 51). What characterises the pilgrim's sense of feeling liminal on pilgrimage is not shedding a social identity, which Turner (cited in Jackson 2009: 6) claimed for the threshold experience, but the relational in-betweenness that such a threshold can produce, where people redouble their efforts to produce new forms of relatedness and,

> augment, supplement, strengthen, enlarge or bolster their sense of self [through clothing, bodies, residences, cars, ideologies, communities,

objects, friends and families] ... What is ritual ... but a way of tapping into the extramundane world in order to augment or make good the degradation of being that accompanies the routines of everyday life? (Jackson 2009: 41)

The draw to this penumbral world of pilgrimage brings people face-to-face with a new everyday world in the wake of some tragedy or unseen affliction where we try to cling to the illusion that "the world is ours to save, to transform, to transcend" (2009: 13).

To make sense of and deal with losses contriving to thwart our lives and their plans, healing must first engage with immediate experience before any story can do its work. We cannot take, therefore, our experiences for granted. If we are not simply to "struggle along" (Desjarlais 1996), places away from everyday habits and constraints are required to rethink even the very acts that have hitherto seemed natural—walking, breathing or sleeping. Abstract existential problems can thus be embodied when pain may resist. Healing, as Csordas writes, at its most human "is not an escape into irreality and mystification, but an intensification of the encounter between suffering and hope at the moment in which it finds a voice, where the anguished clash of bare life and raw existence emerges from muteness into articulation" (2002: 11). As the body expresses pain, literally "pushing it out," new contexts for that pain emerge through the activity of walking in the shared social space of the road, in the places between where the relationship between religion and suffering and religion and salvation may be renewed. In the natural and religious landscape of the embodied pilgrimage, there pilgrims have found themselves at a threshold "at which thought and language falter and mystery begins ... where ... we are fated to live betwixt and between" (Jackson 2007: 153). Insofar as people find such a conclusion on pilgrimage, the journey becomes less an itinerary and more of a crossing over into new more authentic places and simpler experiences.

The Camino is an attractive journey partly because its rules are simple: follow the yellow arrows west to Compostela, walking a short distance every day, providing an orientation to lives experienced as aimless.[5] Simple as these rules are, conflicts are never far away. Jack Hitt for instance writes about a Pamplona banker, "a lifelong Catholic who is earnestly shaken by the vicious history of all organized religions ... Javier is anxious to talk" (2005: 66) with whom he walks for a day. Javier seems so sincere to Hitt, walking with only bare provisions and with a determined stride, and Hitt is quickly exhausted from trying to keep pace—"to Javier all unnecessary distractions violate the spirit of the road. I acquiesce in the presence of someone whose certainty of what he's doing is so thorough and convincing" (2005: 67). Trying to convince Javier to take a quick shortcut outside Estella, Hitt argues that the route marked with yellow arrows is not James's authentic path, that ancient pilgrims would have been more practical, following the wider, straighter road. "These are the yellow arrows. This is the road," (2005: 69) Javier tells him, his voice cracking before acquiescing. Javier and Hitt are strained with each other for the evening, as Hitt had challenged the route itself as laid out, and the core goal to follow the pilgrim path—"I have challenged the authenticity of the yellow arrows" (2005: 69). Hitt has also missed the confluence of the metaphorical and literal road, that the arrows are an aspiration to tradition, simplicity and connection to other pilgrims, Camino ancestors, contemporaries and successors. The following morning, Hitt guiltily realizes that Javier has silently slipped away, unable to share the road with him. The search for authentic relationships is all the more pressing when they can easy fail when, instead of the spontaneous *communitas* of unmediated inter-subjective moments, people end up talking past each other, "missing each other's meanings, and interpreting each other's worlds solely in the light of our own interests and pre-understandings" (Jackson 2007: xxvii).

It is clear, nonetheless, that walking is undeniably more pleasurable as a shared act and few resist the temptation to join together for a while. Many slip into permanent groups, but most accomplish a difficult day's trek in a loose affiliation that helps move them into a more contemplative social space. In the silence of a day's long walk and in the company of sympathetic strangers, the timings, rhythms and inflections slowly pace out new relationships along the ground (Ingold and Vergunst 2008: 1). To trust in the regular sounds of companion's footsteps, the repetitive clack of a *bordón* (walking stick), the sound of one's breathing, is to create a lull, a space whereby, as one pilgrim confided in me, new thoughts and ideas come up from the road itself. The daily walk creates a rhythm to the newness to the day where each night brings a new place and the destination is never in doubt. Often this is more than enough. It must be truly awful to have a secret that one wishes to tell fellow strangers. Rather, for many, the tacit acceptance of a journey completed in comparative quiet is more important where the self expands into the environment, the senses stretching toward distant smells and sounds of the day becoming restorative. Negotiating the unspeakable of what one has left behind often cannot compare to days spent in the easy company of what one pilgrim calls these "existential friendships" (Rupp 2005: 214), temporary friendships (often lasting only days) that compress meaning and worth into contact that is paradoxically both intense and relaxed.

The Limits of Words: Michael

Recalling Simone Weil's image of the person in pain feeling "hammered into one place" (cited in Orsi 2005: 127), trapped by powerlessness and solitude, Orsi captures the predicament of suffering as a dual movement of exposure and confinement that chokes off the lifeworld and ties the sufferer to a "dreadful resonance between heaven and earth" (2005: 145). Confined and exposed, then, making some meaning from existential inertia is less the goal than wounding and companionship. In the painful predicament of his life, Michael, an American pilgrim in his forties, was feeling hammered into one place. It had taken him a week to ask to speak to me privately—dawdling one morning outside our refuge, waiting for me to leave, a common occurrence for pilgrims to join up with desired walking partners—about the decision that had brought him to Spain. The Camino was his solution to this stagnation, a fantasy of an extended trip to Spain, not on a tourist itinerary from city to city, but as a chance to familiarize himself with a putatively authentic Spain. It would also enable him to distance himself from his life and obligations at home. Though he began the trip with several friends, Michael was soon walking alone; this time meant more to him than maintaining what quickly became for him a fragile group harmony. He had come to Spain to address the drain on his happiness and lack of contentment with his life and work, while his walking companions had come to see the sights and enjoy their time immersed in Spanish culture. Despite living what he knew to be a wonderful and potentially fulfilling life, he had never felt himself to be in the right place. He felt followed by a cloud that kept his achievements from helping him to feel excited, keeping him feeling thwarted. Talking to Michael it was clear that the problem was not that his troubles lacked a name, but that they were without form. Even if he had been able to articulate his difficulty, his words would lack their "finer edges" (Bloom 2004: 5).

Hearing difficult stories, being asked to witness, enjoins professional listeners like ethnographers to consider the plural relationships called into play in the telling, the blood in the story can fall on the researcher too. Orsi found such a predicament in listening to women who called on St. Jude to help them:

> while women talked about mastectomies, abandonment, domestic vi-
> olence, adultery and loneliness, I could feel myself being transposed,
> without any encouragement on my part, into other men in their lives,
> not only the protagonists of their stories, but also the doctors, priests
> and counsellors ... being confused with these other categories of per-
> sons can complicate our conversations ... [the] effort to set boundar-

ies was not always successful or possible. The researcher is perceived through multiple frames and becomes the object of displaced resentments and expectations. (2005: 166)

In encounters such as mine with Michael, the porous work of research becomes apparent (Orsi 2005: 176); it was clear that Michael was not concerned for me to collect data, but to assist in some human way. I had once trained as a counselor and, realising Michael's difficulty in communicating his problems, I used this past experience to help him attempt a brief guided visualization exercise. Michael began to face his difficulties head-on as I helped him to acknowledge the anonymity of his depressive feeling by describing his feelings less as emotional processes but as an object. In the course of a half-hour, I asked him to allow his feelings to settle and his emotional state to assume a shape and we improvised a method of embodying his burden, objectifying it and discarding this shadowy drag on his life. Michael eventually described a dense jet-black stone in his palm and, faced with something that had form, external to him, he moved into a position to face the feeling of being burdened. With this new emotional distance from his sufferings, he stood up and threw the stone away in a wild and symbolically liberating gesture. Creating an imaginative gap in his own suffering, he gave form to his ills, freeing himself up to grasp them and dispense with them without having to find a way to "call them out."

In doing this, Michael made a place for himself and, having spent so long feeling dis-placed, he stumbled into the productive fluctuations of non-places (Augé 1995). In escaping the inertia of his home and life, Michael was able to seek a new habitual space and time in the slower pace of the walking pilgrimage. Using Spain as a non-place that did not crowd him with everything that he had left behind in the US, places he had no real connection to, released Michael to experiment with new ways of being. He met new people as a renewed person himself, not feeling that the places he passed through could weigh on him and remind him of what had kept him feeling sad. As a result of this, Spain became a fertile context for the experience of newness and creative activity rather than a feature of the loss of identity that Augé (1995) has argued it always signals—places where meaning is neither possible nor particularly desired. Although this creative impulse has many limits and is driven as much by subconscious impulses and other factors beyond one's control, it still fosters an experience of control. Michael did not take charge of his life; rather his experience of his life had been fundamentally altered.

For several days after this incident, I became involved in a "walking fieldwork" (Irving 2005: 323) where Michael and I started to discuss what he thought the object of the walking might have been. Michael did not name his burden; he did not weave it into existence through a talking cure. Instead, he employed a different tool he had been training in Spain: his body. I was not just an observer; I participated, leading him through these old emotions and, for that time, out the other side. Talking was after the fact of his struggle with this subliminal anxiety in its immediacy. Having faced up to his failing life-project, he could retrospectively put names to what had happened, what had been happening for years. He began to see how he had been experiencing this dread—as an agent controlling his moods and decisions. Cognitively addressing what had happened was not the goal, though; it was merely the result of having experienced his life differently for the first time in so long, by allowing this terrible feeling of failure to be revealed in the "potential space" (Winnicott cited in Jackson 2007: 133) between us. He had faced some unfinished business and the fragile reality of his life became obtainable again.

In his classic monograph, Godfrey Lienhardt describes the Dinka's response to possession (cited in Good 1994: 128–130). Ajak, a young man born without testicles, had almost been killed as a child when his father's sacrifice to the Divinity caused his testicles to descend. He immediately became possessed and this power, having affected Ajak for over twenty minutes, refused to name itself. No one could know its business. It would not "announce itself." Good uses this vignette to compare how pain in modern medical settings similarly refuses to take a name, resisting objectification and insertion into medical narratives. Pain also resists subjectification, though it often lacks a role in our lives as we embrace the fantasy that a future without pain is necessary, possible and desirable. Yet Lienhardt's example is characteristic of a society where people are more deeply integrated into the social fabric. Michael could speak to me precisely because I was a stranger; he could say and do things that required the anonymity of our connection and the charismatic and ephemeral pilgrimage context. Camino pilgrims are not so integrated as in some enduring and ongoing everyday world. The collective rituals they engage in along the route, drinking *aguardiente* spirits at a *queimada* ceremony or burning an item of clothing at Finisterre, the geographic end of the pilgrimage on the Atlantic coast, only loosely produces pilgrim individuals as part of some broader pilgrim collective.[6] Michael felt increasingly pilgrim-like as he immersed himself in his imagination of the culture of the Camino. He did this, however, at the expense of the real relationships he had with his fellow American pilgrims. The ideal of this *communitas*—an unstructured reciprocal feeling of togetherness and equality—was only possible among strangers who were not and who could not be part of his actual life. The idea of giving ills a definite name and setting them forth into a diffuse semiotic chain of worldly discourses seems almost to set them free, without proper charge of them, a potentially dangerous gambit among one's friends at home. Once Michael had done the work he had come to do, he could and did walk away from me when he wished. The raw struggle I witnessed and accompanied did not tie us to any bond that had to outlast our time on the pilgrimage; what had haunted him had been embodied and addressed in what he came to call his "laboratory experience."

Coping with Wounds: John

One of the most apposite examples of walking in order to cope with tragedy came from John, an Irish pilgrim living in England. He set off to trace his sister Myra's journey across Spain exactly one year after her sudden death from an undiagnosed tumour that killed her peacefully in bed the evening of her arrival at the pilgrimage's official endpoint in Santiago de Compostela. With a list of the refuges she had stayed in compiled by her then companions, he walked in her shadow, drawing close to her in her last days, telling other pilgrims about her and about his reason for walking. While neither John nor his sister had obvious religious reasons for walking—she had been a tourist using the Camino as a cheap vacation, while his pilgrimage was centred on mourning her passing—their story animated other pilgrims' pilgrimages. She was para-doxically lauded as an authentic pilgrim, the crucial designation to many pilgrims that justifies the time and effort taken to complete the walk. Her story might be an example of what Clifford Geertz, who famously characterised religion as the "search for the really real" (Geertz 1977: 112), could have called the "frighteningly real." Myra's escape into a refreshing alternative to her work as a hospice nurse represents one pole of motivation for pilgrims rejecting some aspect of modernity in favour of the exotic nature of the pilgrimage. John's Camino represents the other, engaging a deep-felt sense of languishing in a loss that refuses easy categorisation.

For many of us, "the prospect of pain, uncertainty, and despair is off-set by the possibility of again belonging to a world of simple pleasures" (Jackson 2009: 202). The frustrations of failing life-projects—even ones only dimly perceived—must give way in order to strike out and away from the debilitating quotidian that Avery Gordon (1997: 4) character-ises as "furniture without memories" ("that sad and sunken couch that sags in just that place where an unrememberable past and an unimaginable future force us to sit day after day"). Pilgrims like John and Michael go in search of wilder places where "words fail, but meanings still exist, where meanings—unspoken, inchoate, raw and throbbing with life—wait to be found, to be given voice" (Olney in Behar 1996: 134). This sacred old route is just such a place, a frontier experience charged with moral significance (see L. Taylor 2007) that facilitates a confluence with a moral topography of the self, and it is here that pilgrims seek out new understandings of failing lives, livelihoods and lifeworlds in the face of their recent or imminent loss.

Conclusions: Walking as Healing

Walking is a social act with a long history on the Camino. Through walking, one can trace the contours of many stories, uncovering the truth of them in the struggle to find suitable responses. These days, with a declining sense of place in the "great chain of being" or the cosmic order (C. Taylor 1991: 3), pain has become a medical problem and less a moral one (Glucklich 2001: 7). In the past, people found God on the route: these days they are more likely to find nature or themselves. Pilgrims' expectations of meaning are often a wish for alternatives, for a healthy sense of a world capable of being less plastic, a realization that we do in fact live in a world that moves on. Walking for a month produced a fruitful ambiguity for pilgrims travelling longer distances. The walk helped them to think in the rhythms and rhymes that the day brought forth.

John's determined stride across Spain eased as he searched each day for some proof that his sister had been on the route before him. He found messages in hostel registers and proffered them as proof, traces that fellow pilgrims could touch and connect more deeply with Myra. He walked into the helplessness of having lost his sister. John could not know much more about his sister's final days even though he found traces of her life in refuge registers, messages she had left for pilgrims coming after her, notes that she had left, ultimately, for her grieving brother. The pain of his grief began to take shape in how he followed her footsteps. Soon after he returned from the pilgrimage, he bought a small house on the road that he visits regularly, tending to pilgrims he meets, offering them a place to stay or some food. He never mentions his own reasons for being there, just that he had once been a pilgrim himself. Our lives may never achieve a lasting sense of meaning or become more than bearable. One language begets another and any "final vocabularies" (Rorty 1992: 88) are forever closed off. John could not have comprehended his sister's death by walking, and I doubt it became more bearable for him to have lost her. But through his efforts and example of pilgrimage, the story of her death transitioned into the story of her life for those who met him, forged on the Camino—as Orsi (2005) would appreciate— between heaven and earth. John's was a story told by his determined stride, the tears he shed for his sister at roadside memorials and in refuges. For both John and Michael, the steps they took, respectively, to face the loss of a precious life and a lifeworld at risk reinvigorated their own commitment to experience suffering differently when their wounds had become undeniably real.

In assessing the possibilities for altering our relationship with suffering it is useful to revisit the writings of Friedrich Nietzsche. Nietzsche refuses to afford his affliction a status equal with himself; rather, as a dog, it occupies a place reserved for "pets, servants and wives" ([1882] 1974: 249–250), a place where the master is in control. He does not call it by name, but identifies its existential relationship with him; Nietzsche seems to appreciate pain as faithful, entertaining and clever. Pain too often lacks such a clear role in our lives even though it is an experience we all know intimately. Yet it remains a mystery—"whatever refuses to surrender all its secrets to common sense"—and a myth, a veiled truth that refuses "to yield every quantum of [its] darkness to research or to bright ideas. Instead [it] introduces us to unusual states of being which, for a time, we enter into and dwell within" (Morris 1991: 52, 24). The physical pain of wounding—of hard, intense, undeniable hurt in the body—opens pilgrims up to the ironic possibilities of "magical thinking," (Jackson 2007: xxvi), a bodily subjunctive that rediscovers the possibility of possibility itself along Spain's Milky Way and in each weary step to Santiago.

Is it desirable to strive for meaning when hurt or can there be healing in preserving the meaninglessness of personal tragedies (Žižek 2002: 141 n. 56)? Painful places, as Orsi (2005: 200) has noted, do not resolve situations or produce a final meaning. Instead, they produce a space between worlds, "a suspensive space" opened up by the experience of pain. The notion that by entering fully into religious worlds and thus removing oneself to the edge of one's own distressed world, some *personal* meaning is possible or desirable but misses the fact that meaning is produced in inter-subjective experience. Much contemporary production of religious meaning, context and practice disguises a "fear of a total loss of meaning" (Crapanzano cited in Tomlinson and Engelke 2007: 3). The world though, is not to be represented in words without problems, excesses, overlaps, gaps, or losses: "The ultimate questions of being cannot be answered. But insofar as we have no option but to speak, think and act, we are bound to struggle for the kind of language, the kind of thought, the kind of action that does greatest justice to life as it is lived" (Jackson 2007: xi). In other words, life often outstrips our will to describe it and spills out over our attempts at categorizing experience. Making meaning from our lives is often thus an act of magical thinking to compensate for a lack of control.

Too often we are absent to ourselves, bound up in a habitual everyday that erodes the edges of experience. "The wrinkles and creases on our faces are the registrations of the great passions, vices, insights that called on us; but we, the masters, were not at home" (Benjamin cited in Jackson 2007: 3). The reinvigorated everyday of the quotidian trudging, walking, drinking, eating, washing, showering, and sleeping presents pilgrims with an opportunity to embrace a feeling of alienation rather than escape it, where "dys-appearance," a problematic experience of a body-self at its limits (Leder 1990: 83ff.), becomes a means to walk and talk oneself into being a pilgrim somewhere along the road. At some stage, the person I am is left behind and the pilgrim enters the rhythms of the pilgrimage day in a kind of secular transubstantiation. Because our bodies are habitually absent from us, "perpetually outside of itself caught up in a multitude of involvements with other people, with nature with the sacred domain" (Leder 1990: 4), the long pilgrimage is eminently suited to such self-modification. Whether the change is actually permanent or not is less important than the enduring reality and comfort of the memory and thus the possibilities inhering in the fact that change has already happened once.

Most importantly, this serendipitous newness, this possibility in the most habitual of situations—what Arendt calls "natality" (cited in Jackson 2007: 24)—appears in the indeterminate or potential space *between* actors. So little of what pilgrims accomplish can be attributed to will alone: "we *act*, for the most part habitually and unreflectively, moved by deeply embedded dispositions that have far more to do with the struggle for being than the striving for meaning" (Jackson 2007: 23, 25). As the dust settles and we make meaning out of the day's struggle for being, we can appreciate just how much those moments where being has not felt at risk has been in the penumbral company of strangers.

In researching the involutions of existential explorations of life, self, and world, researchers are brought into a world where the interpretation of cultural processes is more successful and faithful when they "join the conversation" and people already in it (Orsi 2005: 170). In following the pilgrims, the research forced me to walk with them as one of them, exploring my own reasons for being among them, discovering for myself the shades of being with and being different that characterized the constant flow of experiences with my companions. For Solnit, pilgrimages act to embody life and individual lives, exhibiting a positive freedom: "The walker toiling along a road toward some distant place is one of the most compelling and universal images of what it means to be human" (2002: 50). The researcher is not immune to drawing toward that image either, as the academic project is at the same time part existential and the authors that inspire the writing and the walking exhibit the researcher's arbitrariness on choice of influences. In the same way, the pilgrims who compose the loose network of informants are much more a product of chance and half-decisions—when to walk, how fast, where to stop each day and how often. The confluence of our trajectories composes the fiction of our combined will on the Camino to walk and to finish and in finishing to feel better for the experience together.

If the Camino is, as pilgrims told Nancy Frey (1998), a "ruta de la terapia [a therapeutic route]," then it is primarily a walking therapy, a somatic mode of healing rather than a way of "exorcising the demons" by naming them. Discarding a model of suffering where ills maintain a simple correspondence with a pain whose task is to provide a context of meaning to the wider world, we can begin to appreciate just how subtle this process of making suffering manifest can be. What terms do we have that can help us refer to this phenomenon of pain produced of existential suffering felt in the body? One such term is somatization; another is psychogenic pain. The first refers to an embodiment of suffering; the second to the biological basis of felt pain that does not seem to have an immediate organic cause. Is it so hard, David Morris asks,

> to imagine that the same brain capable of turning the face blush-red at an indecent joke—the same brain that creates not only its own opioid analgesic but also the infinitely more bewildering product known as human thought—might on occasion fill the hand or foot or lower back with pain? ... [P]ain generated or sustained by the mind needs the body mainly in order to give suffering a location. (1991: 157)

Wounds might not spring from the manifest pain of a specific suffering. Instead, "standing in" as an arbitrary signifier in motion, the *body in motion* is capable of evoking or "speaking for" several wounds that have remained in the realm of the unspeakable. As bodies take on the physicality of the walk, each step past pain and into the numb continuity toward day's end removes the primacy of thought or talk for the triumph of that next step and the shared smiles and glances of mutual recognition among pilgrims at the end of each day's walk.

Notes

This is a revised and updated version of an article that appeared as "Walking Back to Happiness? Modern Pilgrimage and the Expression of Suffering on Spain's Camino de Santiago" in J. Skinner, ed., *Journeys: The International Journal of Travel and Travel Writing*, Special Edition, *Writing the Dark Side of Travel* 11, no. 1 (2010): 107–32.

1. Throughout this chapter, I focus on the activity and experience of walkers, though there are a number of ways of doing the pilgrimage. Many people arrive in Santiago on bikes, by car, bus, or on horseback. A few travel with donkeys (Moore 2004) and one pilgrim has even managed the eight-hundred-kilometre trek on a unicycle. Every kind of pilgrim however, accepts these modes of transport as hierarchical with human-powered walking pilgrims ranked as the most authentic. Only walking and cycling pilgrims can procure the coveted Compostela at journey's end (see note 2). The sense of being authentic is crucial to most pilgrims and can be assessed by refuge workers who refuse entry to all but the walkers in almost every refuge during the day. Cyclists are admitted later each day but car or bus pilgrims—even those who only have their luggage transported while they walk—are forbidden from sleeping in refuges. Thus it is crucial for most to enter the spirit of the archetypal authentic pilgrim in a way that can be recognized as historically genuine and culturally credible by other pilgrims (see Frey [1998: 19ff.] for more on the motorized, semimotorized, and nonmotorized categories of pilgrim; and Bruner [1994] for the semantic distinctions of authenticity in "post-ironic" tourist sites).

2. For instance, in order to walk the Camino, pilgrims must fill out a form to procure a "pilgrim passport" that grants access to the cheap network of traditional refuges populating the route. In filling out the form, pilgrims must choose between three categories of motivation: religious, nonreligious, or both. Not wanting to be denied entry to the refuges or refused the coveted certificate of completion, the Compostela—which one receives in fulfillment of a *pieta causa* or pious motive—many pilgrims tick the religious motivation box. The construction of the pilgrimage as more religious is clear when one examines forms from a few years previous, where religious was only one of five motivations, the other four indicating more secular motivations (i.e., sport, cultural, spiritual, other).

3. The Camino is at the same time a cheap vacation, as pilgrims can spend as little as €20–30 each day for accommodation and food. This is how many Spanish people walk the pilgrimage, for one or two weeks per year, beginning from a town between Léon (two weeks' walk from Santiago) and Sarriá (one week's walk from Santiago, just over one hundred kilometers distance, the minimum required to qualify the walker for the Compostela certificate of completion).

4. There is a tragic echo of Solnit's Sisyphean gyms reaching Camus's Sisyphus. Sisyphus, father of Odysseus, was a murderer and a robber who repeatedly outwitted the Greek gods, first revealing Zeus's tryst with Aegina to her father the river god Asopus, then tricking Hades into testing his own handcuffs until Hermes had to free him. Finally he convinced Persephone into letting him back up from Tartarus onto Earth until Hermes forcibly returned him to the Underworld. For Camus, Sisyphus is able to grasp his fate in his hands in his absurd punishment, to eternally

push his rock up a hill and watch it roll back down again, where Camus enjoins the reader to imagine with him at the foot of the hill that Sisyphus might have found happiness (Solnit 2002: 261; Graves 1960: 216ff).
5. The yellow arrows were the brainchild of one Fr. Sampedro who worked tirelessly to revive the tradition of the Camino that had all but disappeared by the 1950s. The hand-painted yellow arrows marked the trail for all to follow and were soon adopted along the entire route, maintained locally by each parish and *ayuntamiento* (town council). The yellow arrow is another mark of the authentic route and acts to connect the effort of the pilgrim to the effort of each area to help pilgrims. Recent metal signs pointing the way, sponsored by EU patronage of the Camino and the UN World Heritage funding, are thus seen to be top-down impositions that contribute both to an unwelcome worlding (Crain 1997) of the Camino and a perceived loss by pilgrims of the local labor that had previously revived the route. More specifically, the metal signage hints at the encroachment and the omnipresence of the indices of modernity that so many pilgrims have come to the Camino to escape.
6. The *queimada* or *conxuro* is a playful rite of exorcism popular in Galicia where a "witch" makes a concoction of spirits to be imbibed by the audience as everyone shouts "¡Meigas fora! [witches out!]." It is most famously celebrated in O Cebrero, the first town in Galicia in where pilgrims stay.

Bibliography

Augé, M. 1995. *Non-Places: Introduction to an Anthropology of Supermodernity.* London and New York: Verso.
Bashō, M. 1998. *Narrow Road to the Interior and Other Writings.* Trans. S. Hamill. Boston: Shambhala Publications.
Behar, R. 1996. *The Vulnerable Observer: Anthropology That Breaks Your Heart.* Boston: Beacon Press.
Bloom, H. 2004. *The Art of Reading Poetry.* New York: Perennial.
Bruner, E. 1994. "Abraham Lincoln as Authentic Reproduction: A critique of Postmodernism." *American Anthropologist* 96(2): 397–415.
Coleman, S. and J. Elsner. 2003. *Pilgrim Voices: Narrative and Authorship in Christian Pilgrimage.* London: Berghahn Books.
Crain, M. 1997. "The Remaking of an Andalusian Pilgrimage Tradition," in A. Gupta and J. Ferguson (eds.), *Culture Power Place: Explorations in Critical Anthropology.* Durham, NC: Duke University Press, 291–311.
Csordas, T. 2002. *Body/Meaning/Healing.* New York: Palgrave Macmillan.
Daniel, E. V. 1987. *Fluid Signs: Being a Person the Tamil Way.* Berkeley: University of California Press.
De Botton, A. 2002. *The Art of Travel.* London: Penguin.
De Certeau, M. 1977. *The Practice of Everyday Life.* Berkeley: University of California Press.
Desjarlais, R. 1996. "Struggling Along," in M. Jackson (ed.), *Things as They Are: New Directions in Phenomenological Anthropology.* Bloomington: Indiana University Press, 70–93.

Egan, K. 2004. *Fumbling: A Pilgrimage Tale of Love, Grief, and Spiritual Renewal on the Camino de Santiago.* London: Doubleday.

Favret-Saada, J. 2007. "The Way Things Are Said," in A. Robben and J. Sluka (eds.), *Ethnographic Fieldwork: An Anthropological Reader.* Malden, MA: Blackwell, 465–75.

Frey, N. 1998. *Pilgrim Stories: On and Off the Road to Santiago.* Berkeley: University of California Press.

Geertz, C. 1977. *The Interpretation of Cultures.* New York: Basic Books

Glucklich, A. 2001. *Sacred Pain: Hurting the Body for the Sake of the Soul.* Oxford: Oxford University Press.

Gluckman, M. 1970. *Custom and Conflict in Africa.* Oxford: Basil Blackwell.

Good, B. 1994. *Medicine, Rationality and Experience: An Anthropological Perspective.* Cambridge: Cambridge University Press.

Gordon, A. 1997. *Ghostly Matters: Haunting and the Sociological Imagination.* Minneapolis: University of Minnesota Press.

Graves, R. 1960. *The Greek Myths:1.* London: Penguin Books.

Haraway, D. 2007. *When Species Meet.* Minneapolis: University of Minnesota Press.

Hitt, J. 2005. *On the Road.* London: Simon and Schuster.

Ingold, T., and J. L. Vergunst. 2008. "Introduction," in T. Ingold and J. Vergunst (eds.), *Ways of Walking: Ethnography and Practice on Foot.* Hampshire, UK: Ashgate, 1–20.

Irving, A. 2005. "Life Made Strange: An Essay on the Re-Inhabitation of Bodies and Landscapes," in W. James and D. Mills (eds.), *The Qualities of Time: Anthropological Approaches.* Oxford: Berg, 317–30.

Jackson, M. 1998. *Minima Ethnographica: Intersubjectivity and the Anthropological Project.* Chicago: Chicago University Press.

———. 2003. "Foreword," in N. Rapport, *I am Dynamite.* London: Routledge, xi–xiv.

———. 2005. *Existential Anthropology: Events, Exigencies and Effects.* London: Berghahn Books.

———. 2007. *Excursions.* Durham, NC: Duke University Press.

———. 2009. *The Palm at the End of the Mind: Relatedness, Religiosity and the Real.* Durham, NC: Duke University Press.

Kleinman, A. 1997. *Writing at the Margin: Discourse between Anthropology and Medicine.* Berkeley: University of California Press.

Leder, D. 1990. *The Absent Body.* Chicago: University of Chicago Press.

Luard, N. 1998. *The Field of the Star: A Pilgrim's Journey to Santiago de Compostela.* Harmondsworth, UK: Penguin.

Michalowski, R., and J. Dubisch. 2001. *Run for the Wall: Remembering Vietnam on a Motorcycle Pilgrimage.* New Brunswick, NJ: Rutgers University Press.

Moore, T. 2004. *Spanish Steps: One Man and His Ass on the Pilgrim Way to Santiago.* London: Jonathan Cape.

Morris, D. 1991. *The Culture of Pain.* Berkeley: University of California Press.

Nietzsche, F. [1882] 1974. *The Gay Science.* Trans. W. Kaufman. New York: Random House.

Orsi, R. 1996. *Thank You, St. Jude: Women's Devotion to the Patron Saint of Hopeless Causes*. New Haven, CT: Yale University Press.

———. 2005. *Between Heaven and Earth: The Religious Worlds People Make and the Scholars Who Study Them*. Princeton, NJ: Princeton University Press.

Rapport, N. 2003. *I am Dynamite*. London: Routledge.

Rapport, N., and J. Overing (eds.). 2000. *Social and Cultural Anthropology: The Key Concepts*. London: Routledge.

Reader, I. 2007. "Pilgrimage Growth in the Modern World: Meanings and Implications." *Religion* 37(3): 210–29.

Rorty, R. 1992. *Contingency, Irony, and Solidarity*. Cambridge: Cambridge University Press.

Rupp, J. 2005. *Walk in a Relaxed Manner: Life Lessons from the Camino*. New York: Orbis Books.

Schell, M., and D. Schell. 2001. *My Father, My Daughter: Pilgrims on the Road to Santiago*. New York: Journeybook.

Solnit, R. 2002. *Wanderlust: A History of Walking*. New York: Verso.

Taylor, C. 1991. *The Ethics of Authenticity*. Cambridge, MA: Harvard University Press.

Taylor, L. 2007. "Centre and Edge: Pilgrimage and the Moral Geography of the US/Mexico Border." *Mobilities* 2(3): 383–93.

Tomlinson, M., and M. Engelke. 2007. "Meaning, Anthropology, Christianity," in M. Engelke and M. Tomlinson (eds.), *The Limits of Meaning: Case Studies in the Anthropology of Christianity*. London: Berghahn Books, 1–38.

Tweed, T. 2006. *Crossing and Dwelling: A Theory of Religion*. Cambridge, MA: Harvard University Press.

Žižek, S. 2002. *Welcome to the Desert of the Real*. London: Verso.

CHAPTER 6

Shades of Darkness

Silence, Risk, and Fear among Tourists and Nepalis during Nepal's Civil War

SHARON HEPBURN

Shades of Dark Tourism

I went to Nepal to document civilian life in Kathmandu during the conflict between the Communist Party of Nepal (Maoist) and the Nepalese state (1996–2006). I also conducted research on tourism, for two reasons. First, it was a good cover to help protect the people with whom I was talking. Second, it was striking that tourism was carrying on at all and that many tourists thought it was a great time to travel in Nepal precisely because tourist numbers were down. So there was tourism, in which tourists by their own accounts had good journeys; and there was darkness, in which people were dying and fearful. How did these two worlds coexist? The situation did not coincide with scholars' conceptions of what they call dark tourism, the research agenda that stresses tourism *about* darkness. This, in contrast, was tourism *in* darkness. Unlike the usual subjects of dark tourism studies, tourists did not go to Nepal to see war and death, or to experience danger, or to see attractions representing or interpreting the war, as there were none. This chapter explores the tourism *in* darkness in Nepal during the spring of 2002 that seemed blind to much of the darkness. The chapter first discusses how the culture of silence that had emerged throughout Nepal during the war extended to encompass tourists, thus limiting what tourists heard about the conflict zone they were visiting, and influencing their perceptions of it. It then takes the imagery of "shades of darkness" (see Stone 2006) to talk about variations in dark tourism sites. I develop that concept and imagery to talk about the varying ways tourists perceive and relate to the situation in Nepal, and the actual risks of the situation in terms of their individual backgrounds and dispositions.

Modern (and postmodern) practices of travel to sites relating to death and suffering of various sorts, in various ways, are the subject of dark tourism as a research area. One of the earliest steps in this trajectory was Rojek's (1993) account of leisure and travel as escape activity. He described what he called *black spots*, that is, "commercial tourist attractions associated with graves or other sites in which celebrities or large numbers of people have met with sudden or violent death" (1993: 136). Expanding this domain of blackness, renaming it (the heart of) darkness, Foley and Lennon coined the term *dark tourism* to cover travel "for remembrance, education or entertainment" to "sites and events of the last hundred years, which had either been the locations of death and disaster or interpretations of such events for visitors" (Foley and Lennon 1996: 195; see also Lennon and Foley 2000). This definition came after they had adopted an inclusive approach to the topic, but found that led them down "a number of blind alleys" (1996: 195). They do not describe those alleys, but, having excluded them, they defined the parameters of a fruitful area of research. Others took up the project, offering related phrases to describe aspects of the same domain. Blom (2000: 32) considered *morbid tourism* that focuses on sudden deaths that quickly draw crowds, and also attractions related to "morbid" subjects. Tarlow understands dark tourism to be visits to "places where tragedies or historically noteworthy death has occurred and that continue to impact our lives" (2005: 48). Seaton proposes that dark tourism, which he calls *thanatourism*, is travel "to a locality wholly, or partially, motivated by the desire for actual or symbolic encounters with death, particularly but not exclusively, violent death" (1996: 240). Seaton also adds complexity to the model by delineating kinds of attractions such as war memorials, scenes of execution, and war museums. To a lesser degree some have addressed the complexity of visitor motivations (Seaton and Lennon 2004; Tarlow 2005; Wight 2005). These definitions have three things in common, stressed to different degrees: there is a place associated with death or suffering, the originating phenomena is in the past, and the tourist is motivated to visit at least in part by interest in death or suffering.

Other scholars play on the imagery of darkness. For example, in his study of Auschwitz, Miles distinguishes between "dark" and "darker" tourism, the difference being whether the attraction is a site associated with death or suffering, or the site of death itself, and he calls the latter *darker tourism* (2002: 1175). In "Shades of Darkness: Alcatraz and Robben Island," Strange and Kempa (2003: 386) argue that prison tourism is a form of dark tourism, but that there are "multiple shades of penal history marketing and interpretation," and they explore how "multi-hued forms of interpretation have been produced" as these sites evolved as tourist attractions. In a similar way, Sharpley (2005) plays on the linguistic and visual imagery of darkness, and suggests that there can be shades of dark tourism. Sites can be relatively "paler" or "darker" depending on the degree to which visitors are fascinated with death, and the degree to which the site nourishes that fascination. The darkest or blackest site is one in which the visitors have most interest in death and can be absorbed in it at the site. Stone also takes up this imagery and proposes a spectrum of dark tourism sites from the darkest to the lightest. He argues that dark tourism sites "lie along a rather fluid and dynamic 'spectrum of intensity'" (2006: 146) and provides a typology of kinds of dark tourism sites. These range from the lightest—"dark fun factories," to the darkest—"dark camps of genocide." But within these, he suggests that there are many layers (such as authenticity, entertainment value, and political and ideological influence) that contribute to where any site (no matter where on the typology) might be on the spectrum of lighter to darker.

For most tourists traveling to Nepal in the spring of 2002, their journey was not dark tourism in any of the senses above. There was no attraction or site to interpret the war to them. They did not go with the motivation to see death, suffering, or the war. There was no commemoration of an event in the past. Nonetheless, I suggest that considering the situation as "dark tourism" is not a "blind alley" in Foley and Lennon's sense. In this chapter I walk down this alley, along with the tourists who came to Nepal in 2002 and who traveled, knowingly or not, in a situation of widespread death and suffering—darkness—variously experienced and perceived by all involved. Like other scholars, I adopt the imagery of shades of darkness. I do not use the imagery to think about the "attraction," because there was none. Instead, I use the imagery to describe the various ways that tourists and Nepalis experienced and understood travels, life, and risk in a conflict zone.

This chapter is narrative and qualitative and makes no attempt to quantify tourist numbers or the typicality of responses. Building on more than three years of research experience in Nepal prior to the conflict, I made five one-month trips to Nepal during the course of the war, documenting civilian life in Kathmandu and Pokhara. Most information about the situation of Nepalis given here is based on conversations I had in Nepali with people I have known for at least ten years.

Tourism in Nepal during Wars on—and of—Terror

Nepal first issued tourist visas in 1951, and the number of visitors steadily increased until September 2001. In the wake of coordinated attacks by al-Qaeda on the United States on 11 September 2001, security concerns and awareness of the US "war on terror" contributed to tourism's decline worldwide. Nepal's case is interesting in that this external political event coincided with internal political struggles—namely, a civil war and the massacre of most of the royal family—exacerbating the local effects of a worldwide phenomenon. In Nepal, tourist arrival numbers dropped from about 464,000 in 2000 to less than 216,000 in 2002 (MTCA 2003) as many potential visitors either stayed home or went somewhere less troubled.

The events of 2001 in Nepal were the culmination of a decade of political transformation that began in 1990 with the success of a popular movement to establish a multiparty democracy under a constitutional monarch. Maoist members of the Communist Party of Nepal were dissatisfied with the slow pace of structural change occurring under the new system and the persistence of entrenched forms of inequality, and so they launched their People's War in 1996 with the intent to replace the fledgling multiparty system with a communist republic. By the time a peace agreement was signed in 2006, the Maoists had displaced the elected government throughout most of the country. Nearly a half million people had been forced from their homes and land; the economy was in shambles; thirteen thousand people had died as a direct result of the insurgency and thousands more were maimed with countless others missing (Bhattarai, Conway, and Shrestha 2005; Hutt 2004; Shah 2008; Thapa and Hauff 2005).

Most of what I recount in this chapter took place in 2002, six months into a national state of emergency characterized by great political instability and escalating violence. Before this time, the fact of the conflict was not widely publicized in the media, and there was sustained growth in tourism (Bhattarai, Conway, and Shrestha 2005). It was not until the events of 2001 that arrivals declined rapidly. In June 2001, King Birendra and most of his family (the royal lineage) were killed by gunfire while dining together in Kathmandu. Prince Gyanendra was not at the meal and so lived to be crowned king on 4 June. In the midst of the national mood of shock, suspicion, and uncertainty that followed, the Maoists expanded their campaign.

On 26 November 2001, after only six months on the throne, King Gyanendra declared a national state of emergency. Echoing global refrains of the war on terror, the Nepali government promulgated the TADO (Terrorist and Disruptive Activities [Control and Punishment] Ordinance), identified the Maoists as terrorists, and for the first time deployed the Royal Nepal Army to help stop Maoist expansion. King Gyanendra suspended rights to freedom of expression, peaceful assembly, privacy and information, and rights against preventative detention (Hutt 2004: 11). The United States and Britain gave military aid to help Nepal overcome their recently named terrorists. With a well-armed army engaged in the conflict, casualties mounted dramatically. An Amnesty International (2002) report documenting this period notes the widespread use of arbitrary arrest, illegal detention, disappearance, torture, and extrajudicial killing by the Royal Nepalese Army. It notes widespread killing and maiming by Maoists of people not cooperating with their cause. The report expressed great concern about the overall deteriorating human rights situation, and abuses by the army, the police, and the Maoists.

Despite repeated statements by Maoist leaders that tourists were safe, by the end of 2001 Indian visitors had decreased by 24 percent, Americans by 60 percent, British by 45 percent, and Japanese by 63 percent (Anon. 2002; MTCA 2003). Bhattarai and colleagues describe the effects on the economy as hotels were shut, stores closed, and jobs lost: "Regardless of one's views and interpretations of the ongoing cycle of political turmoil and violence, there is little doubt they have engendered a profound sense of public fear, thereby greatly worsening the woes of Nepal's tourism. ... Life revolving around tourism has, in essence, taken a heavy toll" (2005: 684).

Shades of Fear in Dark Times

Like Bhattarai, others have noted the pervasive sense of fear felt by many if not most Nepalis. People felt varying degrees of fear, and, in particular, they felt fear of bodily harm. Over five visits to Kathmandu, friends told me of innumerable specific incidents. An elderly woman who had been my neighbor in the early 1990s was alarmed by the army coming to the door at night, "just coming in, with no respect," to look for Maoists. Another friend and his family received threats from the Maoists and paid "donations" because their son was in the army. A fellow teacher I had known since 1985 had his hand amputated because he had questioned Maoists in the village he taught in and refused to pay a punitive "donation."

Anthropologists working in Nepal during the war have recognized the dangers of overprivileging fear. They note that through it all, other aspects of life go on: people make meals, plan marriages, and enjoy jokes with friends. Pettigrew and Adhikari, who made repeated visits to a village throughout the insurgency, argue that fear is not generic and universal. It is "always contextually situated, differently experienced through time and related to personal circumstances," and that it is "not universal—not everyone is frightened all of the time, and people experience, express and conceal fear differently. Conflict-related fear co-existed, interacted with, exacerbated and diminished other fears" (2009: 403, 405). Yet writing after the war, they feel confident in pointing out that there was widespread fear because "fear (or lack of fear) was the main characteristic which people used to differentiate the insurgency from the pre-and post-insurgency periods" (2009: 405). In her ethnographic work in a village under Maoist control, Lecomte-Tilouine describes what she calls "paralyzing fright" and notes that "one of the first things that was explained to me was that fright left villagers feeling constrained in their freedom of speech and action" (2009: 388). Moreover, what people feared most was bodily harm. Darkness for Nepalis was not continuous and unmitigated. Although they lived in a situation that in the future might become a focus for dark tourism (as classically defined), fear, suffering, death, and injury (the stuff of dark tourism) came and went, in various intensities at various times, creating for them—one might say—a spectrum of lighter and darker experiences of a pervasive darkness.

Although many civilians told me they felt like "a yam between two rocks" (see also Pettigrew 2004), I can say much less about the experience of those who are themselves the "rocks." A young solider I know in Kathmandu feels vulnerable both on and off duty, and worries for his family's safety. But for the Maoists—at least those convinced of the rightness of the cause— the darkness of death might well take on a different hue. Although for many Nepalis the situation was dark and fearful, for many Maoists the situation was surely uplifting and encouraging. In 1995, tourists trekking in the mountains needed permits issued by the Nepali government to show at police posts along their route. Along many trekking routes in 2002, Maoists had replaced the police who were no longer able to defend themselves, and Maoists issued permits (with pictures of Stalin, Lenin, and Mao) and collected fees. Many tourists were worried that insurgents had replaced government authority in their trekking vacation destinations. But for the Maoists, this absence was evidence of their growing power and authority, and a source of revenue formerly claimed by the state they say oppressed them. That the country was in turmoil was a sign of success unimagined for the movement just a few years earlier. Maoists celebrate deaths of Nepali soldiers and martyr their dead comrades. Thereby, the darkness of death becomes a sign of the light ahead in the future regime. For those less convinced of the cause, being a Maoist solider at least ensured food every day, something they otherwise might not have: even at the most basic level, a dark situation can, in relative terms, at times seems bright(er) to any particular individual than the alternatives.

Tourists, Having Decided to Come to Nepal: Spring 2002 in Pokhara

The situation related above was largely unseen by the tourists who have weighed the risks and decided to come here, to the town of Pokhara, in the spring of 2002. When I first approached tourists to talk about their experiences, they often expressed relief that things seemed fine in Nepal, and many thought the travel advisories had been overcautious. Conferring with a colleague about how odd this seemed to me, she agreed and also told me she had met an agent for Doctors Without Borders who had worked in many conflict zones. He was planning to start a medical project in the area of Nepal most influenced by the conflict. He told her that he had never been in a country that was so badly affected by conflict, yet still attracting tourists, many of whom seemed to be little aware of the severity of the conflict. My colleague relates that as he told her this, "he pointed to groups of tourists buying pretty postcards depicting the good old 'smiling Nepalis'" (Judith Pettigrew, personal communication).

The lakeside area of the town of Pokhara has grown over the past few decades to cater to tourists. Unless a tourist had been there preconflict, they would not have known that the streets were eerily empty, and that it is not normal that "you could roll a bowling ball down the main road," as one long-time resident put it. They would see people going about their day: carrying stacks of wood on their back, washing clothes in the lake, or driving a herd of cattle by the restaurant. They would see the sun shining, the Himalayas reflected in the lake, and the food still available on order. Everything would indeed seem bright. And they might reasonably ask what the fuss was about. At my breakfast restaurant by the lake, a tourist would not notice the out-of-uniform policemen sitting at the next table from whom the Nepali staff kept a distance and treated with great reserve and deference. As they showed off their "Maoist visas," the permits collected through various treks as receipts for "donations" to Maoists on the trails, the tourists would not know that the waiter's brother had been killed by Maoists, and he would not tell them that for fear of who might overhear but instead would humor their enthusiasm. And like other waiters, hoteliers, and store owners, when a tourist asks "Where's the war?" they say "Oh, there's no problem here," even though they pay protection money to those police at the next table, in addition to a comparable payment to the local Maoists. The tourists might know that the owner, who I have known for fifteen years, laments the lack of business, but they would not know that he also laments that he has to kill a pig that day "the old way." He prefers to shoot an animal in the head, "but if you walk down the street with a gun like we used to, the Maoists—the place is crawling with them—would be after you for the gun, and if the police see it, they will think you are a Maoist and arrest or shoot you." So he will slit that animal's throat, and it will look to the tourist like "how they do things in Nepal."

One day my friend, a hotel owner, and others told me that some major Maoist activities were expected in the center of town around 5 PM. The Maoists, they told me, had requested that the local government give them virtual control of the town. Although the lakeside is a few miles from the town center, I wondered whether I should return to my room by five. I was the only customer at a fairly upscale café. Some children ran in and out, chased by the waiters: in normal times they would not be let in at all. I was told by the waiter that they were street kids and came from the village to avoid abduction by Maoists,[1] or because their parents had died "like so many these days." I asked a waiter if what I had heard about the takeover was true, and after he had confirmed it I asked if he was scared, to which he answered "of course." Like me he was wondering what would happen; unlike me, he was unable to leave to go to a safer place as the time approached. My present and future looked bright. For me, this was mere interruption. His future—immediate and long term—was uncertain and tinged with memories, knowledge, and a social vision I only know of second-hand through friends in Kathmandu. We both looked out on that beautiful day, in that beautiful place, and it was indeed hard to imagine the troubles hidden there.

Silence, Suspicion, and the Need to Keep Business Going

The troubles are hidden from view and hidden by silence. Although my waiter was candid with me—perhaps because I spoke Nepali and knew about the situation—the usual reticence I witnessed with tourists was part of a wider culture of silence (Gautam 2004) that grew with the insurgency. Maya, a sixty-year-old woman whose family had owned a restaurant and hotel for thirty years, told me "of course we don't talk to tourists about such things; we want them to come. It is safe for them here, and we need them to come. But we also don't talk because we don't know who is listening." In this conversation, she lowered her voice and subtly glanced around to see who might be nearby, behavior I saw repeatedly with many others. Of course that waiter would not tell a tourist his brother was killed by Maoists just last month: who knows who might be listening—perhaps those police at the next table, perhaps an informer—to what he might have to say about that loss and those who perpetuated it? Pettigrew describes how caregivers raising children in a rural village during the war teach them to be silent and cautious, and rehearse them in how to answer questions from soldiers—whether Maoist or government—as it "could be a matter of life and death" (2007: 324). Commenting on this emerging practice of verbal restraint, a Nepali friend I met while living in the United States told me that he was shocked and disturbed by the changes he saw in his native village when he visited in 1998. "We used to sit outside and talk in the afternoon. Now that is gone, that nice part of village life. Now people stay inside." He was admonished by his father to not "walk around just talking about things" and needed no persuading as he knew that just prior to his arrival a village man—the one person in the area who had a phone, and "heard everything"—was killed by Maoists, accused of being an informer.

Silence protects when you do not know whom you can trust. Maya's comments echo what Pettigrew and Adhikari conclude, that "people knew that the Maoist surveillance-society was perpetuated by local collusion. ... Villagers ... betrayed each other. ... There was increasing uncertainty about ... the allegiances and motivations of even the most trusted confidantes" (2009: 404). People were even more fearful of the army and their informers. Lecomte-Tilouine reports this same pattern of silence and distrust. In the Maoist-controlled village she writes about, she found that the

> new complicated communication strategy was ... often based on lies. ... It was as if the revolution had entirely blurred communications. ... It was only at night, or in the forest, that people started to open up, to express their deepest anguish about the two opposing dangers hanging over them. [People would even fear that] their close relations would pass on "reports" to the Maoists and denounce them as "informants." (2009: 399)

If a tourist comes and finds beauty and hospitality rather than fear and suffering, this is partly due to a sensible business strategy, but it is also because Nepalis may well be interacting with tourists in terms of a culture of silence that they share with other Nepalis. This is different from the sort of backstage/frontstage Goffmanesque host/guest interrelationships in tourism. In those situations there is openness among the hosts (Nunez 1989: 271). With the generalized suspicion and fear in Nepal, what is revealed and shown among the hosts themselves is likewise variable, and is strongly censored by the imperative to secrecy. As the darkness proceeds, as the war continues, the tourists' very experience of it is shaped in part by the culture—the culture of silence—that has developed between the people experiencing darkness—or the possibility of darkness—firsthand. The shades of darkness and lightness that are (respectively) concealed from and revealed to the tourist, are the product in part of the adaptations of the host community to their own experiences of darkness.

Back at that restaurant by the lake, on the day of the preannounced Maoist actions, five o'clock passes and six, and seven, and nothing seems different. I decide to take a cab back to my hotel, and we arrive in darkness. As I pay, a policeman of high rank enters the taxi and asks the driver where he is going. By law in these times, police and army officers can requisition any taxi they want on demand. The driver says "I'm going home," and to me he seems afraid. "We'll see," answers the policeman, and they drive away. They are speaking Nepali, and the content and possibilities would be lost on most other tourists. Like other tourists, I go safely to my room, not worried who might knock on the door at night. I close it silently.

Tourists Walking through Shades of Darkness and Light

Many hotels have closed and others stand nearly empty at peak trekking season because many potential tourists have decided to stay home or to go somewhere less dark and less risky. Those tourists who do come have assessed the risks. So who is here? Who has decided to come, despite particular warnings about Nepal and despite generalized security concerns worldwide?

Looking around, there are hardly any white faces (Hepburn 2002). Those white people who are there often think, "We're the only tourists here." They often do not see that the darker-skinned people around them are not all Nepali. Most are Nepali, but many others are from Israel, and some are from India. Nepalis generally use the word "tourist" to refer to white visitors, but often refer to Israeli and Indian visitors simply as "Israelis" or "Indians." I will follow this usage here. Many tourists had indeed thoroughly consulted embassies, travel agencies, and online discussions, and had still decided that it was a reasonable or even ideal time to come. With fewer tourists, lodges were not packed, deals could be had on just about everything, and some previous visitors thought it important to come back and support Nepalis in the collapsing tourism economy. Many told me that they felt quite reassured having read that Maoists had injured no tourists, and that the Maoist leader Prachandra had ordered that no tourist be hurt. They were confident that if they gave money to Maoists, as and when requested, the insurgents would not bother them. Once in Nepal, many were also reassured, they told me, because every Nepali they asked told them that there was "no problem." Once convinced of their own immunity to negative sanctions, some thought the possibility of actually meeting Maoists was an additional perk. Collecting "Maoist visas" was one of the few ways to consume the war materially, and they were a common topic of conversation: people compared them, commenting on the photos of world communist leaders, read the slogans, and told of the encounters that led to them.

Mary and Brian, England

Mary, about fifty years old, who has "been coming here for years" from England, shows me her collection of Maoist visas, given by young men who were "very nice, and told us what they were doing." Although some tourists I met were ambivalent about supporting a violent cause this way, Mary and her husband Brian thought this no worse than contributing to a violent state apparatus, as one does in paying a government visa fee. They were interested in my explanation that the Maoists were renaming districts after ethnic groups, and that these were the districts noted on their receipts; they were interested in "learning more about the situation." Asked if they had fears about traveling, they said they had none as they "know Nepal." Following the advice given at a talk at their guesthouse in Kathmandu about the security situation, they had traveled in groups in some areas due to reports of Maoists and "people pretending to be Maoists and asking for money." As advised, they also hired a local guide who could "keep his ear to the ground about what's going on" because, they were told, "Nepalis will just tell you everything is fine, as to say otherwise is bad for business." They did not mention being told that for a Nepali to talk about the situation in any way might be dangerous due to informers on all sides. Mary and Brian are a particular case, but tell a variation of a story I heard frequently enough: having made the decision to come, they played by the rules and enjoyed a trek as usual, with the added attraction of encounters with "very nice" insurgents wielding weapons. The Nepal they encountered was, by their accounts, not much different from what they had found on previous trips, except more pleasant as there were fewer tourists. They felt they were doing a good thing, contributing economically, supporting a local cause—"It's not for us to judge"—and generally being "open-minded."

Their journey through the shades of darkness experienced by Nepalis around them was—by their own accounts—overall quite bright. Through our conversations over three breakfasts, they recounted the pleasures and rigors of their journey, talked of reunions with Nepalis from past journeys, and were very positive about their experiences, with little mention of Maoists, indicating to me that the political situation had made little impact on their journey. This sort of experience is reflected in the comments made in a "Traveler's Log Book for Annapurna Region" kept in a conservation project office in the tourist area of Pokhara. Steve and Deanon from Canada write, "We had no problem with Maoists"; Brandon and Ang from Canada write, "There weren't any Maoists or Maoist women, and the only guns we saw were in the hands of Nepali soldiers" (who, for Brandon and Ang were apparently a benign presence, rather than a terrifying one, as they are for many Nepalis); Allard and Henry from Holland "felt safe all the time"; Fred reports "evidence of Maoist activities (slogans on monuments, lodges, and red flags) but no one gave us any grief." A few tourists report being "shaken" by encounters with people with guns coming out of the woods who let them pass on after paying a fee.

One hundred and twenty tourists made entries in the Log Book in the first four months of 2002, ranging from a few lines to a few pages in length. Eighty-one of these mentioned the Maoists, if only to note the absence of an encounter with them. That so many mentioned Maoists—despite their apparent absence—indicates a shared consciousness of possibility among the tourists, the possibility of encounter, "grief," or "problems," or even of mortal danger. In short, people writing in the Log Book were aware of the possibility of an encounter with darkness (war, the agents of war, or harm to themselves), and in writing of it they anticipate a reader aware of that same possibility. Almost all encourage their readers to continue without worry: there were perhaps signs of trouble, but little chance that it would touch them. Of the five who noted encounters with Maoists, two (traveling together) enjoyed the ensuing conversation; the other three were "shaken" or found the encounter otherwise unpleasant, either from fear or from their reservations over supporting a violent movement. I know little of the journeys and dispositions of the writers, but, reflecting on the idea of shades of darkness, in terms of what was written, it would seem safe to say that for many tourists there is the idea of darkness, rather like a shadow. They may be aware of something there that casts the shadow. The shadow—the shadow of darkness, the hint of darkness—creates some apprehension, yet it is intangible and cannot touch you. But when the solid object that casts the shadow—the source of darkness—is encountered, as it was for the tourists who were "shaken," it is tangible, seen, and it can touch you. But, in point of fact, they found that touch to be benign. Both the shadow and the source of darkness are fleetingly feared, but then are left behind and noted in a Log Book as nothing for a tourist to worry about.

In an interesting way, Nepalis too are aware of the presence of a shadow of the source of darkness. In Kathmandu, very few people I knew had been hurt by either the Maoists or the security forces. Yet they had all heard many stories, many of them horrific. And the intermittent contact they had—the head counts at night by the army, for example— kept up an alertness to the possibility of fears being realized. Similarly, based on interviews with eighty-five villagers, Pettigrew concludes:

> The majority of the time, people's greatest fears are not realized, such as death, abduction or injury to themselves or their families, but the possibility is always there. The potential always exists for punishment for actions interpreted or re-interpreted as unacceptable. (2007: 313)

Lecomte-Tilouine suggests that having heard of brutal actions "in people's imagination, the limits of the Maoists' possible actions were boundless" (2009: 392). If tourists can be thought of as being aware of a shadow they can ignore until its source materializes, many Nepalis can be thought of as also being aware of the shadow but in a more charged, fearful way as—counter to the risks to the tourists—the appearance of the source of the shadow to Nepalis brings the possibility of the sort of horrific things they have heard about. There is darkness itself, its source, and its shadow: each differently known, perceived, recognized, and talked about by both Nepalis and tourists.

Tourists addressed other concerns in the advice they wrote in the Log Book: concerns about temperature, altitude, routes, speed of walk- ing, and even the caution to get to the Neeru Guest House in Marpha— "the most amazing apple crumble," they warned, "Be careful, it sells out very quickly." In fact, the general tone was that things are as usual with whatever is going on among the locals well in the background. A trekker might well be more worried about the supply of dessert than the pos- sibility of violence.

Anne, Canada

Although Mary and Brian and others had not otherwise encountered war at home or in their travels, some white tourists did experience Nepal against quite a different background. Anne is a forty-seven-year-old Canadian nurse and has traveled mostly through voluntary work. She reports that she was not at all scared to visit Nepal. Volunteering as a nurse in Iraq during the Gulf War, she had worked in a Kurdish camp and described traveling by helicopter "strapped to the gun part as there was no seat," and other adventures. Although she assigned such adventures to the past, to her relative youth, she says that now she thinks the risks for any individual are small. Furthermore, "it's unfamiliarity that makes things seem risky," and that lack of familiarity can make places seem like "a big amorphous blob of badness." She had traveled in the Arabian Peninsula at times when negative stereotypes of the people dominant in North America were particularly pronounced, and yet she found warm, hospitable people—"but you don't hear that kind of thing," she added. Nonetheless, although she had traveled in Israel, she would not visit that country during 2002, nor would she go to the United States, simply because she saw these countries as anti-Arab rather than due to any perceived risk. Rather than visiting and taking advice on how to deal with the situation from guides, hotels, and others in the tourism industry, Anne sees the landscape as similar to ones elsewhere. There are shades of gray—"not just the bad things, and not just good times," she says, and, as in many other places, there are ways of being in Nepal that let you see what you might see without a war, and experience your travels in a way as untouched as possible by local troubles. Or, she continues, "you can accept that life goes on shaped by difficulties, and take an interest in that." Anne concluded that if she encountered violence in Nepal, at least as a nurse she would be able to help someone, thereby moving from thinking of risks to herself to recognizing the risks that others live with. Anne came to Nepal having lived and traveled in other places during times of violent conflict, and having observed other foreigners in such situations. Cast in my terms, I would say that like me, she sees that people can take steps to ensure that their experience is, in terms of the shades of darkness, bright. But they can also allow that there are shades between darkness and brightness. And you can recognize that the shadows are there, seen by others, and maybe yourself, and still recognize that life goes on in the various ways that it does.

Hermann, Germany

Hermann, forty, from Germany, has been to Nepal many times and is here now on a break from volunteer work in India, resting and convalescing in a cooler place. Like Anne, he responds to my question "Did you have any fears about coming?" suggesting an obliviousness to risk:

"I'm not afraid of injury or being hurt: that is not the point. I'm thinking that people must have changed here, away from the dignity they had." Hermann was in Nepal in November 2001 when the state of emergency was declared, most civil liberties suspended, and curfews enforced by gunshot in the cities: "There were army in the street with guns, and I look at their faces and they are just stupid young boys. ... If something would start to happen, they would just start shooting." He repeats that he is not afraid of being hurt. His fear is for what he saw happening in Nepal, that "the tension of the situation must affect people and that would be my reason not to go ... because of what people would be like: how could they act normally, like in the past?" And Hermann is right: the Nepalis do not engage the tourists "normally," but within the constraints of a culture of silence. Hermann sees that the form of his encounters with Nepalis would be the product of what people are living. Hermann recognizes the army presence, that people must be "tense" and that something might "start to happen" and so he can be said to recognize the possibility of death and the presence of suffering. But his fear, he said, is not darkness, death, or injury for himself but for how the darkness others experience will be refracted through his encounters, distorting them. He noted that he saw that for many tourists this was not a problem; they were simply here on vacation and got on with what they came to do. Tourists, like Mary and Brian, perhaps, knew people would not be able to be relaxed and honest, but as long as the guide had "his ear to the ground" and knew of the dangers, the fact that they were walking in areas of scared people was not an issue. Quite different in attitude, Hermann "sees the darkness," and sees that people will be changed by it. He does not deny the darkness, he just decides not to engage with the effects of it.

Sally, England

Sally is an English psychotherapist taking a few days of vacation before working with victims of torture. She tells me that from her preparation to work with the Center for Victims of Torture, she is aware of the increasing number of abductions by the army and the Maoists and their common use of torture. She knew that levels of violence have increased since the state of emergency began, and had heard that some threats had been made against foreigners. In short, she knew about the darkest parts of the national situation, had comparative experience, and only visited because a friend here whom she "trusted absolutely" said it would be "safe enough." Having said she was not worried about coming during the conflict, she turned to other worries: "I might get ill from this giardia" (an intestinal parasite commonly contracted in the area) or from SARS disease. She "was worried about having a strange man from Bhutan come knocking at my door at 11 PM trying to get me to go to Bhutan," which had happened to her last time she was in Nepal. Sally worried about getting things stolen, perhaps her "passport and mascara." She worried that her husband would forget to water the lawn at home in England and worried about changing money. She worried that her "leg might collapse," or that she "might fall off a cliff in a car, or be run over, or be stuck and not able to leave for months." Although fully aware of the grimness of the situation, her few days on vacation before working were not shadowed by fear of violence. Rather, it was the risks of the physical environment for someone approaching sixty that worried her, and the practical details of life in Nepal and at home in England. As with Nepalis, fear of the conflict is not her only concern. Like many other tourists, once assured that it would be "safe enough," she does not worry about being a victim of the war herself. Unlike other tourists though, she will be confronting evidence of the darkness in an intense way. Sally works with victims of torture in England, and hears of atrocities on a weekly basis. I can only guess, but I would guess that like in England, she will not "take it home with her" after a day's work, just as she does not take "it" (the darkness) on her short holiday with her. Like Anne, the nurse, she is familiar with darkness and, like Anne, she sees the shades of gray and the different ways to engage with the presence of darkness.

Israelis and Tourists

Large numbers of Israelis leave for long backpacking journeys after finishing their conscripted national military service. I talked to some young Israelis, just out of the army, and some older ones who were traveling after a period of work or education. Almost all of the men I spoke with had been in combat positions that brought them high prestige but also accompanying levels of high risk. Women had served in various positions—cooking, paramedic training, or secretarial work—which brought them into situations of higher and lower risk at different times. Most had experienced acute levels of risk and seen much darkness during military service in contexts where they themselves had been the enemy to be shot at. No Israeli I talked to expressed concern about the Maoists and in fact, my questions brought laughs that I think were prompted by my naiveté. One man, obliquely referring to his past military experience, explained to me: "At least no one here particularly wants to shoot us." A woman pointed out that she feels no less safe here than in walking down the street in Jerusalem, her home. In Israel, it might have been risky and dark, but in Nepal the risk and the dark were incidental and not integral to their experiences. I heard no indication that the conflict was an attraction drawing Israelis to Nepal, however.

Indian tourists continued to come to Nepal; to see the mountains, go on pilgrimage, and go shopping. Worldwide caution and the civil war seemed lesser concerns than the rigor of their journeys in general. The big decline in Indian tourists came in January 2001 when Hirithik Roshan, a Bollywood star, allegedly said that he hated Nepal and the Nepalese people. In the days that followed, Air India stopped flights to Nepal, and cinemas and Indian businesses were attacked. I stayed in hotels that were nearly empty because Indian tour buses had turned back to safety, and I saw effigies of Roshan hung and burned. Public denials and apologies for misunderstanding "cooled things off." Perhaps the terror attacks on the United States and Nepal's state of emergency diverted national concerns from India and its popular stars. In any case, Indian tourists continued to come in 2002, though in smaller numbers, when many others were staying away.

Though internally diverse, like the white tourists, the Indians and Israelis come to the area of conflict with a different shared range of experiences. For instance, an Israeli man Avi expressed sympathy for, and empathy with, both the young Maoists he has heard of, and the young soldiers he has seen: "Children even younger than we were drawn into a national campaign." Rather than seeing "stupid young men" as Hermann had, he saw his counterparts of a decade earlier. It is unlikely that Hermann and Avi would have shared each other's perceptions. I have mostly described white tourists in this chapter, and tried to briefly recount their different perceptions. They share some common traits, and are distinctly different in some ways from other groups who, for example, might have served on the Gaza Strip or been potential targets of violence due to a Bollywood star's comment. I have focused here on white tourists, but have briefly introduced Israelis and Indians to indicate how very diverse group perspectives and experiences can be in life, and at the Pokhara lakeside in 2002, and thus in a site of darkness.

Conclusion

Dark tourism is about death, suffering, and atrocities, and Nepal during the conflict had all three. Nepalis experienced that darkness, and the fear around it, in different ways, at different times, and in different contexts. I have recounted how one adaptive strategy, a culture of silence, in part shaped how many tourists experienced the situation. The tourists' experiences were also shaped by perceptions they brought with them by preparatory reading and consulting, by the reasons they travel, and also by their own life histories and values. The diversity within all these backgrounds and predispositions contributed to their diverse experiences traveling in the Nepali darkness. If there is darkness, then here there are shades of darkness of experience and perception on multiple, interacting levels.

Nepal was a conflict zone in 2002, but even so would not be a site of dark tourism according to Foley and Lennon's understanding of the term, and as a subject it does not fit well within the range of research generated by the common definitions of dark tourism. There was no attraction set up to display or interpret the situation;[2] visitors on the whole came despite the war, not because of it. There was no commemoration of events in the past.

The scholarly considerations of shades of darkness discussed above point to differences that sites might have in intensities of associations with suffering and death after the suffering and death they represent have ended. This chapter has been an attempt to partially describe a site and the people involved as the darkness was unfolding. I point to the different ways people actually in the site—Nepali and otherwise—experience and are touched by death and suffering.

Pettigrew and Adhikari contend that fear is "always contextually situated, differently experienced through time and related to personal circumstances" (2009: 403). So, too, is the experience of dark things as they happen, as they shadow us, as we hide them and hide from them, reflect on them, and protect ourselves and others from them. To set out a scale of dark or darker, paler or darker, or more or less intense aspects of a situation is useful when talking about a fixed site. But if the motivations of visitors are considered, another layer of relative shades of darkness can be seen to shape these sites. And if there are visitors with widely ranging experiences of other instances of darkness, then the layers of various spectrums of lightness-darkness will start to pile up. If we could bring back the people who experienced the darkness as it happened, to add to the mix and swirl of hues and shades, what we will have is the practical necessity of discarding the scales and typologies, and describing from multiple points of view the shades of darkness, light, shadows, multihued forms of interpretation, and grey that coexist and are produced at any particular dark place, at any moment. The idea of a typology breaks down because in the case of Nepal, each aspect of the situation—each shade of fear, of darkness—during the conflict was contingent on context and the multiple shades of experience that formed it.

This partial description of one time in the conflict, in a place of death and suffering, does not fit the research paradigm of the fruitful dark tourism project. But it is offered to hint at the sorts of complexities that surround dark situations as lived, to point to questions to be asked when we study and create their later representations and interpretations. It is also offered as an account of tourism *in* darkness rather than tourism *about* darkness. Perhaps, then, there can be dark tourism without an identifiable "attraction"?

Acknowledgments

This research was funded by the Social Sciences and Humanities Research Council of Canada. I thank the editor of this volume, Jonathan Skinner, as well as Kathryn White, Judith Pettigrew, and Francois Thibault for their careful reading and helpful comments. I take responsibility for any errors of fact or interpretation.

Notes

This is a revised and updated version of an article that appeared as "Shades of Darkness: Silence, Risk, and Fear among Tourists and Nepalis during Nepal's Civil War" in J. Skinner, ed. (2010) *Journeys: The International Journal of Travel and Travel Writing*, Special Edition, *Writing the Dark Side of Travel* 11, no. 1 (2010): 133–55.

1. Most accounts I heard indicated that Maoists do not abduct children until they are in their teens.
2. In some sense I, the anthropologist, was an interpretive "attraction." For each hour I talked with a tourist about their experiences, I spent at least an hour talking about mine, and answering their questions about the conflict.

Bibliography

Amnesty International. 2002. *Nepal. A Deepening Human Rights Crisis: Time for International Action*. London: Amnesty International.
Anon. 2002. *Fiscal Years, 2000–2002*. Kathmandu: Ministry of Finance.
Bhattarai, K., D. Conway, and N. Shrestha. 2005. "Tourism, Terrorism and Turmoil in Nepal." *Annals of Tourism Research* 32(3): 669–88.
Blom, T. 2000. "Morbid Tourism—A Postmodern Market Niche with an Example from Althorp." *Norwegian Journal of Geography* 54(1): 29–36.
Foley, M., and J. Lennon. 1996. "Editorial: Heart of Darkness." *International Journal of Heritage Studies* 2: 195–97.
Gautam, N. 2004. "Maoist Movement and Development of Silence Culture: A Case Study of Dang District in Mid-Western Nepal." MA thesis, Tribhuvan University, Kirtipur, Nepal.

Hepburn, S. J. 2002. "Touristic Forms of Life in Nepal." *Annals of Tourism Research* 29(3): 611–30.

Hutt, M. 2004. "Introduction: Monarchy, Democracy and Maoism in Nepal," in M. Hutt (ed.), *Himalayan People's War*. Bloomington: Indiana University Press, 1–20.

Lecomte-Tilouine, M. 2009. "Terror in a Maoist Model Village, Mid-Western Nepal." *Dialectical Anthropology* 33: 383–401.

Lennon, J., and M. Foley. 2000. *Dark Tourism: The Attraction of Death*. London: Continuum.

Miles, W. 2002. "Auschwitz: Museum Interpretation and Darker Tourism." *Annals of Tourism Research* 29: 1175–78.

MTCA. 2003. *Nepal Tourism Statistics*. Kathmandu: Ministry of Tourism and Civil Aviation.

Nunez, T. 1989. "Touristic Studies in Anthropological Perspective," in V. L. Smith (ed.), *Hosts and Guests: The Anthropology of Tourism*. Philadelphia: University of Pennsylvania Press, 265–80.

Pettigrew, J. 2004. "Living between the Maoists and the Army in Rural Nepal," in M. Hutt (ed.), *Himalayan People's War: Nepal's Maoist Rebellion*. Bloomington: Indiana University Press, 261–83.

———. 2007. "Learning to Be Silent: Change, Childhood and Mental Health in the Maoist Insurgency in Nepal," in H. Ishi, D. N. Gellner, and K. Nawa (eds.), *Nepalis Inside and Outside Nepal: Political and Social Transformations*. Delhi: Manohar, 307–48.

Pettigrew, J., and K. Adhikari. 2009. "Fear and Everyday Life in Rural Nepal." *Dialectical Anthropology* 33: 403–22.

Rojek, C. 1993. *Ways of Escape*. Basingstoke, UK: Macmillian.

Seaton, A. V. 1996. "Guided by the Dark: From Thanatopsis to Thanatourism." *International Journal of Heritage Studies* 2: 234–44.

Seaton A. V., and J. Lennon. 2004. "Thanotourism in the Early 21st Century: Moral Panics, Ulterior Motives and Alterior Desires," in T. V. Singh (ed.), *New Horizons in Tourism—Strange Experiences and Strangers Practices*. Wallingford, UK: CABI Publishing, 63–82.

Shah, S. 2008. "Revolution and Reaction in the Himalayas: Cultural Resistance and the Maoist New Regime in Western Nepal." *American Ethnologist* 35(3): 481–99.

Sharpley, R. 2005. "Travels to the Edge of Darkness: Towards a Typology of Dark Tourism," in C. Ryan, S. Page, and M. Aicken (eds.), *Taking Tourism to the Limit*. Oxford: Elsevier, 217–28.

Stone, P. R. 2006. "A Dark Tourism Spectrum: Towards a Typology of Death and Macabre Related Tourist Sites, Attractions and Exhibitions." *Tourism* 54(2): 145–60.

Strange, C., and M. Kemper. 2003. "Shades of Dark Tourism: Alcatraz and Robben Island." *Annals of Tourism Research* 30(2): 386–405.

Tarlow, P. 2005. "Dark Tourism: The Appealing 'Dark Side' of Tourism and More," in M. Novelli (ed.), *Niche Tourism: Contemporary Issues, Trends and Cases*. Oxford: Butterworth-Heinemann, 47–58.

Thapa, S. B. and E. Hauff. 2005. "Psychological Distress among Displaced Persons during an Armed Conflict in Nepal." *Social Psychiatry and Psychiatric Epidemiology* 40(8): 672–79.

Wight, C. 2005. "Philosophical and Methodological Praxes in Dark Tourism: Controversy, Contention and the Evolving Paradigm." *Journal of Vacation Marketing* 12(11): 119–29.

CHAPTER 7

Beyond Frames

The Creation of a Dance Company in Healthcare through the Journey of Brain Trauma

JENNY ELLIOTT

Many creative notions are accidentally tripped over by the artist. I had my own tripping experience: a weekly repetitive neck and hand motion that took place as I stood outside the locked glass door of a Brain Trauma Rehabilitation Unit: freezing cold, ringing the doorbell, lurching my neck forward and from side to side to peer deep through the familiar landscape on the other side of the glass panes with the intention of being noticed. On a weekly basis I repeated these zoo-like actions, begging entrance and permission to begin my weekly on-ward dance class. The patients wanted out, and I wanted in.

The repetitiveness of the doorbell and peering motion coupled with the consistent ignoring of my presence outside the ward door by passing healthcare staff attached itself to me as a negative embodied experience of rejection that in some way defined and catapulted me through the next crucial stage of investigating my dance residency within a healthcare environment (Varela, Thompson, and Rosch 1991). These very ordinary, everyday experiences of on-ward dance classes benefited from my reflective dance practice transferring from the physical, to the sensing, to the absorbing, and deposited within my dancing body.

The portrayal of "Arts in Health" programs that are currently emerging often present a lively image of the perceived integration/partnership of arts with healthcare. The reality however is that many artists working within healthcare settings can feel isolated and struggle to give meaning to their practice within such clinical environments (Elliott 2008). This chapter journeys through the negative embodied actions of a dancer at ward level to an artist retreat in the middle of Ireland, returning to the core of the rehabilitation ward experience of the nurses and patients, the development of a dance company, and a public dance performance. All of these experiences have been woven together and finally articulated through a PhD study. The journey structure adopts my dance practice framework as the traveling companion through which certain elements of the very intimate research journey of my personal and professional dance experience and that of the PhD research participants are articulated.

Before proceeding with the reader to the artist retreat, I pause to reflect on the traumas integrally linked within this journey. They are not comparable, but the encountering of these two sets of traumas with each other within the locked environment resulted in an intense four-week creative explosion and public articulation of a portion of life shared by the dancer, a group of men with enduring brain trauma, and the nurses who cared for them.

Beyond Frames

The first glimpse of the traumas involved in this explosive, creative encounter is from the dancer's perspective because it comes from my firsthand experience and is translated as a recurring rejection that impacts on the delivery of my healthcare practice. Rejection is recognized as an inherent part of the professional processing of the dancer's craft and embodiment particularly for the dancers who have chosen the path of performance as their first steps on the professional ladder. The World Wide Web bursts with personal reflective advice from other artists/dancers on how to deal with the trauma of rejection as delivered by the casting theater/dance director. However, little advice or literature exists either on the Web or elsewhere that provides any sense of understanding or management of the very real rejection or acceptance of the professional dancer whose nontherapeutic professional practice is located within a healthcare community. The familiar experience of rejection for the dancer and other artists in health as they remain on the concrete step that acts as a metaphorical stage outside the ward can cut as deep as audition rejection and affect the dancer's sense of value and purpose, particularly as it can be experienced on a daily basis (Elliott 2008). I liken my experience of motioning outside the locked ward, dancing in time to the tune of the side glances of the institutional culture, to the acute memory in the pit of my stomach of standing outside the door of the dance audition, waiting to go in to demonstrate my value and worth to the dance director (Freyd 2005). Wolfram (1994) has suggested that the feeling of the audition experience is a vestige of the fight or flight instinct of primitive humans.

I can confirm the presence of these instincts in my own experience of delivering my practice within certain secure hospital wards.

The experience of rejection as the dancer on the ward step is just part of the professional tapestry that forms the backdrop to my current fifteen-year dance residency with the charitable organization Arts Care, an organization that supports artists-in-residence across a diverse range of healthcare settings in Northern Ireland. Similar patterns of experience, almost parallel threads, have been woven into the same tapestry by other artists. My weekly experience on the front steps of the ward can be viewed as a reflective embodied dance experience at the beginning of my PhD evaluative film (Elliott 2008). I rooted the structure of the evaluative film text in Rye's (2004) experimentation of different film documentation techniques such as the split screen and repetitive image with the belief that it best captured and evaluated the live experience of the participants.

The conversion of my embodied response to the environment and culture in which I practice into a choreographic realization in my dance studio is the primary coping strategy I have employed over the years to deal with the many challenges and celebrations of being a dancer within a psychiatric setting. Another strategy I employ to address this sense of weekly and sometimes daily rejection is to convert the experience into an exercise of self-awareness, accepting, as one online source suggests, that rejection can often lead to the growth of the performer propelling them to work more at their craft and to a better level of understanding (Anon. 2009). The source advises the reader not to let the rejection waste your dreams. As I stand on that concrete auditioning step weekly in those minutes of waiting, my childhood dream of being a dancer revisits me as a flashback that never fails to inspire.

The decision to go on a retreat was precipitated by my growing recognition of the negative impact that the daily routine and culture of my sustained residency had on my creativity. One of the ongoing struggles for artists is accessing time to explore, imagine, reflect, and create in the middle of other life happenings. Accessing such real time is crucial to the delivery of a meaningful creative professional practice and development of artistic excellence (Remender and Lucareli 1986). I also had a strong desire pre–PhD study to seek, through investigative practice of my Laban dance training (Laban and Lawerence 1974), ways of asking, resolving, and creating dance-based frameworks of methodology, analysis, and evaluation of my personal dance experience. Dunagan (2005) and Langer (1953) perceive the dancing body as a human agency that builds and stores knowledge, thus forming a network of data that facilitates one's ability to make sense of the world. I felt that the ability to explore deeply and make sense of my own dance experience would provide a foundation on which to investigate and evaluate the other's experience of dance.

The focus for now shifts to the individual's experience of sustaining a brain trauma. This is plucked from the perspective of one of the patients from the neuro-rehabilitation unit. His experience, for the purposes of this chapter, represents the story of the majority of men with enduring brain injury who reside within the neuro-rehabilitation unit of my residency. I will call him "Paul" because of the uncanny resemblance of his startlingly blue eyes to those of the actor Paul Newman. This middle-aged man with an enduring major brain trauma resides in a long-term neuro-behavioral rehabilitation unit. Paul's blue eyes, coupled with a strong jaw, rest on a body that has been permanently lowered to function daily in a wheelchair. He has a reputation for being "a bit of a ladies' man," a reputation apparently that persisted unscathed through his Traumatic Brain Injury.

Traumatic Brain Injury (TBI) is an acquired brain trauma that occurs with sudden injury to the head. The damage may be focal—confined to one area; or diffuse—involving injury to more than one part of the brain. The degree of disability acquired as a result of the TBI depends on several factors such as the severity of the injury, age, and the general health of the individual. The resultant disabilities may range from mild to severe depending on the extent of the head injury (Gronwall and Wrightson 1995). Common disabilities include problems with cognitive functioning, sensory processing, communication, and behavioral or mental health problems.

Paul—who spends most of the day with his right hand fisted, propping up his chin in front of the large screen TV in the ward—experiences and struggles with most of the common disabilities linked to his enduring brain injury. He is very amicable and sticks his tongue out as a voluntary greeting, which is generally followed by a cheeky, wide-grinned, toothless smile. His obsessive attempts and failure to stand up from his wheelchair make him look like he is swimming in space. As Paul endeavors to find his central balance, two staff move forward almost mirroring his swimming movements in an attempt to "rescue" him before he falls to the ground. The hands of two nurses clasp his armpits and Paul is lowered in a somewhat ungainly manner into his wheelchair to adopt again his embodied wheelchair form.

The nursing staff expire breath as they release his weight. Paul "inspires" breath and his lower body stiffens in resistance as he is sucked by the wheelchair sponge into submission. These repetitive movement encounters between Paul and the staff become, through my long-term observation, an embodied coding for evaluating the patient/nurse relationship within this institutional culture. In Paul's moment of independent movement outside of his chair, even in its unbalanced state, I get a glimpse of the energy, determination, and strength in this man with the traumatized mind and body. The "rescue" of Paul from his attempts of independent movement can at times appear like restraint and at other times can take on the image of a sensitive dance contact improvisation task involving three dancers full of gesture and expression. Villella (2003) locates the human action in gesture and expression, passing through the medium of predetermined positions extending to the aesthetic (Nadel and Strauss 2003). His suggestion that the resulting forms create the foundation of dance aligns closely with my personal definition of dance and the concept of dance employed in my practice.

The Warm-Up: The Open Door of the Retreat

It was a glorious spring day as I juggled along the pitted Irish roads. The sustained motion of my car as it negotiated the uneven road blurred the clear green hedgerows of the narrow entrance to the artist retreat, set far back from the road, deep in County Monaghan. I had never before been to the retreat, but many artists told me wonderful, inspiring stories of their perceived renewal and positive creative processing there.

The sense of the dancer taking time to draw away from their dance placements to explore their own dance is central and essential to many artists' practice, but is something not regularly accessed by the professional dancer who is often a social and collective animal by nature. The primary experience of the retreat was withdrawing from the daily collective framework of my dance practice to spend time in my personal dance, to find meaning and to rediscover my dancing, to retread my journey with dance. This retreat was to be about dance just for the sake of dancing. Sheets-Johnstone (1979), in exploring the meaning of dance, promotes a return to the lived experience as an essential step to discovering the uniqueness and vitality of the art form. For Fraleigh and Hanstein (1999), dance is not a precise or singular activity but contains a family of meanings such as creativity, style, context, and self-knowledge. My retreat was to be about just such an imprecise, impromptu integration of my dancing body and dancer self.

I settled in a warm room with dark, stained wooden floors, white-painted shutters, and a breathtaking view of the lake. The word *asylum* comes to mind in its truest sense. A "sanctuary," a "safe haven" is a somewhat different interpretation than the asylum of my practice from which at that point in time I was retreating. The contrasts in these environments could not have been more obvious. I was to return regularly during my days in the retreat dance studio to the space that lay between these contrasts, wrestling with concepts of potential fusion facilitated by creativity, freedom of self-expression, and the unfolding of self-knowledge, management, human rights, and well-being. The artists' retreat allowed me to examine the crucial creative knowledge of well-being, self-management, and expression that I suggest could be translocated to the 160 green acres and the many wards of the psychiatric campus by developing a vibrant cultural community that contributes to existing programs of health and well-being (Elliott 2008). My argument danced in the retreat studio steered away from the direct therapeutic benefits of arts in healthcare (Staricoff 2004) into a cultural discourse regarding the employment of the arts within such environments as a tool or cultural right (Blacking 1982).

Moriarty (2003) locates participation in the arts within the individual's absolute human right to access creativity as an integrated part of life experience. The building of Moriarty's argument stating the first value of the arts to be the provision of an opportunity for individuals to explore ideas, feelings, hopes, and fears that are difficult to articulate in other circumstances reverberates with central concepts of my practice in health, where dance provision provides a platform for negotiating and relating the different elements of the participant's life experience. Moriarty's debate about defining the contribution of the arts in our lives from a human rights perspective offers useful instruction for perceiving the function of the cultural arts such as dance within healthcare programs.

On the first day of the retreat, I ventured across the courtyard of the old house past a row of well-worn but buzzing art studios. I see the concrete steps to the entrance of the dance studio in the distance, and my excitement builds. The narrow dance studio is located above the large, open art studio below. It had rained the night before, and, as I began to ascend the slippery steps to the studio, I felt like I was making my way to heaven. This was such a contrast to the concrete step outside the neuro-rehabilitation unit: my feet were light, and I was heady. There was an excitement as I ascended the steps. I felt very grown–up as a dancer.

My background in dance is as rickety and unpredictable as the old shutters in my retreat bedroom. I trained originally as a radiographer to satisfy my mother's desire for me to have a decent job. It was there in the X-ray departments of my early youth that I encountered and negotiated the stiff, clinical culture of general medicine. Deep frustrations about my career in radiography and a longing for my dance contributed to my decision to follow my childhood dream and embark on a Laban Community Dance Training Programme that was piloted in Northern Ireland in the late 1980s.

Having completed my dance training, I practiced part-time contemporary dance in education and was invited by the charity Arts Care to undertake a six-month residency within the psychiatric site, where I remain fifteen years later as the dancer-in-residence.

As I enter the retreat dance studio, framed flashes of sunlight stream across the long, narrow studio. The only literature knowledge that I permitted to accompany me to the studio was Laban's Principles of Movement to assist me in building an analysis framework for my dance experience (Laban and Lawrence 1974) and the words of Lu Ch'ai:

> Some set great value on the method, whilst others pride themselves on dispensing with method. To be without method is deplorable, but to depend on method entirely is worse. You must first learn to observe the rules faithfully; afterwards, modify them according to your intelligence and capacity. The end of all method is to have no method. (Lu Ch'ai in Janesick 2001: 932)

However, like every dancer, I was well aware of the ephemeral aspect of the dance experience that, according to Fraleigh and Hanstein (1999), is often expressed as a voiceless, nonmaterial activity involving improvisation that can never be held onto or repeated and can thus present difficulties in terms of constructing serious study.

In order to lay the much-needed foundations of meaning through the ephemeral nature of the exploratory research dance experience, I referred throughout the dance process to my body knowledge built through years of personal dance and professional practice. My "personal dance" refers to the layers of dance experience that I engaged in since childhood such as jazz, disco, and contemporary dance accessed mainly through school productions and youth clubs. I invite the reader to now come with me through a sample of reflective narratives and escapes that depict how the dance conceived in the retreat studio guided me through some of my confusions.

The stillness of reflection and personal creativity afforded to me in the retreat provided the much-needed creative space through which to investigate options for defining and resolving the inadequacies of traditional methodology. The abstract from the poems below offer some insight into the journey I undertook daily at the retreat dance studio. I began each session by dancing and awakening my senses. I brought large sheets of paper, charcoal, pencils, and my camera with me to the studio. As I danced I began to articulate, through the different media, my reflective knowledge of the different elements of that dance experience. That knowledge focused on the relationship with self and other environment, dance skill building, and emotional responses. These themes became the foundation stones that generated my PhD methodology and evaluation tools. The whole experience of combining different art media through which to articulate experience impacted on the transcribing of my final PhD thesis text. My method of personal expression prompted me to include visual art, film, poetry, clay sculpture, and performance articulations as integral parts of my final text submission. The clearing of my inner and outer spaces at the retreat informed my critical thinking and assisted in the activity of locating my PhD study within the paradigms of communicative learning (Mezirow 1990).

The reflections below relate to the experience of my solo personal dance as I seek to underpin relevant concepts in the initial stages of my research project:

My Solo Dance at the Dance Studio, Annamakarrig

The Dance Studio: 11:30 am
… The streams of light through the window
Nourish,
energise,
focus
I am encouraged to move
Always that first expression
I am alone
in this process
The existing source of light
amidst the narrowness
motivates me.
The light source internalising
Coming from Interchange of
internal and external space
Lines blur
Creativity awakens Motivation stretches
… the sunlight streams in fields
going far
beyond the frames of the window
to distant space
Confusion vanishing. …

The dance studio: 11:45 am Warm-Up
Music begins
and I move
In space
Intimate

self connection
Inviting
… My body moves freely
Sensing the textures of the floor
Drawn by the sunlight
making shape and form
So nourished
Accessing creativity. …

Theme Development
I let my head and arms move shape form
gesture amalgamate. …
I desire to record this awakening
I use the charcoal
begin to create
the movement images
from my centre,
across the large pages
scattered on the floor,
There is liberation there. …

These extracts from my reflective diary offer an insight into the intimate elements and directions of my solo dance experience. The artist retreat acted as a creative catalyst. It soon became clear that the combination of experiencing, reflecting, and intuition leading to an external expression of my inner space through art forms such as visual art, sculpting, and dance within my own creative retreat was to underpin a reflective, qualitative inquiry model that was mirrored by the experience of all the participants—including audience and myself in the study (Dunagan 2005; see also Illustration 7.1). These three charcoal inspired images of the solo dance emerged in the retreat to inform different aspects of the research design, constructing creative signposts that ultimately led to the development of an appropriate creative-based methodology that expressed the dancer and the participant within a lived frame of experience.

Reflective practice in the dance experience and subsequent visual representations revealed the following series of embodied thoughts as danced through in the retreat:

- Initial confusion
- Appropriate creative space
- Impact of environment
- Relationship
- Feelings and responses—unfamiliar, good, vulnerable

Dance A. Initial encounter with creative process through free dance experience expressed in the abstract.

Dance B. The dance emerges into the aesthetic to begin to make shape and form; Laban choreographic considerations begin to surface; weight, time, and flow.

Dance C. Form and shape locate within meaning, developing the lived frame concept of theory and choreographic practice with dancer and participant held central to that experience.

Illustration 7.1. Seeding of themes for conceptual framework of PhD study expressed through solo dance and a series of charcoal drawings. Drawings by Jenny Elliott.

- Awareness of existing resources
- A place where internal and external amalgamate
- Multimedia recording of experience
- Relevance of capturing "the now" of the dance

This series of embodied thoughts gained from the retreat experience, and further solo creative processing in my home studio, resulted in the development of both qualitative and quantitative constructs. The quantitative framework, "The Laban-Based Functional and Expressive Quality of Movement Measurement Framework" that evolved out of the retreat experience, is based on some of the above elements and is a five-point flexible scale from 0 to 100 percent (0, 25, 50, 75, 100). It contains nine measurable elements that emerged from my practice and materialized through the retreat experience (Elliott 2008). These constructs and themes, coupled with my ongoing dance practice, reflection, and a comprehensive literature review, delivered the conceptual basis and eventual characteristics for the development of the quantitative "Functional and Expressive Quality of Movement Measurement Framework Based on

Laban's Analysis of Movement." This framework measures both the expressive and functional elements of dance movement. The themes from the framework also emerged as a foundational framework for analyzing the film recording data and producing the subsequent evaluative documentary text (Elliott 2008) across the broader tapestry of my PhD study.

I close the dance studio door at the retreat to return a couple of weeks later to the concrete step outside the neuro-behavioral rehabilitation unit and the locked door that is typical of the many locked doors throughout the corridors of mental health. I catch a glimpse on the other side of the glass of blue-eyed Paul propping the same chin up in front of what appears to be the same television program. Nothing appears to have changed. This is the first day of the on-ward six-week prestudy pilot where the dance-based methodology and evaluation tools generated in the liberated space of the retreat dance studio are to be initially tested. Different elements of the ward routine that interrupted the flow of the on-ward dance class were observed by the participants and later translated into movement sequences. This translation at times surfaced through humorous exchange but more often from reflection on the darker perspective of lost identities surrendered to cognitive dysfunction and the presence of permanent disabilities. The residents often commented on their sense of hopelessness and the difficult ongoing journey of coming to terms with the daily need to depend heavily on others to survive. The loss of identity and independence are two well-documented challenges of brain trauma (Landau and Hissett 2008).

> I felt as if everything had been taken from me. Now at times I cannot remember who I was before my accident. I think I am coming to terms with it and then it hits me hard again. Nothing could describe it. I feel good in the dance as if my body is able to move again and I often express bits of what happened to me. It is good to have it out in the open. (resident with brain injury)

The pilot program experience revealed a snapshot of the creative community potential within the unit and what could be made possible if the residents and staff members bought into my vision of a dance company. I held firmly to my vision of creating a dance company with the staff and residents: this would shift identity perceptions from "patients" to "dance students," turning patients on settees into active, vital dancers with the ability to translate their story through dance performance. The result would be a theater of hope in the heart of the local community. The pilot program offered the hope of achieving this by providing the staff and unit manager with the opportunity to critique and reflect insightfully into what the male residents could deliver in terms of dance skill building, creation, and performance production: "I find it hard to believe that these guys can put so much effort into this class. We can't get them to do anything other than lie about wanting to watch TV and smoke" (senior unit staff member).

The Arts Care Studio where the first three weeks of the four-week study takes place is a large, old, weather-worn Portacabin. The studio is our own "Tardis" for making journeys in time and space: it looks small on the outside but on the inside it opens up a world of creative exploration and journeys to unknown territories of self-expression, negotiation, resolution and discovery. To date, it is the only designated dance studio space within a healthcare environment in the world. It is an unusual home for dance, but it serves its purpose well.

I can hear the patient bus draw up outside the studio door. This is the first day of the intense, four-week PhD project; three weeks in the dance studio and one week of rehearsals in the theater. The duration of the working dance day for the participants involved four hours of contemporary dance training broken down into morning and afternoon sessions with short breaks and lunch. The intensity and length of the daily sessions were both demanding and challenging, taking into consideration the sedentary lifestyle of the ward. The framework of daily engagement for the four-week project was modeled on Maldoom's (2004) community method of contemporary dance practice in education. This model offers participants an opportunity to learn the technical and performance skills of contemporary dance. The result of this experience would be the creation of a performing dance company with a strong and egalitarian identity.

The daily exchanges between the staff and the residents had a fatigue about them with responses that often seemed dismissive and well rehearsed. Disparaging humor was at the heart of our proceedings. Higgs and Titchen (2001) reflect on the very real challenges for the nurse in developing and sustaining a professionalism that focuses on crafting a meaningful care relationship. Their focus on the role of the arts in this development falls within the "Art of Healing—Staff Dance Training Programme" that was offered as an integral part of the PhD study experience. This program offers healthcare staff an opportunity to explore their own creativity, build dance skills, and learn how to transfer an embodied creative experience into their professional healthcare delivery.

The experience of the dance training program proved a valuable educational tool as the four-week dance project progressed in relation to the staff's ability to support the resident participants as well as develop their own professional craft knowledge through creative exploration and production (Elliott 2008; Higgs and Titchen 2001). One of the findings to arise from the study focused on how as the dance project progressed, the relationship between the participating residents and staff became more democratic and less antagonistic. This highlighted the need for the staff to avail themselves of programs of art participation within their working lives from the perspective of professional development, workplace well-being, and cultural rights (Moriarty 2003). There have been few published recommendations for rightful art engagement for healthcare staff within their professional experience. Hastings (2005) recognizes the importance of embracing staff in the wider arts in healthcare experience, encouraging a social model of arts engagement for staff, patients, and visitors throughout healthcare environments. The experience of the staff on the PhD study, as well as further dance training opportunities, reveals the transformative potential of arts participation for personal motivation, relationship development, and professional knowledge (Elliott 2008, 2009a, 2009b).

> I used to see my patient as just another brain injury but now, through participating in the dance, I see a person who had a life and family before his brain injury. Taking part in the dance has opened up a new type of communication for me. Now, when I am carrying out my physical duties of care on the ward, I have real conversations with the men. The physical touch of care has also become more meaningful through dancing with my patients. (staff participant)

Over the next three weeks, the Arts Care Dance Studio door opens at 10:30 AM every day when the bus arrives. The seven resident and three staff participants become increasingly committed to the concept of becoming a dance company and work hard on training their bodies through the Principles of Laban Movement. The physical and cognitive disabilities range from moderate to severe. After the warm-up, the choreography is explored and an aesthetic begins to emerge that is both challenging and mystical. Arms and legs frozen through broken neurological pathways are encouraged and supported into shape, form, and direction. The movements repeated over and over are digested and expressed by the physiological, anatomical, emotional, and spiritual dancing body. Movement rests within all of these elements to become embodied and honored by the individual's abilities and aesthetic (Fraleigh 1996). Over the three-week period the studio dance experience is captured, mapped, and analyzed. The sedentary lifestyle of the on-ward experience slips out of sight during the daily four hours of dance skill building and theme exploration.

Nurses' uniforms are traded for T-shirts and tracksuit bottoms, and the residents arrive wearing the same dance uniform. Over the weeks of the study, identities of "staff" and "patient" metamorphose into "dancer," and a dance company slowly emerges. A turning point is reached after just three weeks into the project: a creative democracy has emerged. Even the residents with more severe cognitive dysfunction are demonstrating an ability to retain and recall their choreographic movement patterns and become less dependent on staff assistance.

Regular reports from the unit manager indicated that levels of potentially high-risk outbreaks on the ward had been greatly reduced and more easily defused over the project period. Positive mood levels increased resulting in staff and residents reportedly "getting on better." An overall increased mobility resulting in greater independent movement by wheelchair user participants was also reported by the ward staff. The emergence of the creative identity has been shown to create a valuable space and being that is critical to reconsiderations and the reconceptualization of self and relationships—two areas most fractured through brain trauma (Elliott 2008). Maldoom's work makes a case for the delivery of creative opportunities to reidentify this relationship in his dance in education work (Maldoom 2006). He states that true growth and knowledge can only be achieved for both teacher and pupil when democracy has a chance to flourish. Maldoom argues that democracy and nourishment within such relationships are successfully facilitated through creative engagement, the exploration process, and production. The significance in this, according to Maldoom, is that it encourages the individual through creative critical thinking, practice, exploration, and achievement to see and respond to others differently and constructively outside of their traditional identity and reputation.

The Cool Down: The Performance and Fall Out

Week 4 of the project and the participants experience a shift from the dance studio to rehearsals in the local community theater. As always, on entering through a theater door, the first thing encountered is a cold darkness similar to the darkness experienced on the ward step. The unfamiliar darkness greets the rehearsing performers like a veil of fear. I often liken my personal experience of entering unlit theater spaces to a ride on a ghost train. In fact, it was obvious from the participants that their first encounter with the theater space was indeed scary and awesome. The thick sound of the theater light switching on brought a welcome relief to the participants' quickened breath.

The journey through the three-week process stage of the project resulted in the performance work "Beyond Frames." This demanded, where possible and as requested by the group, the exploration and the brave revisiting of the dark experiences of the accidents that had resulted in the patients' permanent brain dysfunctions. Fragments of life recalled before and after brain injury were subtlely and startlingly articulated through choreographic production. The intention was not therapeutic, but the art form of dance provided a vehicle through which the residents traveled through their own personal territories, expressing their version of what one participant described as "an explosion in a coal mine when all goes black and life tumbles down round you. ... You become trapped and life is never the same again."

Through the expressive dance experience, the residents began to gain control and make informed, insightful decisions about affecting and defining their life within residential care (Farkas et al. 2005; Guss 2005; Heinssen, Liberman, and Kopelowicz 2000). This was primarily facilitated by the shared discussions with the staff participants in the dance workshops and made evident in the performance. In this very public arena, the residents and staff utilized with creative confidence their dance knowledge as a dialogue through which they present their political and life views publicly. Taking the theme of "Beyond Frames," the dancers focused and shifted the stereotypical perceptions of people in wheelchairs and disability through shape and movement flow. By switching support in the dance from resident to nurse, the audience members were challenged to consider their own perceptions of disability, democracy, and aesthetic in the dance.

The performance offered the potential to offend audience members as the men commented on surviving life with a brain injury through their dance choreography (MacBeath 2006). The study acknowledges the value of risk taking and the potential to offend politically within the domain of subversive choreography and public performance. The findings of the study demonstrate that risk taking and political statement within a supportive environment serves staff and service users with a creative autonomy that supports and encourages concepts of self-government as promoted within current emancipatory health education and patient-centered care programs (MacBeath 2006; McCormack 1998). "I really enjoyed watching the audience's faces as we spun the wheelchairs and used the almost scary video images of brains and scarred faces to state the reality of brain injury" (resident participant).

On the open stage, participants used performance to articulate the multiple complexities and negotiations of life with brain trauma. Some audience members admitted finding the visibility and physicality of the dancers with brain injury challenging but enlightening: "I found seeing people with disabilities performing publicly challenging, but it has made me think about disability in a different way. This would all have been hidden if it was not brought out in the performance" (audience reflection).

The power of the performance was summed up by Micky's ability to stand up straight before the audience, managing his swivel movements, and focusing way above the audience's heads into distant front space. As he moved backward, with the last gesture of his choreography, his foot caught on a moving wheelchair. He stumbled but was able to quickly regain his stature. This time there were no obscene words released. What the audience witnessed, along with all the other dancers, was an empowerment and control in Micky that clearly demonstrated a discipline and renewed body knowledge. In the postperformance discussion, family members in the audience reflected on how proud they were of their relatives who took part in the dance performance: "I was able to see my son coming through again for the first time since his accident. I was very proud. I didn't know that he was capable of doing anything like this" (mother of one of the residents).

We leave the performance with a single row of dancers locking hands standing and seated in their wheelchairs, bowing in front of an excited audience. Family members, consultants, and other staff members flood the stage following a standing ovation to offer their praise and thanks. The bodies that greeted me now, upright and focused, had been strewn horizontal across the settees on the first day of the pilot study, staring aimlessly into space. This moment cannot be taken away from them. It is theirs and will remain an embodied memory in their being (see Illustrations 7.2 and 7.3).

Further Development of Kompany Maine

It is with the gift of professional recognition and autonomy that the artist contributes to developing a cultural life in healthcare settings that ultimately serves the human rights of the individual working or availing of the healthcare (DCAL 2000). On completion of the graduate research, staff and service user participants requested that Kompany Maine continue to develop in both concept and practice. We established an in-residence dance company within their healthcare setting. Kompany Maine continues to flourish with weekly rehearsal classes and project-based dance programs. The residents and staff have sustained their commitment to the contribution to the arts within the local and wider community through the development of a repertoire of dance performance

Illustration 7.2. "Beyond Frames," a PhD journey with research participants. Photo by Jenny Elliott.

Illustration 7.3. "Liberation from Frames," a reflection in charcoal. Drawing by Jenny Elliott.

with sociopolitical themes. Kompany Maine's promotion of inclusive community practice through their dance programs has been recognized within the community, and in 2006 they were awarded the Unison Prize and were runners-up in the Renee MacIntosh Award for their contribution to enhancing quality of life programs specifically in residential care settings.

The concept of developing creative identities within healthcare settings, such as resident dance companies comprising staff and service users, can assist in generating fresh visioning of holistic, inclusive, and empowering programs of care within healthcare environments. For those service users such as blue-eyed Paul and belligerent Micky who remain committed to the development of Kompany Maine, the evidence of sustained improvement in many areas of their life, including social interaction and functional movement, attests to the worth of this dance work—a journey out of darkness. The residents' independence and improved quality of life within residential care warms each and all of us involved in Kompany Maine.

The ongoing funding by Health Promotion Services in the Trust where I remain the resident dancer, and the recent accreditation status awarded by the local university to the Art of Healing Staff Creative Dance Programme, demonstrate the level of integration and recognition community dance practice has achieved within the Northern Ireland healthcare context.

Notes

This is a revised and updated version of an article that appeared as "Beyond Frames: The Creation of a Dance Company in Health Care through the Journey of Brain Trauma" in J. Skinner, ed. (2010) *Journeys: The International Journal of Travel and Travel Writing*, Special Edition, *Writing the Dark Side of Travel* 11, no. 1 (2010): 156–77.

Bibliography

Anon. 2009. "Dealing with Rejection." *The Acting Source.* Retrieved 26 February 2010 from http://www.theactingsource.com/index.html.

Blacking, J. 1982. "A Case for Higher Education in the Arts: Research into Higher Education Monographs," in K. Robinson (ed.), *The Arts and Higher Education.* Guildford, UK: Society for Research into Higher Education, University of Surrey, 26–28.

DCAL. 2000. *Unlocking Creativity: A Strategy for Development.* Report for Department of Culture, Arts and Leisure Northern Ireland; Department of Education; Department for Employment and Learning; Department of Enterprise, Trade and Investment; and Invest Northern Ireland. Belfast: DETI.

Dunagan, C. 2005. "Dance, Knowledge and Power." *Topoi* 24(1): 29–41.

Elliott, J. 2008. "Dance Mirrors: A PhD Journey Embodying, Actualizing and Operationalizing a Dance Experience in Healthcare." PhD dissertation, University of Ulster, Jordanstown.

———. 2009a. "Developing a Laban-Based Dance Community within Healthcare Environments." *Movement and Dance* 28(1): 10–11.

———. 2009b. "An Evaluation Report on The Art of Dance Training Programme for Healthcare Staff." Unpublished manuscript.

Farkas, M., C. Gagne, W. Anthony, and J. Chamberlin. 2005. "Implementing Recovery Orientated Evidence-Based Programs: Identifying the Critical Dimensions." *Community Mental Health Journal* 41(2): 141–58.

Fraleigh, S. 1996. *Dance and the Lived Body: A Descriptive Aesthetics.* Pennsylvania: University of Pittsburgh Press.

Fraleigh, S., and P. Hanstein. 1999. *Researching Dance: Evolving Modes of Inquiry.* London: Dance Books.

Freyd, J. 2005. "What about Recovered Memories?" Retrieved 26 February 2010 from http://www.dynamic.utegon/jjf/whatabout.html

Gronwall, D., and P. Wrightson. 1995. *Head Injury: The Facts.* Oxford: Oxford University Press.

Guss, F. 2005. "Re-Conceptualizing Play: Aesthetic, Self- Definitions." *Contemporary Issues in Early Childhood* 6(3): 233–43.

Hastings, L. 2005. "Evaluating Participative Arts Projects in Healthcare Settings." MA thesis, University of Ulster, Jordanstown.

Heinssen, R., R. Liberman, and A. Kopelowicz. 2000. "Psycho-Social Skills Training for Schizophrenia: Lessons from the Laboratory." *Schizophrenia Bulletin* 26(1): 21–46.

Higgs, J., and A. Titchen. 2001. *Practice Knowledge & Expertise in the Health Professions.* Oxford: Reed Educational and Professional Publishing.

Janesick, V. 2001. "The Choreography of Qualitative Research Design: Minuets, Improvisations and Crystallization," in N. K. Denzin and Y. S. Lincoln (eds.), *Handbook of Qualitative Research.* London: Sage, 923–48.

Laban, R., and F. Lawrence. 1974. *Effort: Economy of Human Movement.* London: Macdonald & Evans.

Landau, J., and J. Hissett. 2008. "Mild Traumatic Brain Injury: Impact on Identity and Ambiguous Loss in the Family." *Families, Systems and Health* 26(1): 69–85.

Langer, S. 1953. *Feeling and Form: A Theory of Art Developed from Philosophy in a New Key.* New York: Charles Scribner's Sons.

MacBeath, J. 2006. *Leadership as a Subversive Activity.* ACEL Monograph Series, 39. Melbourne: University of Melbourne, ACEL/ASPA.

Maldoom, R. 2004. *Rhythm Is It.* Berlin: Boomtown Media.

———. 2006. "Presentation on Community Dance and Education in Berlin." Unpublished manuscript.

McCormack, B. 1998. "An Exploration of the Theoretical Framework Underpinning the Autonomy of Older People in Hospital and its Relationship to Professional Nursing Practice." PhD dissertation, University of Oxford.

Mezirow, J. 1990. *Fostering Critical Reflection in Adulthood.* San Francisco: Jossey-Bass.

Moriarty, G. 2003. "The Faith to be More Fully Human" in J. Hoadley (ed.), *Image and Imagination: Writing from the Making Space Conference*. Belfast: Stranmillis Press, 86–89.

Nadel, H., and M. Strauss. 2003. *The Dance Experience: Insights into History, Culture and Creativity*. Hightstown, NJ: Princeton Book Company.

Remender, P. and R. Lucareli. 1986. "In Search of Artistic Excellence: The Social Construction of Artistic Values." *Studies in Art Education* 27(4): 209–12.

Rye, C. 2004. "Living Cameras." PhD dissertation, University of Bristol.

Sheets-Johnstone, M. 1979. *The Phenomenology of Dance*. London: Dance Books.

Staricoff, R. 2004. *Arts in Health: A Review of Medical Literature Research*. Arts Council Report 36. London: Arts Council England.

Varela, F., E. Thompson, and E. Rosch. 1991. *The Embodied Mind*. Cambridge, MA: MIT Press.

Villella, E. 2003. "Foreword: Why Dance?," in M. Nadel and M. Strauss (eds.), *The Dance Experience: Insights into History, Culture and Creativity*. Hightstown, NJ: Princeton Book Company, xi–xiii.

Wolfram, E. 1994. *Your Dance Resume: A Preparatory Guide to the Audition*. San Francisco: Dancepress.

CHAPTER 8

The House on the Hill

An Analysis of Australia's Stolen Generations' Journey into Healing through the Site of Trauma

FIONA MURPHY

Revisiting the Site of Trauma

The train rumbles through the sunburnt landscape as Mary and I sit together, for the most part in silent rumination. This journey, from one of Australia's major urban centers to a small country town in rural New South Wales, was one where Mary would begin the process of confronting the material traces and ruins of her childhood suffering. It was a journey she and her close friends, all members of Australia's Stolen Generations, considered critical to their personal journey of healing and notions of forgiveness and conciliation. Having spent a number of months conducting research with the women in the New South Wales Sorry Day organization, they extended a personal invitation to me to accompany them on this important journey to revisit the site of their former institution. Accompanying Mary on the train engendered the understanding that in journeying towards the site of trauma and hurt that was the former Aboriginal children's institution, the women were reckoning with the ghosts of traumatic time past in the hope that personal healing would be forthcoming. For the final hour of the journey, it seemed as if Mary had become a little girl again as she recounted the startling tales of a fractured childhood and spoke to me about the institution, describing it in minute detail. With every bend rounded, Mary would sigh. The move deeper into the countryside was signaled by the increased blackness of the scorched earth from recent bushfires, and I heard her say to me in withered tones that we were nearly there, nearly there now. I felt all objectivity slip away. I wanted to cry for her and with her. Instead, I sat frozen, all senses dimmed and sensibilities eclipsed by Mary's fear.

With some minutes to go, we passed a hill, and Mary pointed to it saying that the institution was not too far from it. She told me she felt terrified about going back as the train pulled into a nondescript country town station.

The history of the Stolen Generations is a long one, and continues to be marred by acrimonious debates. On 26 May 1997, the Australian Human Rights and Equal Opportunity Commission (HREOC) tabled one of the most shocking and painful reports that Australia had ever seen. The *Bringing Them Home* (BTH) (Dodson and Wilson 1997) report was the result of months of consultations across Australia and established that from 1910 until the late 1970s, between one in three and one in ten Indigenous children were forcibly removed from their families. The Commission listened to nearly six hundred stories of removal, abuse, loss, continuing pain, and trauma, and had access to nearly a thousand more in written form. What followed were months of intense debate on the nature of the removals, the policies, and whether what had happened was genocidal in intent (see Manne 2001; Read 1999; Moses 2004). Stolen Generations were called upon across the continent to tell their stories, to allow Australians from all backgrounds to bear witness to the crimes and tortures of a past both known and unknown (Haebich 2000). Amid the flurry of telling came newspaper articles, autobiographies, documentaries, films, and a keener sense among many members of the Stolen Generations that they had to address both their individual and collective traumas. Testimony, memorialization, reparations, and reunions on the sites of former institutions were all seen as legitimate routes for healing and eventual reconciliation.

The trope of the journey then figured large in my research with members of Australia's Stolen Generations. Pathways to healing were constructed as the need to undergo necessary journeys of bearing witness; journeys to the state archives in order to uncover personal histories; journeys to reconnect with a place that should have been called home; journeys of calling and protesting for forms of reparation; and finally, the subject of this article, journeys to former Aboriginal children's institutions to confront the space and place of traumatic experience. Underpinning these multifarious and often very individual kinds of journeys was a strong sense of both the interplay between the journey into healing and the place of healing, as well as a growing cognizance of the politicization of trauma and suffering. The act of storytelling, of piecing together the "broken stories" (Jackson 2002) of their past, crisscrossed the intent of many of these journeys, blurring and bridging the boundaries (Jackson 2002: 58) between private and public worlds, as well as divergent emotional categories such as fear, trauma, creativity, hope, and healing.

In reconceptualizing this journey to a former Aboriginal children's institution accompanied by a large number of Stolen Generations and their families as a journey of healing, this chapter reflects on questions connected to journeying, traumatic experience and sites of trauma, and the yearning for healing. Configured as a journey of mourning and healing by the women, the reunion at the Cootamundra Aboriginal girl's home precipitated debate, dialogue, and even controversy among the women themselves, other members of the Stolen Generations, and the local townspeople who had become aware of the reunion through the role of the local reconciliation committee in the town as well as some newspaper reports.[1] Reunions such as this one at the sites of former Aboriginal Children's institutions started to occur with some frequency after the BTH Commission, mostly supported by different organizations such as local reconciliation groups, the National Sorry Day Organisation, or Link Up.[2] Over the course of my fieldwork, I attended two of these reunions (this one and another in Alice Springs, Central Australia), and also interviewed members of the Kinchela Boys Home Group (also based in New South Wales). The Kinchela Boys Home Group organized their own reunion soon after the release of the BTH report, and many of them also described this journey as a "healing" experience.

Broadly, then, these reunions on the site of trauma have been deemed healing for trauma survivors and indeed for the broader polity.[3] Unlike other sites of memory and trauma, however, such as Port Arthur in Tasmania (Tumarkin 2005) or even ANZAC war memorials (Inglis 1998) that maintain a strong presence in the National Australian imaginary as places of pilgrimage and mourning, Aboriginal children's institutions often only exist as sites of trauma within Indigenous Australians' imaginaries—particularly those of the Stolen Generations. Thus, while constructed as sites of trauma that need to be memorialized by members of Indigenous communities and interested non-Indigenous Australians, such places of pain have not, as yet, been fully consigned to national and collective history and memory as important places of remembrance.

The spatial and emplaced nature of trauma, however, plays a key role in the construction of traumatic memory and possible future healing and reconciliation. Sites of trauma, I contend, converse with a gamut of affective experiences, therefore anchoring practices of memory, forgetting, mourning, and history making in the material residue of trauma. Much of the writing about trauma points to the survivors' difficulties in mediating between the extreme and the everyday and of the problematics of "traumatic identity." In so doing, several authors unpack the complexity of the temporal dimensions of traumatic experience, as well as the political and collective construction and negotiation of trauma (Miller and

Tougaw 2002; Farrell 1996; Fassin 2007. Yet, very little of the literature speaks to the spatial and emplaced nature of traumatic experience (see Tumarkin 2005). Attending a reunion at the site of the former institution engendered in a palpable way this interplay between the extreme and the quotidian, creating a sense of recognition of how spatially anchored traumatic experience is. The journey to the institution, then, allowed me to ask some important questions about the relationship between journeying, place, traumatic experience, and witnessing.

For some of the women I traveled with, this was their first time returning, and for others—mostly the women who had invited me—it was their second or third return trip. Members of the Stolen Generations with whom I spoke, those who had attended this particular reunion and others who had attended previous ones, constructed the reunion as an attempt to move into a space of healing, or as Mary told me, "It is an attempt to find peace, some peace from the ruins and torment of that place." The "reunions," then, were the first step for many in garnering personal experiences of trauma into a single narrative and in exposing a fractured past in a very public way. For many of the women whom I traveled with to Cootamundra, the reunion was an attempt of sorts to attribute meaning to the process of removal, to recover a deeper significance to their life experiences. The women told me that the reunion held the possibilities of transformation and, for my part as researcher, I wondered how journeying to these sites made the women feel: at the same moment so afraid yet somehow so empowered as witnesses to the story of their own past. What is crucial about the physical return to the site of trauma, then, as I see it, is the engendering of a sense of witness, a movement to a space of mastery over one's own past experiences.

Furthermore, the reunion allowed the women to reconnect with one another, the women they identified with as sisters, and it helped those children and grandchildren present to confront their mothers' lost childhoods and understand the trauma trails that moved through their own lives. One of the women explained it as follows:

> I feel close to my story here. My whole world now has become this world of the Stolen Generations. Sure there is pain here, but it was also my home, there is purpose in coming back, I feel better now, I can tell my story when I go home. I'll be stronger for this, I know I will.

My respondents, particularly Mary and her close friend Emily, wanted to share with me some sense of how Cootamundra as a place, a town, an institution, a home, and indeed a prison, had played a crucial formative role in their life experiences. As I made the journey with Mary through the scorched landscape of time present and past, I was aware that in coming back to the institution for a second time, she was just beginning to confront the trauma trails moving through her life and world. As the train passed through the countryside of her past, Mary's memories of the institution, the loss of her family, the death of her younger sister, her brutal rape, and her many attempts at running away came flooding back.

Understanding who they might have been had the removal policies never been instigated has thus become an aim of many members of the Stolen Generations. This understanding necessitates great creativity and moral imagination on the part of members of the Stolen Generations who inhabit a liminal space between non-Indigenous and Indigenous communities. Part of the process of revisiting former institutions is to reimagine and even remake the traumatic past in order to carve out a self free from suffering and pain. Accompanying the women allowed me to question the social power of traumatic place and to attempt to understand how members of the Stolen Generations negotiated their ghosts while confronting the material traces of their suffering. This physical return allows a confrontation of sorts with the ruins of place and decay of self driven by traumatic memory. For many members of the Stolen Generations, then, sites of former institutions have become what Deborah Bird Rose calls "wounded spaces" (Bird Rose 2004: 34). The space and place of former institutions are firmly embedded in the Australian Aboriginal imaginary as places of trauma and woundedness. Acknowledging this has been an important step for both members of the Stolen Generations and the wider populace in moving toward a space of healing. Moving around the site with the women exemplified the emotional potency of the physical site of trauma in enabling memory, mourning, and healing.

Reconstructing the Ruins of Memory

> Cootamundra was our home, and when we returned most of things
> we knew weren't there, we asked them not to remove some of the
> things like the well and the morgue. The dining room they made into
> a chapel, and lots of other changes. The first time we went back, we
> were very upset. All I could see when I first went back was matron up
> front. We had beautiful rose gardens, they took it all out, and lovely
> white pebbles leading up to matron's office. We asked them to keep it
> as it was but they didn't, they took them all out.
>
> —Emily, Ethnographic interview: 2003

The question of how journeying to the sites of former Aboriginal children's institutions could prove healing for members of the Stolen Generations figured large in my thinking prior to the reunion. It was only when I walked around the actual site with the women that I developed a keener sense of how deeply anchored the gamut of affective experiences were in this site of trauma. Walking around the site of the former institution with the women was both engaging and illuminating; it was also an experience awash with a quiescent mournfulness. As we moved through the site, I laughed with the women as they pointed to places of play and happiness and cried with them when they showed me places of punishment and abuse. A number of the women were unhappy that the new owners of the site had not kept certain aspects of the institution intact, claiming that even though these places were intertwined with memories of punishment, their preservation was key to the ability of the site to signify the true story of Aboriginal child removal.

Indeed, many of my respondents felt that addressing their past traumas through a personal confrontation with the material traces of their past suffering (see also Edkins 2003; Tumarkin 2005) proved more fruitful than "traditional" therapeutic methods such as counseling. Their articulation of this belief points to the complex intertwining of traumatic memory and the site of trauma. This individual and collective "bearing witness" (see Felman and Laub 1992) at the site of former suffering is a mode of reassembling traumatic experience in order to begin the long personal journey of healing. Present at the material place of trauma are the ghosts of traumatic time past. Indeed, as such, our ghosts and particularly those ghosts tied to the place are entities with whom we can imagine having a relationship with, quite unlike our traumas that can only be addressed, compensated for, and eventually healed. The women articulated this implicitly as they told one another ghost stories, stories of abuse, and stories of suffering as we moved through the site, thereby situating themselves as "witnesses" to the past, to the place of suffering, and to one another. This conversation and physical presence at the place of suffering allowed many of the women to circumvent clinical forms of therapy and activate their own healing through meaningful activities such as storytelling, bearing witness, and memorializing.

Amid furtive and lonely glances we continued, and while older fingers traced the outlines of a place where beatings and abuse invaded their lives, the story of what happened to these women was gradually pieced together. Mary and her friends directed one another around the site in an edifying and gentle manner, recalling stories and events mired in sadness. I walked with them slowly past a place where they told me the bodies of young children who had died had been put—discarded, but forever remembered and felt by the women as an abiding sense of loss.

I had heard about this place many times and suddenly it was before me, banal and ordinary; and I had to try my hardest to imagine it engulfed by the distant, resonating pain and suffering of its former residents. The institution is a place of overwhelming ordinariness for the neophyte visitor. For the women, however, it is a place beset by traumatic memory, a place borne of suffering, and yet in the same moment, a place that could be called home, one that continually bespeaks the loss of being a stolen child. Negotiating the traumatic past with the women ignited an effusive energy that encouraged us to walk further into the labyrinthine depths of this traumatic place. The women's angry response to the parts of the site that had been destroyed, renovated, or allowed to fall into disrepair signaled the important relationship that traumatic memory holds in relation to ruins. Ruins, Norman Klein (2008) reminds us, signify what is deemed worthy of remembrance or not. For the women, it was clear that certain parts of the site held an excess of meaning, bubbling up as they moved through it, temporally and spatially. The ruins evoked the scars of forgetting: the women's story and stories challenged this shadowland of amnesia. It also proved to me that this wounded site was in a very real sense a "placescape" (Casey 1993), one where the boundaries and connections between body, experience, and place proved coterminous and fluid. The institution, for the women, had made them into who they are today; its ruins, its buildings, its places of punishment, and the rawness of their memories (even after thirty years) illuminated the umbilical relationship between the story, people, and place of Aboriginal child removal.

Moving through the site also elucidated the sense of "sacredness" that many of the women attached to this place of suffering. The journey was described by some of the women as a "sacred one," and conversations about the site and possibility of memorializing it were also shrouded in a vocabulary of "sacredness." It was quite clear from the life of the institution, however, that it was really only members of the Stolen Generations and the broader Indigenous community that had imputed this sense of sacredness into this place of removal and force. This is not an uncommon theme in other studies of "sites of trauma," mainly places of mass death and trauma, where both survivors and tourist-visitors point to the numinous and sacred qualities of these sites, particularly evident in debates around Holocaust memorialization (see Young 1993) and the memorialization of Ground Zero (see Sturken 2004). The notion of sacredness in its connection to place operates at several levels, moving through political, religious, secular, and personal idioms. Smith (1987: 1–10) reminds us that "sacred places are made, not discovered," an argument that connects to the women's experiences here as they fight to have the place of their childhood recognized, even sanctified by the presence of a memorial.

Chidester and Linenthal (1995) also point to the manner in which sacred space is an arena where power relations are reinforced and played out. For members of the Stolen Generations, numerous debates about memorializing their past suffering—whether on sites of former institutions or in "Reconciliation Place" in Canberra—point to the complexities of history making as it is linked to the increasingly politicized uses of traumatic experience. While some scholars feel that sites of trauma automatically invoke feelings of "sacredness," others emphasize the need to move forward, to let what has become for some "hallowed ground" reemerge as part of the quotidian, and to reincorporate it into the mundanity of everyday life (Sturken 2004). Debates around memorializing Ground Zero furnish us with many examples of the desires of those living in the neighborhood around the September 11 site to expunge the aura of sacredness from the site. For many, their greatest fear was that they would end up living in a museum, and that their daily lives would be forever entwined with the events of September 11 (Sturken 2004). While the traumas and atrocities of September 11 and the Holocaust differ hugely from the experiences of Stolen Generations in terms of their personal impact and their broader politicization, I refer to the debates around memorialization, and particularly the idea of sacredness, to highlight the complexities of creating out of a place of trauma, a space of remembrance and memorialization. Sites deemed sacred then are nearly always sites of contestation. Significantly, the women at Cootamundra were more attached to the parts of the institution that had been destroyed or left in ruins even as the daily life of the institution as a Bible College went on. The site nonetheless remains a strong testament to the experiences of the stolen children, and continues to chide at least some of the local townspeople from its position on top of a hill overlooking a seemingly innocuous rural town.

Dare to Differ

Since the publication of the BTH report, the Stolen Generations story has become a cipher for the story of national redemption. The Rudd 2007 national apology to the Stolen Generations has become a ritual counterpart of this. Due to widespread media and academic attention, and the process of what Bain Attwood (2001: 183–212) calls "narrative accrual" (the manner in which individual stories of removal have become coalesced into one overarching narrative), many individual members of the Stolen Generations feel they cannot publicly tell their story if it deviates from some of the more publicized experiences. I was often told in hushed tones varying versions of "the" story of Aboriginal child removal. Unwilling to diverge from the developing public story of removal, the narrators would frequently ask me not to repeat to other members of the Stolen Generations what they had told me. Others refused to tell me anything: telling me their experiences were very different from the stories I was used to hearing. Such stories often featured individual personal relationships to the manager of a particular institution or indeed, the complex relationship to the institution as both a place of suffering but also the only place some of my research participants felt they could call home. Stories they felt could offend, hurt, or even anger other members of the Stolen Generations.

There are, then, clearly some stories that can only be retrieved and told from a particular place or site (Basso 1996; Tumarkin 2005). Being present in a particular place allows the enactment of particular memories and stories. Place, whether numinous or nebulous in its evocation and description, allows a connection with the force of memory. Strolling around the site with the women opened a space where different versions of the stolen children's story emerged. Emily, a close friend of Mary, invited me to walk around the site with her while the other women were contentedly sipping lukewarm coffee. Asking me to come and see some of the places where they were most at ease as children was Emily's attempt at telling me a different version of the story of being a stolen child. It was a story that evoked in a palpable way the loss that some of the little girls felt when they reflected on their mothers under their special tree and the closeness they felt to one another growing up.

But Emily also wanted to tell me about her relationship with the matron. This was not a story that she felt she could tell me in front of some of the other women who had little good to say about those who ran the institution. Taking me to the place where dreams about mothers were cultivated under the little Aboriginal girl's favorite tree, Emily spoke about the matron in a tender and caring way. She told me that the matron had often expressed a wish to adopt her, for her to be her little girl—the child with whom she could continue to share her problems and concerns about the institution and the other children. She had kept in touch with the matron up until her death, and had even attended her funeral. In fact, Emily often reflected on her closeness with her to me, but always in private away from the other women who would consistently stress their fractured and sometimes angry relationship with the matron.

Emily's story illuminates the investment made by many trauma survivors in the site of trauma as a site of memory and an anchor for hope and eventual healing. The intricate and involuted work performed at these material settings of trauma and memory centers on the recovery and restitution of a "stable" traumatic past where site and victim enter into a reciprocal process of meaning making and reconciliation. Kenneth Foote (1997: 5–6) argues that sites of trauma very often play an active role in their own interpretation and the act of meaning making. Using as an example the crematoria of death camps, Foote argues that these remnants of violence demand that the visitor begins the business of interpreting, and subsequently meaning making. The women, however, as former residents, went beyond this; they were beginning the process of *re*interpreting, of ascribing in great emotional intensity new meanings to the story of removal. The business of reinterpretation signals the palimpsest nature of Indigenous sites of trauma as places where layered cartographies of loss are made visible through Indigenous performance and storytelling. Whether we evoke these places in the language of Casey (1993) as "placescapes," or Tumarkin (2005) as "traumascapes," what remains most critical to the conceptualization of sites of trauma is the sense of how entangled they are with individual, communal, and often national investments in History (writ large), memory, and mourning. The value of these particular sites in the Australian imaginary is yet to be fully realized; they exist for now only on the margins of collective memory. The women's stories and experiences of the "reunion," while fraught (and perhaps also conflicted), indicate the mosaic nature of the profound link between suffering and place. They also indicate that "History" must include multiple voices and variant narratives, that the story of the Stolen Generations is a multivalent and polysemous one, and that the reactions of the women whom I accompanied to the site of the former institution are complex and layered, shifting between individual and collective responses to suffering and its politics.

Rescuing the Fragments of Memory

Cootamundra is my home, but through my travels around New South Wales with my job, I have learned that my town and its name is a name which strikes terror in the hearts of Aboriginal people. Cootamundra is akin to Auschwitz in the minds of some Aboriginal people.

—Opening welcome to meeting by member of the local reconciliation group, Fieldnotes 2003

From the site of the institution, our next stop that day was a meeting with the local community reconciliation group that had played a key role in organizing the reunion. The meeting was held with the intention of discussing both the women's experience of returning to the town as well as the possibility of a memorial to the women placed either in the town in a visible location or up at the institution. Parting from the institution, fatigued by deep emotion and a choking humidity, we got back into our cars to make our way to the meeting. My companions sat silently as we drove back to the town. It had been undoubtedly a day of ups and downs, of intense smothering sadness, and hysterical laughter; a day of darkness ensnared by an umbilical thread through traumatic time and space. As we drove towards the town, we looked out the window in dramatic silence as the car followed the undulations of a small country road, allowing the vista of eclipsed time to close in on us. Arriving back into the busy country town, we shake ourselves back into being, ready for the meeting ahead. It is a busy Saturday afternoon; mothers and daughters rush around, arms full of shopping bags, while impatient fathers sit slumped in the front of waiting cars. The meeting about the memorial is, I agree with the women, a piercing positive from a town wanting to open its doors onto a past hitherto ignored.

As we sit around in a circle, the meeting opens with a traditional "acknowledgment of country," now a common reconciliatory practice in contemporary Australia.[4] Standing at the top of the room is the non-Indigenous gentleman who collected us from the train the previous day. His nervousness penetrates the atmosphere in the room, and we all sit in silence. He speaks a well-rehearsed acknowledgement of country in an Aboriginal language that none of the women understand because of their long absence from Aboriginal Australian worlds. I stare about the room at the blank and fatigued faces; the welcome is infused with irony. I feel uncomfortable, only because I feel that in spite of the best intentions, the welcome circles around what has been lost and what for most of the women sitting in the room will never be recovered. The welcome is translated into English. The man at the top of the room shakes as he continues, and I scribble down his words as fast as I can in a feeble attempt to capture not only what I feel is his grace, his tacit plea for forgiveness, but also his embarrassment. He sits down amid applause, and I glance across at him sitting red-faced in shame.

The women are asked to speak next about what it felt like for them to come back to Cootamundra. Mary is the first to speak. She is angry as she speaks about how difficult it was to make the journey back; she tells of how, when they were growing up, she and the other girls were not allowed into the cinema or the swimming pool. She tells of her rape and abuse, and of how the police did not pursue the investigation. The participants in the room sit in uncomfortable silence. Emily is the next to speak; she tells of lost dreams, lost families, of broken spirits and rejection from both Aboriginal and non-Aboriginal worlds. Another woman cries out that still she was one of the lucky ones; she did not suffer physical or sexual assaults in the same way as some of the others. Emily concedes that this may be the case, but she nonetheless suffered in her own way. Other voices emerge, a cacophony of sad and tortured stories of life in the institution telling us of how difficult it was to be there but yet how difficult it was to leave. One woman tells us how she came back to live in the town; she felt she had nowhere else to go. The meeting proceeds, and Sarah speaks out. She describes the first afternoon that we arrived in the town. Walking around the town on her own, she spotted a mural on the main street. It was a mural depicting the town in its minutiae painted by some local schoolchildren. Sarah tells us that the mural is a wonderful illustration of the town's story and history. But it tells a history marked by absence; the mural did not include an image of the institution. Some of the local townspeople speak up; they tell us that for the children who painted the mural, the home was not part of *their* history. In fact, they tell us most of the young people do not even know about the institution. After the meeting, some of the women ask me to go and take some photos of the mural. I stand in front of it. It is cartoon-like, and filled with popular memory. It evokes the richness of country town life. I shoot it from a few angles, but it does not change what it tells me, it does not change the knowledge that the tide of forgetfulness has tried to wash away the histories of those little girls taken from their families and communities.

The mural and the absence of the girl's home became a topic that Sarah and some of the women I worked with frequently referred to during my time in the field. For Sarah, and her sister Mary, it was something that symbolized the feelings of absence and loss that they felt their entire lives. Sarah articulated it thus:

> I was really hurt when I saw that the story of the institution, our story was not present in the mural. It means there is no place for us in their hearts. We do not matter. They have asked why we keep coming back here. What we want from them. They don't seem to recognize that this town was ours for a long time too. But they never accepted us back then. I guess there is no reason why they would now either. The memorial is great, but it is not the same as the whole town—their children and grandchildren remembering spontaneously this story, this, our very very painful story.

Illustration 8.1. Memory holes: A town's view of its own past. Photo by Fiona Murphy.

The mural indicated the wider absence, the Orwellian (1961) "memory hole" in the broader Australian collective's approach to Indigenous histories. It also fueled further debate among the women on the salience of the Stolen Generation's story for the town. The women wanted their everyday existence in the former institution to be publicly remembered. Lack of recognition and remembrance among the majority of the townsfolk crystallized the perilous nature of attempting to reconstruct their narratives for many of the women. The institution had been metaphorically abandoned as a site of remembrance, forging on in its new existence as a Bible College. Not valued as a site of memory or a place of history, Cootamundra Aboriginal Girl's home, constructed by members of the Stolen Generations as a site of woundedness and trauma was, through the mural, once more made invisible.

Sites such as these, as well as sites of massacres and other colonial traumas, mark out Australia's landscape as scarred and haunted by the force of a violent past (see Bird Rose 2004). Henry Reynolds (1999:

177) reminds us that Indigenous communities have stringently marked
out sites of massacres as important sites of commemoration and remembrance for decades, but these sites do not exist with the same spectral force
on the non-Indigenous Australian landscape. In recent years, through the
reconciliation movement, the process of recognizing in memorial form
these scars on an otherwise beautiful landscape have become critical to
the relationship between Indigenous and non-Indigenous communities.
Memorials on other former institutions such as the Colebrook memorial in Adelaide, South Australia (see Read 2008), and the Myall Creek
Massacre memorial (see Johnson 2002) in Northern New South Wales
are two success stories that signify the vanishing borders between Indigenous and non-Indigenous forms of remembering the colonial landscape
(see Goodall 1996). The scaffolding supporting the move to memorialize in this fashion for the Australian collective as a whole remains as
yet attenuated by disagreements and controversial debate about the nature and factual accuracy of Australian colonial history (see Windshuttle
2002; Moses 2004).

Former Aboriginal children's homes, some now memorialized by
plaques or monuments, are constructed by members of the Stolen Generations as witness objects, places that tell and retell the history of Aboriginal child removal in a transformative way. The mural, however, did
not recognize the institution as part of the town's social, historical, and
contemporary fabric. Indeed, with such an absence carved into its very
heart, the mural reiterated the link between the way forgetting is so enmeshed with traumatic experience, the art of memory, and the social
decay of place. During our visit to the institution the women had openly
expressed their disappointment that some parts of their former "home"
had not been preserved. Here, facing the mural painted by local schoolchildren, I found confirmation that the institution had become part of
what Tony Birch (1999) has called Australia's "landscape of abandon-
ment." On some level, the women's concerns recalled Keith Jenkin's
(1991) question, "Whose history counts?" and points toward the ambiguous nature of history and social memory as they manifest on a local
and, indeed, national level. It further signposts the complex relationship
between local forms of social and familial memory and "History" writ
large on the national stage.[5] In coming together on the site of the former institution, the women were, I believe, challenging the monolithic
narrative engendered by media and academic studies, as well as local
forms of social memory and history. Along with the women, I saw how
the mural as an artifact, an object of interest in the middle of the town,
could have "unintended historical after-effects" (Seremetakis 1994: 10)
unless attended to. The debate about the mural and the positioning of

a memorial commemorating the women's experiences highlighted how important the women deemed the business of memory making and place making to be.

Final Reflections: Memorializing the Site of Trauma

A memorial now stands on the site of the former institution. It was officially opened in 2006 in conjunction with the local reconciliation committee. For some of my respondents, it was a moment that articulated the beginning of recognition. For others, it was a disappointment; they wanted the memorial to stand elsewhere. Regardless of the mixed attitudes of some of the women, the memorial bespeaks the birth of a stronger sense of recognition and solidarity from the small town. Not without its complexities for members of the Stolen Generations, the story of revisiting the site of trauma and of its subsequent memorialization has become a story of healing, a journey into the past set, then, in stone to issue liberation from an unsure and painful future. The idiosyncratic, highly individual, and contingent nature of healing, however, has meant that many members of the Stolen Generations understand, define, and interpret their "moving forward" quite differently, and thus in practice enact a very different relationship to processes such as memorializing and journeying to sites of former institutions.

For Emily, the memorial provided a critical encounter with the possibility of healing; she continues to revisit the institution, the memorial, and some of the local townspeople. Sarah, unhappy with the memorial, has never returned to the town, and told me that she will never go back to what for her is a "place of suffering." As an artist, however, she continues to revisit the institution, painting it and its surrounding landscape over and over again. One of those paintings hangs in my apartment, so I too can revisit this burnt landscape whenever I think of my research participants, thereby reinforcing my scholarly interest in the contingent and temporally layered nature of history, memory, and revisiting. Mary, the most vocal of the women, continues to publicly tell her story and was also an active participant in the memorial process in Cootamundra; she has deemed the whole process of revisiting the institution and being involved in the memorial process as having led her into her personal place of healing. Through the stories of Mary, Emily, and Sarah, then, and for the many other women I met on the reunion, the social power of traumatic place exists as a site of memory making with the potential for healing and moving forward to a place where their personal stories of removal no longer weigh so heavily.

In setting out the experience of the women as they move through the former institution into the town to meet with the local reconciliation group, I hope to have illuminated the kinds of transformation possible in journeying both into one's past as well as towards one's future through the site of trauma. The story of the mural and the debate about the memorial anchored the women's journey within the complexities of both place and history making, perhaps even shadowing for some time the existential immediacy of revisiting the actual institution. Nonetheless, the entanglement of "trauma time" with historical and sacred time ignited the women's ability to successfully mourn—both individually and collectively—a past that had hitherto been silenced. In journeying to the site, and moving about it, the women were enabling the construction of a traumatic place into a sacredly charged place (see Coleman and Elsner 2003) in the Stolen Generations imaginary. Revisiting, remembering, hoping, healing, and moving forward individually and collectively were key tropes permeating the women's articulations of their journey back to the former institution. Some felt the reunion had brought healing, others felt it was just the beginning, but regardless of the different outcomes, all the women agreed that the "return" had been a watershed moment in their lives as members of the Stolen Generations.

The focus on the potential therapeutic or healing value of sites of trauma has been the subject of some critique in the trauma literature, deemed responsible for eliding the politico-historical importance of such sites (see Nagle this edition; Tumarkin 2005). The ethnographic data, however, in this chapter shows that a focus on the healing powers of sites of trauma cannot in fact be possible without considering the complex interplay between the politicization of trauma, the vagaries of historical remembering on national and local levels, as well as the sacralization of place. The women described herein, in making a personal pilgrimage to the site of their former institution, also traversed and negotiated the sociopolitical discourse and challenge of reconciliation, history making in postcolonial terms, and the question of reparations. Moreover, while journeys to sites and places of trauma have been deemed healing, some survivors of trauma as well as visitors to these sites have offered complex and often contradictory emotional commentaries on this experience.

In returning to the former home and in dealing with past memories, in confronting their ghosts, both individually and collectively, the women enabled the process of mourning to begin. By so doing, they began to construct a story for themselves and others about what it means to be a survivor of trauma and a member of the Stolen Generations.

For a number of the women, the presence of their children and grand-children signaled an important attempt by the next generation to face the suffering of their parents and grandparents. The material place of trauma, then, overcrowded with ghosts, embeds its woundedness into the landscape; by its very existence, it demands to be witnessed, to tell the story of those who once passed through.

Notes

1. Cootamundra is located in rural New South Wales and is situated in the federal division of Riverina. The Cootamundra Girls Home, originally a local hospital, was opened in 1911 and maintained by the Aborigines Protection Board until 1968. The majority of my respondents had attended the institution during the 1960s. At this time the institution was run by a woman called Matron Hiscocks. At the time of writing, the institution was being used as a "Bible College," and is now known as Bimbadeen Christian College.
2. The National Sorry Day Organisation, the organization I conducted my research with, was founded as a result of the Bringing Them Home Report. Its central focus is the organization of "Sorry Day" every 26 May, as well as existing as a support organization for Stolen Generations. Link Up was founded in 1980 by Carol Edwards and Peter Read and is currently present in a number of states across Australia. It is an organization that provides a large range of support for members of the Stolen Generations, counseling, and family reunification in particular.
3. Survivors of other traumatic events have also reported that returning to the site or place of trauma had been an immensely difficult yet healing part of their process of grieving and moving on. September 11 World Trade Center survivors have been widely interviewed about their experience of returning to the pit where the towers stood. See http://www.survivorsnet.org/resources1.html.
4. The idea of giving a "welcome to country" or "acknowledgement of country" in the traditional language of the local Aboriginal group has become a practice very much adhered to largely due to the reconciliation movement. Traditionally, different Aboriginal groups would request permission from the original owners/ custodians before entering a new land (country). Once granted, they would acknowledge with respect these owners. During the reconciliation movement, many non-Indigenous groups began to formally open meetings and events with an acknowledgement of country that is a brief acknowledgement of the traditional owners of the place where the meeting was being held. A "welcome to country" is also frequently given by a member of the local Aboriginal community, usually an elder, and often in the local Aboriginal language (as well as English) at the beginning of various events and meetings.
5. See Gillian Cowlishaw (2006) where she considers the notion of the "new Aboriginal history" and its impact on subjectivities and social relationships in everyday reality, critical to the role of history making on local and national levels visible within this piece.

Bibliography

Attwood, B. 2001. "'Learning About the Truth': The Stolen Generation Narratives," in B. Attwood and F. Magowan (eds.), *Telling Stories: Indigenous History and Memory in Australia and New Zealand*. Crows Nest, NSW: Allen and Unwin, 183–212.

Basso, K. 1996. *Wisdom Sits in Places: Landscape and Language among the Western Apache*. Albuquerque: University of New Mexico Press.

Birch, T. 1999. "Come see the Giant Koala." *Meanjin* 58(3): 61–72.

Bird Rose, D. 2004. *Reports from a Wild Country: Ethics for Decolonisation*. Sydney: UNSW Press.

Casey, E. 1993. *Getting Back into Place: Towards a Renewed Understanding of the Place World*. Bloomington: Indiana University Press.

Chidester, D., and E. Linenthal. 1995. *American Sacred Space*. Bloomington: Indiana University Press.

Coleman, S., and J. Elsner (eds.). 2003. *Pilgrim Voices: Narrative and Authorship in Christian Pilgrimage*. New York: Berghahn Books.

Cowlishaw, G. 2006. "On 'Getting It Wrong': Collateral Damage in the History Wars." *Australian Historical Studies* 37(127): 181–202.

Dodson, M., and R. Wilson. 1997. *Bringing Them Home: National Inquiry into the Separation of Aboriginal and Torres Strait Islander Children from their Families*. Sydney: Australian Human Rights and Equality Commission Publication.

Edkins, J. 2003. *Trauma and the Memory of Politics*. Cambridge: Cambridge University Press.

Farrell, K. 1996. *Post-traumatic Culture: Injury and Interpretation in the Nineties*. Baltimore: Johns Hopkins University Press.

Fassin, D. 2007. *L'Empire du Traumatisme, Enquête sur la Condition de la Victime*. Paris: Flammarion.

Felman, S., and D. Laub. 1992. *Testimony: Crises of Witnessing in Literature, Psychoanalysis, and History*. London: Routledge.

Foote, K. 1997. *Shadowed Ground: America's Landscapes of Violence and Tragedy*. Austin: University of Texas Press.

Goodall, H. 1996. *Invasion to Embassy: Land in Aboriginal Politics in New South Wales, 1770–1972*. St. Leonards, NSW: Allen and Unwin.

Haebich, A. 2000. *Broken Circles: Fragmenting Indigenous Families 1800–2000*. Fremantle, WA: Fremantle Arts Centre Press.

Inglis, K. 1998. *Sacred Places: War Memorials in the Australian Landscape*. Melbourne: Melbourne University Press.

Jackson, M. 2002. *The Politics of Storytelling: Violence, Transgression, and Intersubjectivity*. Copenhagen: Museum Tusculanum Press.

Jenkins, K. 1991. *Re-thinking History*. London: Routledge.

Johnson, D. 2002. *Lighting the Way: Reconciliation Stories*. Annandale, NSW: Federation Press.

Klein, N. 2008. *History of Forgetting: LA and Erasure of Memory*. London: Verso.

Manne, R. 2001. *In Denial: The Stolen Generations and the Right*. Melbourne, VIC: Black Inc.

Miller, N., and J. Tougaw (eds.). 2002. *Extremities: Trauma, Testimony, and Community.* Urbana: University of Illinois Press.

Moses, D. 2004. "Genocide and Settler Society in Australian History," in A. Dirk Moses (ed.), *Genocide and Settler Society.* New York: Berghahn Books, 3–49.

Orwell, G. 1961. *Nineteen Eighty-Four.* New York: New American Library, Signet Classics.

Read, P. 1999. *A Rape of the Soul So Profound: The Return of the Stolen Generations.* St. Leonards, NSW: Allen and Unwin.

———. 2008. "The Truth That Will Set Us All Free: An Uncertain History of Memorials to Indigenous Australian." *Public History Review* 15: 29–46.

Reynolds, H. 1999. *Why Weren't We Told? A Personal Search for the Truth About Our History.* Harmondsworth, UK: Penguin.

Seremetakis, C. N. 1994. *The Senses Still: Perception and Memory as Material Culture in Modernity.* Boulder, CO: Westview Press.

Smith, J. 1987. *To Take Place: Toward Theory in Ritual.* Chicago: University of Chicago Press.

Sturken, M. 2004. "Grounding September 11: The Aesthetics of Absence: Rebuilding Ground Zero." *American Ethnologist* 31(3): 311–25.

Tumarkin, M. 2005. *Traumascapes: The Power and Fate of Places Transformed by Tragedy.* Carlton, VIC: Melbourne University Press.

Windshuttle, K. 2002. *The Fabrication of Aboriginal History*, vol. 1, *Van Diemen's Land 1803–1847.* Sydney: Macleay Press.

Young, J. E. 1993. *The Texture of Memory: Holocaust Memorials and Meaning.* New Haven, CT: Yale University Press.

CHAPTER 9

Exploring Landscapes after Battle

Tourists at Home on the Old Front Lines

JENNIFER ILES

The Western Front was a strip of land a few miles wide that ran from the Channel to the Swiss frontier. The battles fought over this area of ground during the First World War (1914–1918) were so intense that whole villages were reduced to "handfuls of smoke-grimed dust" (Oxenham 1918: 34), woods were blasted into blackened stumps and in places entire sections of topsoil disappeared, exposing the white limestone substratum underneath. Once labeled by Wilfred Owen as the "topography of Golgotha," today much of the Front's terrain has been reclaimed and restored. Yet it is a landscape that as Shepheard comments, still "remains thick with the memory of that time" (Shepheard 1997: 204–5). Although in the contemporary Western world we tend to "perceive" landscape as a perspective of views and vistas, it has deeper and more complex dimensions (Bender 1993: 1). Rather than landscape being some form of inert container or an empty backdrop, embedded in its earth are personal biographies, social identities, and memories of previous movement (Tilley 1994: 27). It is as Shields remarks, the "memory bank" of society (2000: n.p.). And it is the landscape of the Western Front, resonant with traumatic historical association, that remains a key site in the British memory bank.

Today the battlefields, military cemeteries, and memorials of the Somme and the Ypres Salient—the areas of the front lines where the majority of the British and Allied soldiers were stationed and fought—are visited by hundreds of thousands of tourists every year. Although largely neglected by tourists for the first two decades after the Second World War, the Western Front now occupies a central place in the British historical imagination and has become a popular visitor destination. All kinds of people are attracted to the area. There are the military enthusiasts and historians; genealogists; schoolchildren; others may have a literary interest in the war, moved by the work of "trench" poets such as Isaac Rosenberg, Siegfried Sassoon, and Wilfred Owen; some have undertaken the journey solely to accompany spouses or friends; and there are also the merely curious. In tandem with the region's growing appeal, new museums and visitor centers are still being opened, memorials are still being constructed, and new ceremonies to honor the dead continue to evolve.

As Piekarz (2007: 153) notes, war and the tourism industry are deeply entwined. Battlefield tourism, located within the larger grouping of touristic experiences described by Lennon and Foley (2000) as *dark tourism* and alternatively by Seaton (1999) as *thanatourism*, has materialized as an important form of tourist activity (Prideaux 2007: 17). Indeed, for Smith (1996) war is actually an important stimulus to tourism, and despite its horrors, or because of them, it probably constitutes the largest single category of tourist attractions in the world (Smith 1996: 248). As she comments, warfare "reaches the heart of a culture and touches the soul of every inhabitant on both sides" because whether a war is lost or won, it will always entail the tragic sacrifice of lives (Smith 1998: 205). Yet as Baldwin and Sharpley observe, it is unlikely that battlefield visitors themselves would feel happy being categorized as "dark tourists" or "thanatourists" (2009: 190) because both these terms have negative connotations that hint at a ghoulish interest in the macabre (Sharpley and Stone 2009: 249). Although an element of morbid curiosity may exist to some extent, many visitors either go on battlefield tours or pilgrimages that suggest that their main aims are a combination of historical understanding and emotional experience (Baldwin and Sharpley 2009: 190–91).

In many respects battlefield tourists on the Western Front explore a landscape that today visually reveals relatively little of the bloody carnage that took place during the war. Long empty of its former military occupancy, its geography requires significant decoding to understand its hidden narratives (Gough 2001: 231). In the years after the Armistice was declared in 1918, the dead were gradually cleared from the land and reburied in military cemeteries, the roads and flattened villages were rebuilt, and farming and natural regrowth eventually returned the area to local communities. On his return to the former front lines in the 1930s, the author Mottram exclaimed, "There is still, in a corner of one of the lower meadows, a great pile of rusty barbed wire. Otherwise all semblance is gone, irretrievably gone" (1936: 44). In addition, over the last thirty years the construction of new industrial parks, theme parks, and housing developments have steadily encroached upon the old battlefields

184 • *Jennifer Iles*

and destroyed many of them. In his guide *Walking The Salient* (1999) the military historian and tour guide, Paul Reed expresses his frustration with the relentless nature of new construction work carried out around the Ypres Salient area:

> But even in my lifetime the Salient has changed; another house was built, a factory unit thrown up or some aspect of the town meddled with. Life must go on, and it did. And it made following the men of those times more and more difficult. (Reed 1999: 6)

Yet despite the ongoing disappearance of many of the scars of battle, even for first time visitors who may have little historical knowledge about the events of the First World War, the presence of the thousands of cemeteries and memorials dotted around the fields, towns, and villages cannot fail to impress on them that they are traveling across a terrain which was once composed of "fields of carnage" (Douie 1929: 217). For British tourists, the Western Front has become a sacred landscape of remembrance, and its battlefields and memorials are now regarded as the equivalent of shrines and holy sites (Winter 2009: 611). The behavior of visitors at both formal sites on the landscape and informal ones where no landscape preservation has been undertaken indicates a deep ritual response to the symbolism and meaning of these places (Price 2005: 4). At memorials visitors often touch the inscribed names of those who died or insert paper poppies in the crevices between the stone panels; at historically charged places such as the Sunken Lane near Beaumont Hamel where two companies of the Lancashire Fusiliers were cut down in seconds at the start of the Somme Offensive on 1 July 1916, people create shrines of poppy crosses which are renewed on a regular basis (Price 2005: 4).

Allied to the emotive power of the battlefields is a sense of belonging that remains an important aspect of visitor experience. The previous history of action and the historicity of the lived experiences by British and Dominion soldiers play a significant part in the continuing emotional attachment of British visitors to the area. The military historian Michael Stedman has said of its enduring appeal, "This is where so many of our roots lie. … A whole generation passed through this place" (Stedman and Skelding 1999: 74). The foreign countryside of the Western Front has effectively become established in what Anderson (1991) has called "the imagined community" of British nationhood. Yet, it is a nationhood that is English rather than British in character. As Andrews notes, while the practice of tourism raises awareness and reinforces ideas of national identity, the relationship between tourist experience and nationalism is a tangled one (2010: 28). Tourist sites and experiences are often densely layered with complex narratives of social, cultural, and political history (J. Harrison 2010: 72). Former battlefields are no exception and are, as Saunders observes, composed of a palimpsest of multivocal, overlapping, and often contested landscapes (2001: 37).

This chapter will focus on the commemorative landscape of the Western Front and will engage with the theme of the articulation of emotion, memory, and national identity in the context of British touristic travel to the battlefields. In particular I will weave these three thematic aspects into a discussion of the relatively recent development of a popular visitor site on the Somme—the Lochnagar Crater near the village of La Boisselle. The ethnographic detail upon which my arguments rest is based on a continuing study of battlefield tourism to the Western Front which began in 1997 (Iles 2006, 2008). I begin by examining the place of emotion and empathy in tourists' engagement with the battlefield landscape. In my discussion I also include the role of my own emotional responses during the course of conducting ethnographic fieldwork, because they were integral to developing my understanding of the ways in which visitors identify with the commemorative landscape. I then explore how the notions of Britishness and Englishness are bound up with the emotional attachment to the battlefields before moving on to discuss the commemorative and contested landscape of the Lochnagar Crater. As Bremer contends, the inherently social nature of meaningful sites makes them vulnerable to contestation by different groups of people (2006: 27). The crater, which is now an important site of commemoration on the battlefields, is subject to various tensions and conflicts raised by both tourists and the local population who may be at odds regarding its historical association and symbolic meanings.

Empathy and Emotion

Following the publication of Urry's work, *The Tourist Gaze: Leisure and Travel in Contemporary Societies* in 1990, many researchers have explained tourist behavior as an activity that is primarily carried out through the medium of vision or the gaze (Franklin 2003: 83; see Jakle 1987; Macnaghten and Urry 1998; Rojek 1995; Crawshaw and Urry 1997). While research continues to build on Urry's notion of the gaze, however, new directions acknowledge that tourism is a multidimensional and complex practice and that the tourist is more than a disembodied sightseer. Increasing attention is now being paid to the embodied and performative nature of tourist activities (see Bowman 2005; Coleman and Crang 2002; Crouch and Lübbren 2003; Edensor 1998, 2000,

2001; Franklin and Crang 2001; Iles 2006, 2008; Kirshenblatt-Gimblett 1998; Tucker 1997). This approach recognizes that tourists continue to mediate and make sense of the world through their bodies, through social interaction, imagining, "doing," and feeling (Crouch 2002: 209). Although authors such as Jakle (1987) might contend that visitors or sightseers only occasionally consciously insert themselves as potential actors into the actions of a scene because "place as picture" is their primary objective, I would argue that in visits to the Western Front, tourists are required to be appreciative of the ambience of the area in order to identify and empathize with its symbolic, commemorative spaces. In my own investigations I found that the more familiar I became with the landscape of the Front, the nature of the battles fought there, and the behavior and attitudes of the people who travel to its now quiet fields and villages, the more I was struck by this sense of deep sense of empathy that the emotionally heightened spaces of the battlefields engender.

As Hastrup acknowledges, fieldwork is not a one-way process in which ethnographers remain external to their objects of study (1992: 119), and in recent years there has been an increasing appreciation of the subjective and reflexive nature of much research (Widdowfield 2000: 199). For Okely (1992: 16), at the heart of the practice of reflexivity is an examination of the more intangible inner experiences of the senses. The researcher learns not only through the "verbal and the transcript" but also through the sights, sounds, smells, tastes, as well as the emotions of the field. Although Geertz (1988) is dismissive of the claim that ethnographers acquire a special empathy through fieldwork and emotional involvement, Sanders (1998: 196) affirms that it is integral to "being there." For Sanders, intimate familiarity with a setting and with the people who inhabit it requires more than simply observing and participating in their activities. Real understanding comes when the ethnographer attends to and shares the emotions that are felt by those in the field. Further, as Anderson and Smith maintain, the inclusion of "affect" in the work of researchers is useful way to illustrate the manner in which social relations and spaces are mediated by feelings and sensibility, particularly in settings where the emotional is routinely heightened (2001: 8).

The battlefield landscape, eloquently described by the war poet Edmund Blunden in his poem, *Report on Experience*, as having a "peculiar grace," is marked by mass death.[1] While some of the remains of dead soldiers lie buried beneath the "green coverlets" of the military cemeteries, others, which have been estimated at a figure of over a hundred thousand, still lay scattered beneath the fields (Saunders 2001: 46). When walking across a terrain that remains full of the detritus of war, as a researcher it is easy to drop a skeptical guard. Along similar lines, the historian

McPhail in her work *The Long Silence* acknowledges, "However honest and dispassionate we wish to be we cannot read about the Great War without applying its circumstances to ourselves, our own families and communities or thinking of similar events awaiting the survivors and their children" (1999: 8). Because my own images of the war had been fashioned by the recollections of my grandfather, to my mind the conflict had taken on the aspect of being an "an old man's war." During my first visit to a military cemetery on the Front, the realization that it was very much a "young man's war" soon began to dawn on me as I passed the rows of headstones with the ages of death clearly inscribed on the white Portland stone—aged nineteen, aged eighteen, aged twenty-one, aged twenty-three, aged twenty-six. Only occasionally did I come across a headstone that recorded the death of a soldier who was over forty.

Having had my own affecting encounters with the evocative nature of the Western Front landscape, my awareness and appreciation of the emotive topographies, or as Raymond Williams states, the "structures of feeling" (1977: 132) of the tourists who journeyed there, also became sensitized and sharpened. During my fieldwork encounters it became clear that visitor experience remains dominated by an intense degree of emotional engagement. Many visitors have often found themselves to be deeply touched by the evocative nature of the area as their comments left in the visitor books of the military cemeteries and memorials reveal. Remarks such as "so many mothers' sons—such a shame"; "sad to see so many young lives lost and so far from home"; "to see the granddad I never knew" are typical examples of the thoughts expressed by those who, as Belloc mused, perhaps felt "overwhelmed by the sanctity of a place on which men have done this or that a long, long time ago" (1958: 167). The geographer Relph (1976) also acknowledges the role of affect and emotions in the understanding of a sense of place. He recognizes that in order to embrace the richness of meaning attached to a site, people are required to develop a sense of "empathetic insideness," or a willingness to be open to its significance and to feel it and to know it, to see into and appreciate "the essential elements of its identity" (1976: 49). And it is this sense of "empathetic insideness" that is one of the keys which repeatedly draws people back to the battlefields.

An interest in family history appears to be the initial impetus for many repeat visitors when they first made the decision to tour the Western Front. As Samuel comments, today we live in an expanding historical culture in which history as a mass activity has probably never had so many followers (1994: 25). With the distance in years since the Armistice was declared in 1918, the level of family connection has widened considerably, and the majority of people presently looking into their family history will inevitably find a relative who saw active service in the First World War.

According to Reed, at least 50 percent of his clients have visited the Front specifically to find a grave or to follow the footsteps of a relative who fought there (P. Reed, communication, April 2000). By retracing their ancestors' movements across the battlegrounds, visitors are given the opportunity to reinforce their sense of family pride and acquire some kind of affirmation of their own self-identity. One repeat tourist disclosed that as both sides of his family had relatives who served in the war, he felt that he "grew up with the Western Front." Although he made his first visit late in middle age, once he discovered the place where one of his uncles was killed, "that was it, I never looked back" (A. Potton, communication, March 2003). But this empathic appreciation of the emotional dimensions of the landscape also embraces tour guides too. A guide who now lives on the Somme maintains that his interest in the war is "a lifelong thing" and his work "is more than a job—the day it comes to just pointing left and right I'll pack it in, I honestly will" (V. Piuk, communication, June 2000). Some take the opportunity to interact with the dead. One guide routinely reads the Lord's Prayer in the military cemeteries, not for the benefit of present-day visitors but for the soldiers who often called out to God as they lay dying. Another commented that she frequently lit up a cigarette as she was walking through the rows of headstones because she knew "the boys wouldn't mind, they would enjoy it" (I. Jones, communication, April 2002).

Battlefields Forever England

Intensifying the poignancy of the old front lines is the almost tangible sense of shared ownership between Britain and France that began during the war and has continued to this day. Writing about his wartime experiences at the Front, Mottram noted that it "became a part of Britain, to be defended" (1932: 72). There were in fact so many soldiers in some areas of the Front that they "far exceeded the local inhabitants" (Mottram 1936: 2). Enhancing this perception of possession were the similarities between the French countryside around the Somme and the landscape of southern England that were noted by many soldiers returning from the battlefields. In 1930 Henry Maskell wrote that "it was a typical Wealden landscape. … The hedgebanks were yellow with primroses and in the spinney … the bluebells mingled into a dreamy sapphire glow (1930: 13).

Today traces of the soldiers' vernacular tongue remain entwined in the historic and spatial configuration of the Western Front. Much of the terrain abounds with the wartime names the soldiers gave to particular places, ensuring an enduring British presence in the region and offering to present-day British tourists the comfort of familiarity and a sense of home (Andrews 2010: 35). Tourist guides and history books still use English names for places and land features, and on the Somme, for example, guides will routinely point out features such as the Sausage and Mash valleys and High Wood. But the most visible signs of the lasting British presence are the hundreds of Commonwealth War Grave Commission (CWGC) military cemeteries.[2] The CWGC's green and white signs pointing to cemeteries that bear names such as "Windy Corner," "Blighty Valley," "Flat Iron Copse," and "Owl Trench" also imbue the landscape with a perception of Britishness and belonging. As Harrison observes, "the surest way to take possession of a place and secure it as one's own is to bury one's dead in it" (R. P. Harrison 2003: 24).

Within the cemeteries are inscribed the individual names of the dead. For the many thousands of unidentified soldiers who lay under headstones marked "Known Unto God," their names can be found carved on the walls of the monuments to the missing. The immense and cathedral-like Thiepval Memorial on the Somme, for example, bears the names of approximately seventy-three thousand British and Allied soldiers who died in the Somme sector before March 1918 and have no known grave. The memorials to the missing and the cemeteries, some of which are so large that they resemble a well-kept suburb of small back-to-back terrace houses, commemorate the populations of whole communities. The historian Laqueur ruefully notes that "the pyramids pale by comparison with the sheer scale of British commemorative imposition on the landscape" (1994: 155).

This sense of British "ownership" of the battlefields is particularly noticeable in the Somme area (Gough 2007: 699). Unlike the Ypres Salient, which has been subject to considerable industrial and residential development, its topography largely remains as it was in 1916; in some places, the villages are even smaller today than they were before the conflict began in 1914 (Robertshaw 2006: 90). One consequence of this stasis is that despite the steady increase in the numbers of British tourists over the past thirty years, there has been relatively little interest shown by the French in offering tourist facilities to battlefield visitors. This gap in the market, however, has been slowly filled by the growing number of British people who have decided to live on the Somme permanently and make their living through offering services such as running bed and breakfast establishments, battlefield visitor-friendly tea rooms, and guided tours.

Paradoxically, the landscape that tourists come to experience is not perceived to be British in character but English (Lowenthal 1991: 213). Furthermore, as Mabey notes, it is naturally a rural English landscape that has become the leitmotif of British national identity, even though England has been an industrial and urban nation since the nineteenth century (1993: 64). Rupert Brooke's lines, taken from his sonnet, "The Soldier," "If I should die, think only this of me: / That there's some corner of a foreign field / That is forever England," were written in 1914 with an uncanny prescience of many of the ideas of an imagined Englishness and homeland that still permeates the Western Front landscape. What men were fighting and dying for, Spender suggests, was "some very green meadow with a stream running through it and weeping willows on the banks" (1974: 140). In the minds of the soldiers, freedom was "a feeling for the English landscape" (Spender 1974: 140). This image of a piece of foreign soil that was to be "forever England" was carried through in the design of the military cemeteries. The cemeteries, or "God's acres at home," are lovingly kept by the CWGC gardeners. Their design was under the overall direction of Sir Frederic Kenyon, director of the British Museum, who was appointed adviser to the commission in 1917. Kenyon recommended that the cemeteries should recreate a pastoral idyll, reminiscent of a mixture between an English country garden and a village churchyard. The grieving relatives and friends would at least be comforted in the knowledge that although the dead could not be brought home for burial, they were interred within the boundary walls of a familiar-looking landscape. The commission's intentions were achieved with remarkable success. A veteran who returned to the battlefields in 1938 gave the following response in a letter to *The Ypres Times:*

> All the cemeteries are as we should wish them to be. ... The headstones are becoming dulled by time, roses and tree lupins adorned each little plot and in every sense it was an English garden. (Roses for Memory 1938: n.p.)

Comments written in the cemetery visitor books indicate that present-day visitors experience the same sentiments:

> A beautiful English garden, rest in peace.
> Fields forever England.
> A little corner of France forever England.

However, as Morris notes, the decision to inter soldiers in cemeteries that employed an English garden style in their design in order to symbolize the "home" of Britain has to some degree negated the identities and involvement of soldiers from other parts of Britain as well as its former colonies (1997: 426). The area's cold and inclement winter weather has meant that the graves that belong to West Indian, West African, and South African soldiers have no plants typical of their countries, although there has been a limited use of "native plants" in other sites. Australian graves in France, for example, are planted with wattle and blue gum tree, Canadian graves with maple trees, and Indian cemeteries have marigolds, flag irises, and cypresses (Morris 1997: 425). Yet this "horticultural discrimination" has attracted little criticism even from Commonwealth countries themselves. Comments in the visitors book at Villers-Bretonneux Military Cemetery on the Somme, which contains the Australian National Memorial to commemorate Australian soldiers who died in both France and Belgium during the war, appear to express mainly positive responses towards the soldiers' last resting places, for example:

> A wonderful memorial for these heroic men.
> To those Australians who sacrificed themselves—thank you. To those who now care for you, thanks.

Nevertheless, despite the iconography of the cemeteries as being spaces of "Englishness," Gough notes that on the Somme there is actually little evidence of an English place of commemoration for English battlefield tourists (2007: 699). Although, as he observes, on a national level there are constructions memorializing the Welsh, Scottish, and Irish participation and losses, and on a local and regional level there are numerous commemorative sites, such as the Sheffield Memorial Park, there are no specifically English sites and emblems of remembrance (2007: 699). There is one important site of commemoration on the Somme, however, which sets out to encapsulate a melting pot of different identities—regional, English, British, and beyond, and this is the Lochnagar Crater, privately owned by an Englishman.

The Lochnagar Crater on the Somme

The Lochnagar Crater, which is approximately two kilometers from the Thiepval Memorial, was caused by the detonation of a mine at 7:28 AM on 1 July 1916 near the village of La Boisselle, which marked the beginning of the Somme Offensive. The mine was the largest of several that were exploded under the German front lines that morning, and the blast created an immense hole with a diameter of approximately three hundred feet and a depth of seventy feet (Middlebrook and Middlebrook 1991: 123).[3] Cecil Lewis, then a Royal Flying Corps pilot, vividly described the scene as he was flying above Thiepval:

> The whole earth heaved and flared, a tremendous and magnificent column rose up into the sky. There was an ear-splitting roar, drawing all the guns, flinging the machine sideways in the repercussing air. The earth column rose higher and higher to almost four thousand feet. (Lewis 1936)

Despite the detonation of the mines, however, the attack in this particular sector on the Front was not successful, and the British troops suffered heavy losses. It is not known how many British or German casualties there were in the immediate vicinity, but heavy fighting took place and it is believed that there are about six hundred Germans who still lie entombed in dugouts beneath the field nearby. Although the Somme offensive went on to last for four months, it has always been defined by the events of the first day. That day was the bloodiest twenty-four hours in the history of the British Army when its modest first-day gains cost nearly sixty thousand British and Allied casualties, of whom nearly twenty thousand were killed or died of wounds (Simkins 1993: 8). But as Middlebrook and Middlebrook (1991: 7) point out, it was not simply the numbers of British dead that has made the Somme such an emotive battlefield, but the composition of the units that went into battle there— it was the first great battle to involve the volunteer mass citizen army raised in response to Lord Kitchener's call shortly after the outbreak of war in 1914. Although the epicenter of British emotional attachment to the Western Front was for many years the Ypres Salient in Belgium, as Gough observes since the 1960s it has been the Somme that appears to have exerted the greatest impact on the popular historical imagination (2007: 699).

The present owner of the crater, Richard Dunning, was also drawn to the emotive nature of the French battlefields. Although Dunning acknowledges that he used to have only a mild interest in the war, his reading of John Masefield's book, *The Old Front Line* (1917) while waiting for a coach in the Greyhound bus terminal in Chicago in 1968 proved to be the start of his abiding fascination and growing sense of attachment to the region. His original intention was not specifically to buy the crater but to purchase any small plot of land on the former old front lines. For nearly four years during the 1970s he wrote over two hundred letters to local mayors, solicitors, and newspapers in the Somme area enquiring about land for sale before he was unexpectedly presented with the opportunity to buy the crater from a local farmer who at the time was in the process of applying for permission to have it filled. Dunning received

the deeds for the property on 1 July 1978, and from the outset, his intention was to preserve the site as a memorial and to honor "the memory,
the courage, the sacrifice of the lads who were there" (Dunning 2000b).

Since its purchase and rescue from certain oblivion, the crater has
gradually evolved as a major site of tourism and commemoration, and
today it is a busy place with an estimated two hundred thousand visitors a year.[4] Over the years various memorials have been erected around
the crater's lip including several plaques and memorial benches as well
as a small cross which marks the spot where the remains of a British soldier were found near to the crater in 1998. A large oak cross functions
as the focus of commemorative activities. One of the latest additions to
the site is "Angela's Garden," a small plot set behind the soldier's cross.
It is intended to provide visitors with "a quiet place of contemplation"
away from the busier parts of the site around the entrance (Dunning
2008).

Despite the addition of the benches and the garden, which to some
extent may symbolize the imposition of a sense of order and harmony in
a menacing landscape, the crater remains a stark reminder of the brutality of battle. As Saunders (2001) notes, this landscape is dominated by
"the missing" (Saunders 2001: 46) and the emptiness of the crater mirrors both the absence of those men and alerts us to the fact that nature
was the war's victim too. Tourists who write comments in the visitors'
book often seem to struggle to find adequate words to describe their
impressions, illustrating Gough's observation that "language strains to
depict the calamity and depravity of modern war" (2008: 221): "No
words can capture this"; "This crater speaks louder than any words I
could speak"; "I look at the hole, I think and then cry."

While some British visitors associate Lochnagar as a piece of British
terrain—as illustrated by this comment written in the crater's visitors'
book, "Let's keep this place a little corner of Britain"—to some extent it
embodies some of the geographical imagining of Englishness and homeland found in the military cemeteries. Angela's Garden, for example, was
constructed in order to "create a peaceful garden of 'English' flowers."
Although the crater is not as meticulously tended as the military cemeteries, it nevertheless requires considerable upkeep to control the persis-
tent growth of brambles and shrubs. Like an English landscape that, as
Lowenthal observes, is subject to "an English creed that all land requires
human supervision," the land around the site also needs to be vigilantly
tended and controlled (1991: 218). However, in its dual role as a place
of memorialization and also as a reminder of war, a balance has to be
struck between maintaining the site as a garden of remembrance on the
one hand and on the other, preserving its "unspoilt, wild nature."

One aspect of its wild nature that causes considerable concern is the mud. The glutinous, chalky Somme mud described in the *British Official History* as taking on an "aggressive, wolf-like guise, [which] like a wolf could pull down and swallow the lonely wanderer in the darkness" remains an ongoing problem (cited in McCarthy 1993: 163). The tramping of thousands of feet on the narrow path around the crater's perimeter has left it pitted and uneven, and after a frost or when it rains its surface becomes as slippery as ice. Various initiatives to make the site safe for visitors and to protect it from further wear and tear have included the chiseling of steps around some sections of the path as well as the construction of wooden duckboards at the entrance. The addition of the duckboards also serves the further purpose of alerting visitors that they are entering a sacred site. Dunning is anxious that the crater should be approached with the same reverence as the military cemeteries and hopes that a neater, more formal entrance will convey the message to visitors, especially school children, that "this is a special, sacred place" and that they should "treat it appropriately and respect others who wish to sit quietly and reflect on the momentous events that happened here" (Dunning 2002).

One of the busiest times of the year at the crater is the period around 1 July. Although the anniversary of the beginning of the Somme Offensive is not widely observed in Britain, an increasing number of British visitors now attend the official and unofficial remembrance ceremonies that are held at various sites on the old Somme battlefields throughout the day. Lochnagar hosts the first ceremony, and it begins at precisely 7:28 AM when the firing of a maroon simulates the blowing of the mine in 1916. At the first remembrance ceremony that took place on the morning that Dunning received the deeds of the property, only one other person was in attendance to lay the single wreath. Today, the ceremony regularly attracts over thousand people. Although Dunning states that he did not intentionally set out to create a "different" type of ceremony from the official services that take place elsewhere, he admits that he has nevertheless "created something that is unique and special" (R. Dunning, communication, July 2010). Of central importance is the avoidance of any rigid protocols. He recalls that several years ago at the ceremony held at the Thiepval Memorial, he noticed that the presence of the veterans was almost disregarded:

> I remember looking at the VIP enclosure and seeing all the top brass, the politicians and officials together with their wives, in the shade with chairs and cold drinks. Nothing greatly wrong in that but then I looked back and saw a group of veterans standing together on the far side, in the blazing sun with no chairs. (Dunning 2000a: 21)

Despite the high numbers of people in attendance, the service is structured so that it has a more intimate and personal ambience than the official ceremonies, some of which are attended by royalty, politicians, and civic dignitaries. At the crater, however, the only people who are treated as VIPs are "the old boys and their families" (R. Dunning, communication, July 2010).

The rituals that have slowly developed over the years have been carefully designed to build up an emotive tension "which has the effect of peeling away people's protective layers, one by one" (R. Dunning, communication, May 2000). As Baldwin and Sharpley observe, battlefields are places that can draw out and expose strong emotions even over the deaths of now-distant figures (2009: 193). At the ceremony's climax, the participants are given poppy petals to scatter over the crater's rim, which Dunning describes as a cathartic and healing process:

> The ceremony makes Englishmen cry. Even the most hard-bitten BBC war reporter has been seen to break down and weep, along with a large number of the congregation. Emotions rarely run so intense. (R. Dunning, communication, May 2000)

Adding to the poignancy of the ceremony is its dramatic location, high on a ridge and on the edge of an enormous mine crater. The task of remembering is not taking place in some distant, built-up area away from where the fighting took place, or within the neat and manicured space of a memorial or military cemetery, but at the location where the physical damage wrought on the landscape remains clearly visible. After the ceremony, the crater's rim and base remain tinged with the bright red of the scattered poppy petals, creating a symbolic and highly emotive image of blood, death, and loss.

A further aspect of the service that singles it out from many other remembrance ceremonies is that it does not only to speak to a British audience. All the dead of the Somme including the French and Germans are remembered with an emphasis on equality of sacrifice. To this end, some sections of the ceremony are conducted in English, French, and German and both the local villagers and German visitors are made welcome. Its inclusive nature, though, does not always pass without incident. Most dark tourism sites, including battlefields, as Seaton reminds us, are historical ones and are bound up with important and sensitive issues of personal identity for present-day visitors (2009: 97). On occasions, disputes that have long been settled can suddenly reignite causing further controversy and discord (Seaton 2009: 99). Dunning is aware that the presence of Germans in the ceremony "does upset a few people" (R. Dunning, communication, July 2010), but he is anxious that their

196 • *Jennifer Iles*

participation should continue. However, according to a local tour guide, after one particular ceremony all the wreaths laid during the service were set alight and destroyed. Among them was a large spray of flowers placed by a group of German police who had been invited to play the "Last Post." The following message, thought to have been written by the perpetrators, was left in the visitors' book: "We saw the Germans were here yesterday and their natural colours. When will we ever learn?" (V. Piuk, communication, July 2010)

There have also been tensions arising from the attendance of French officials at the ceremony. In recent years the local Sous-Prefet indicated his wish to attend and promptly imposed a strict order of protocol that Dunning was advised to comply with.[5] This resulted in the presence of the French official party becoming the main focus of the ceremony instead of the remembrance of "the lads themselves, the so-called 'ordinary men'" (Dunning 2009). The issue moved Dunning to make the following statement indicating his intention to return the ceremony to its original purpose:

> It may be that Lochnagar is the victim of its own success as it is now considered a major remembrance ceremony on the Somme but at what point, and on whose say-so was it deemed to be an official ceremony on private land? … The Lochnagar Ceremony will always be dedicated [to the veterans] so this matter of protocol will have to be resolved in the coming months. (Dunning 2009)

Further strains have arisen regarding financial support for the upkeep of the site. The crater has no entrance charge or official source of funding and depends upon individual generosity and fundraising. One major avenue of raising money was provided by a member of the Friends organization who for several years sold hand-painted ceramics near its entrance. However, following the member's apprehension by the French police in 2008 and a subsequent court ruling, any further fundraising efforts on site are now deemed as illegal because Dunning does not have a license to trade. Although Lochnagar has become an important and popular site of tourism and commemoration for both the French locals and British visitors, as Dunning observes, the French authorities currently regard it "in the same way as a market stall" (Dunning 2009).

The crater is a living tapestry of various practices, imaginations, and emotions. It is a tourist site that fascinates and appalls at the same time; it is a place of individual and communal remembrance; and it also seeks to be a convivial spot that invites the visitor to sit and watch and talk and think. The conservation, management, and interpretation of significant commemorative spaces such as Lochnagar can be a complicated matter because the different sets of stakeholders who have an interest in the site exert their own and sometimes mutually exclusive interpretations of its heritage and meaning (Gough 2008: 222). For Dunning, its ability to function as a memorial that allows people to connect with it on several potent levels is its greatest strength:

> There is nowhere quite like it in France, or indeed the world. It has that rare quality that not only can it instantly and powerfully evoke the terror and sacrifice of war but it can also show that now we can create a special, unique place of peace and quiet reflection, of friendship and fellowship with anyone who shows up there. (Dunning 2002)

Conclusion

As has been asserted, the preservation of historical sites such as the battle landscapes of the Western Front is layered with complexity (Gough 2004: 252). For British tourists, many of whom have ancestral links to the area, the old front lines represent a living link to the past. However, as Kirshenblatt-Gimblett notes, a site can be limited in its ability to tell its own story (1998: 167), and in order to gain a true appreciation of the landscape, visitors are required to develop a sense of empathetic involvement so that they can properly identify and understand its significance (Relph 1976: 49). Tourists are not really going for "What am I looking at?" but "What am I trying to understand here?" As poignant reminders of past suffering and tragedy, battlefields are, as Prideaux (2007: 18) notes, capable of evoking deep sentiments. While endeavoring to embrace the ambience of the Western Front and to comprehend the experiences of the men who fought there, many people, including myself, have found their visits to be dominated by an intense degree of emotional engagement that can initially take them by surprise. The importance and meaning that sites such as Lochnagar are able to wield and their ability to evoke profound reflection among some battlefield tourists is captured in the following comment written in the Lochnagar Crater's visitor's book:

> Many thanks for preserving such a piece of land to enable us to pay our respects. We had a most moving service and two minutes silence that meant an awful lot to us.

In view of the emotional and affecting impact of landscapes such as the Western Front, the categorization of visits to battlefields under the general umbrella of "dark tourism" tends to be misleading because the word *dark* implicitly suggests a morbid curiosity in death and disaster.

Although authors such as Smith defend war-related tourism, contending that it is honorific in intent rather than maudlin (1996: 263), as Baldwin and Sharpley suggest, the term nevertheless links battlefield tourists in the same category as those who travel to see sites of murders and executions (2009: 190).

In addition, the blanket categorization of all visits to places or events associated with death as dark tourism may overgeneralize and hide the multifaceted nature of battlefields as well as the variable ways in which they are consumed and contested by the different groups who engage with them (Sharpley and Stone 2009: 250). Places such as the Lochnagar mine crater are required to embrace a wide range of narratives, expectations, and often emotive and strongly held views. Because it is a commemorative site and a setting where blood and soil have a symbolic poignancy in relation to ideas about national identity and shared memory, it does not lend itself to be approached with dispassion (Price 2005). For Saunders (2004), differing perceptions of place find their most extreme expression on battlefields, particularly those that have involved international, multiethnic armies (Saunders 2004: 8). Although the ceremonies at the crater are designed to promote reconciliation among the previous warring forces that brought about the destruction of the landscape, remembrance does not always result in forgiveness but can sometimes stoke resentment (Williams 1977: 188). As Sharpley and Stone contend, there are no simple, unproblematic definitions of dark tourism (2009: 250), but this in turn presents a rich and fascinating ground for further research on tourists and their experiences.

Notes

1. Edmund Blunden's poem "Report on Experience" appears in his memoir, *Undertones of War* (1928).
2. Before 1960 the CWGC was known as the Imperial War Graves Commission.
3. The second mine crater that was blown at La Boisselle was filled in many years ago. The mine crater blown at nearby Beaumont Hamel still exists but is difficult to access.
4. This figure is according to the official website of the Lochnagar Crater. Retrieved 27 November 2010 from http://www.lochnagarcrater.org/.
5. In France the administration of a district is assigned to a sous-prefet who assists the departmental prefet.

Bibliography

Anderson, B. 1991. *Imagined Communities: Reflection on the Origin and Spread of Nationalism.* London: Verso.

Anderson, K., and S. Smith. 2001. "Editorial: Emotional Geographies." *Transactions of the Institute of British Geographers* 26(1): 7–10.

Andrews, H. 2010. "Contours of a Nation: Being British in Mallorca," in J. Scott and T. Selwyn (eds.), *Thinking Through Tourism.* Oxford: Berg, 27–50.

Baldwin, F., and R. Sharpley. 2009. "Battlefield Tourism: Bringing Organised Violence Back to Life," in R. Sharpley and P. R. Stone (eds.), *The Darker Side of Travel: The Theory and Practice of Dark Tourism.* Bristol, UK: Channel View Publications, 186–206.

Belloc, H. 1958. *Selected Essays.* Ed. J. B. Morton. London: Penguin Books.

Bender, B. (ed.). 1993. *Landscape: Politics and Perspectives.* Oxford: Berg.

Bowman, M. 2005. "Looking for Stonewall's Arm: Tourist Performance as Research Method," in J. Hamera (ed.), *Opening Acts: Performance in/as Communication and Cultural Studies.* Thousand Oaks, CA: Sage, 102–33.

Bremer, T. S. 2006. "Sacred Spaces and Tourist Places," in D. J. Timothy and D. H. Olsen (eds.), *Tourism, Religion and Spiritual Journeys.* London: Routledge, 25–35.

Coleman, S., and M. Crang. (eds.). 2002. *Tourism: Between Place and Performance.* New York: Berghahn Books.

Crawshaw, C., and J. Urry. 1997. "Tourism and the Photographic Eye," in C. Rojek and J. Urry (eds.), *Touring Cultures: Transformations of Travel and Theory.* London: Routledge, 176–95.

Crouch, D. 2002. "Surrounded by Place," in S. Coleman and M. Crang (eds.), *Tourism: Between Place and Performance.* Oxford: Berghahn, 207–18.

Crouch, D., and N. Lübbren (eds). 2003. *Visual Culture and Tourism.* Oxford: Berg.

Douie, C. 1929. *The Weary Road: The Recollections of a Subaltern of Infantry.* London: John Murray.

Dunning, R. 2000a. "Another Special Anniversary Ceremony at the Lochnagar Crater Memorial, Somme," *Western Front Association Bulletin* 58: 21.

———. 2000b. *Friends of Lochnagar Newsletter* 31.

———. 2002. *Friends of Lochnagar Newsletter* 36.

———. 2008. *Friends of Lochnagar Newsletter* 53.

———. 2009. *Friends of Lochnagar Newsletter* 55.

Edensor, T. 1998. *Tourists at the Taj: Performance and Meaning at a Symbolic Site.* London: Routledge.

———. 2000. "Staging Tourism: Tourists as Performers." *Annals of Tourism Research* 27: 322–44.

———. 2001. "Performing Tourism, Staging Tourism." *Tourist Studies* 1(1): 59–81.

Franklin, A. 2003. *Tourism: An Introduction.* London: Sage.

Franklin, A., and M. Crang. 2001. "The Trouble with Tourism and Travel Theory?" *Tourist Studies* 1(1): 5–22.

Geertz, C. 1988. *Works and Lives.* Stanford, CA: Stanford University Press.

Gough, P. 2001. "That Sacred Turf: War Memorial Gardens as Theatres of War (and Peace)," in J. Fidler and J. M. Teutonico (eds.), *Monuments and the Millennium.* London: James and James, 228–36.

———. 2004. "Sites in the Imagination: The Beaumont Hamel Newfoundland Memorial on the Somme." *Cultural Geographies* 11: 235–58.

———. 2007. "'Contested Memories: Contested Site': Newfoundland and its Unique Heritage on the Western Front." *The Round Table* 96(393): 693–705.

———. 2008. "Commemoration of War," in B. Graham and P. Howard (eds.), *The Ashgate Research Companion to Heritage and Identity.* Abingdon, UK: Ashgate, 215–29.

Harrison, J. 2010. "Belonging at the Cottage," in J. Scott and T. Selwyn (eds.), *Thinking Through Tourism.* Oxford: Berg, 71–92.

Harrison, R. P. 2003. *The Dominion of the Dead.* Chicago: University of Chicago Press.

Hastrup, K. 1992. "Writing Ethnography: The State of the Art," in J. Okely and H. Callaway (eds.), *Anthropology and Autobiography.* London: Routledge, 116–33.

Iles, J. 2006. "Recalling the Ghosts of War: Performing Tourism on the Battlefields of the Western Front." *Text and Performance Quarterly* 26(2): 162–80.

———. 2008. "Encounters in the Fields: Tourism to the Battlefields of the Western Front." *Journal of Tourism and Cultural Change* 6(2): 138–54.

Jakle, J. 1987. *The Visual Elements of Landscape.* Amherst: University of Massachusetts Press.

Kirshenblatt-Gimblett, B. 1998. *Destination Culture: Tourism, Museums and Heritage.* Berkeley: University of California Press.

Laqueur, T. 1994. "Memory and Naming in the Great War," in J. R. Gillis (ed.), *Commemorations: The Politics of National Identity.* Princeton, NJ: Princeton University Press, 150–67.

Lennon, J., and M. Foley. 2000. *Dark Tourism: The Attraction of Death and Disaster.* London: Continuum.

Lewis, C. 1936. *Sagittarius Rising.* London: Peter Davies.

Lowenthal, D. 1991. "British National Identity and the English Landscape." *Rural History* 2(2): 205–30.

Mabey, R. 1993. "Landscape: Terra Firma?" in N. Alfrey (ed.), *Towards a New Landscape.* London: Bernard Jacobsen, 62–69.

Macnaghten, P., and J. Urry. 1998. *Contested Natures.* London: Sage.

Masefield, J. 1917. *The Old Front Line.* London: Heinemann.

Maskell, H. 1930. *The Soul of Picardy.* London: Ernest Benn.

McCarthy, C. 1993. *The Somme: The Day-by-Day Account.* London: Arms and Armour Press.

McPhail, H. 1999. *The Long Silence: Civilian Life under the German Occupation of Northern France, 1914–1918.* London: I. B. Tauris.

Middlebrook, M., and M. Middlebrook. 1991. *The Somme Battlefields: A Comprehensive Guide from Crécy to the Two World Wars.* London: Penguin.

Morris, M. S. 1997. "Gardens 'For Ever England': Landscape, Identity and the First World War British Cemeteries on the Western Front." *Ecumene* 4(4): 410–34.

Mottram, R. H. 1932. *Through the Menin Gate.* London: Chatto and Windus.

———. 1936. *Journey to the Western Front: Twenty Years After.* London: G. Bell and Son.

Okely, J. 1992. "Anthropology and Autobiography: Participatory Experience and Embodied Knowledge," in J. Okely and H. Callaway (eds.), *Anthropology and Autobiography.* London: Routledge, 1–28.

Oxenham, J. 1918. *High Altars: The Battlefields of France and Flanders as I Saw Them.* London: Methuen.

Piekarz, M. 2007. "Hot War Tourism: The Live Battlefield and the Ultimate Adventure Holiday?" in C. Ryan (ed.), *Battlefield Tourism: History, Place and Interpretation.* London: Elsevier, 153–69.

Price, J. 2005. "Cultural Landscape of Sacrifice, the Problem of the Sacred Ground of the Great War 1914–1918." *Proceedings of the 2005 UNESCO Forum/WAC Inter-Congress on Cultural Landscape in the 21st Century, 11–16 April 2005.* Newcastle-upon Tyne, UK: Newcastle University. Revised June 2006. Retrieved 2 September 2010 from http://conferences.ncl.ac.uk/unescolandscapes/files/PRICE jon.pdf.

Prideaux, B. 2007. "Echoes of War: Battlefield Tourism," in C. Ryan (ed.), *Battlefield Tourism: History, Place and Interpretation.* London: Elsevier, pp. 17–29.

Reed, P. 1999. *Walking the Salient: A Walkers Guide to the Ypres Salient (Battleground Europe).* Barnsley, UK: Leo Cooper.

Relph, E. 1976. *Place and Placelessness.* London: Pion.

Robertshaw, A. 2006. *Somme 1 July 1916: Tragedy and Triumph.* Oxford: Osprey Publishing.

Rojek, C. 1995. *Decentering Leisure: Rethinking Leisure Theory.* London: Sage.

"Roses for Memory." 1938. *Ypres Times,* January: n.p.

Samuel, R. 1994. *Theatres of Memory,* vol. 1: *Past and Present in Contemporary Culture.* London: Verso.

Sanders, C. R. 1998. "Animal Passions. The Emotional Experience of Doing Ethnography in Animal-Human Interaction Settings," in S. Grills (ed.), *Doing Ethnographic Research: Fieldwork Settings.* London: Sage, 184–98.

Saunders, N. 2001. "Matter and Memory in the Landscapes of Conflict: The Western Front 1914–1999," in B. Bender and M. Winer (eds.), *Contested Landscapes: Movement, Exile and Place.* Oxford: Berg, 37–54.

———. 2004. *Matters of Conflict: Material Culture, Memory and the First World War.* London: Routledge.

Seaton, A. V. 1999. "War and Thanatourism: Waterloo 1815–1914." *Annals of Tourism Research* 26(1): 130–58.

———. 2009. "Purposeful Otherness: Approaches to the Management of Thanatourism," in R. Sharpley and P. Stone (eds.), *The Darker Side of Travel: The Theory and Practice of Dark Tourism.* Bristol, UK: Channel View Publications, 75–108.

Sharpley, R., and P. Stone. 2009. "Life, Death and Dark Tourism: Future Research Directions and Concluding Comments," in R. Sharpley and P. Stone (eds.), *The Darker Side of Travel: The Theory and Practice of Dark Tourism.* Bristol, UK: Channel View Publications, 247–51.

Shepheard, P. 1997. *The Cultivated Wilderness: Or, What Is Landscape?* Cambridge, MA: Massachusetts Institute of Technology Press.

Shields, R. 2000. "Memory and Place: The Importance of Attending to Absence in Place-Based Research." *ASA Conference: Participating in Development: Approaches to Indigenous Knowledge,* 2–5 April. London: SOAS.

Simkins, P. 1993. "Introduction," in C. McCarthy, *The Somme: The Day-to-Day Account.* London: Arms and Armour Press, 7–13.

Smith, V. 1996. "War and Its Tourist Attractions," in A. Pizam and Y. Mansfeld (eds.), *Tourism, Crime and International Security Issues*. Chichester, UK: Wiley, 247–64.

———. 1998. "War and Tourism: An American Ethnography." *Annals of Tourism Research* 25(1): 202–27.

Spender, S. 1974. *Love-Hate Relations: A Study of Anglo-American Sensibilities*. London: Hamilton.

Stedman, M., and E. Skelding. 1999. *Great Battles of the Great War*. Barnsley, UK: Leo Cooper/Pen and Sword Books.

Tilley, C. 1994. *A Phenomenology of Landscape: Places, Paths and Monuments*. Oxford: Berg.

Tucker, H. 1997. "The Ideal Village: Interactions through Tourism in Central Anatolia," in S. Abram, J. Waldren, and D. Macleod (eds.), *Tourists and Tourism: Identifying with People and Places*. Oxford: Berg, 91–106.

Urry, J. 1990. *The Tourist Gaze: Leisure and Travel in Contemporary Societies*. London: Sage.

Widdowfield, R. 2000. "The Place of Emotions in Academic Research." *Area* 32(2): 199–208.

Williams, R. 1977. *Marxism and Literature*. Oxford: Oxford University Press.

Winter, C. 2009. "Tourism, Social Memory and the Great War." *Annals of Tourism Research* 36(4): 607–26.

Notes on Contributors

Simon Cooke is a Research Fellow in English at Wolfson College, Oxford. He completed his PhD dissertation, "Voyages of Recovery and Renewal: Travellers' Tales of Wonder in Contemporary Literature—Chatwin, Naipaul, Sebald," at Justus-Liebig-University Gießen in 2010, and is currently preparing it for publication. He is also coauthor, with Richard Humphrey and Ansgar Nünning, of *Essential Study Skills for BA/MA in British and American Studies* (Klett: 2007).

Keith Egan was the Leach/RAI fellow (2009/10) at NUI Maynooth. Keith graduated in 2007 from NUI Maynooth with his PhD in anthropology for a thesis entitled "In Defense of the Realm: Mobility, Modernity and Community on the Camino de Santiago." He has conducted research at various Christian shrines across Europe as part of a NORFACE research consortium.

Jenny Elliott is dancer-in-residence with Arts Care at Knockbracken Healthcare Park, Belfast Health and Social Services Trust. In 2008, Jenny completed a PhD researching the impact of a Laban-based dance program on people with an enduring brain injury and the healthcare staff who care for them. The core element of the PhD text was the use of performance and film documentary to capture the participants' experience of an arts-based activity. She is also the Artistic Director of Orbit Dance and Kompany Maine, two integrated-ability dance companies that have evolved out of her dance residency.

Sharon Hepburn is Associate Professor in Anthropology at Trent University, Canada. She spent four years in Nepal, doing research on aspects of tourism, identity, the senses, and—most recently—civilian life during the armed conflict between the Communist Party of Nepal (Maoist) and the Royal Nepal Army. Part of this work has been published in *Annals of Tourism Research* ("Touristic Forms of Life in Nepal"), *Fashion Theory: The Journal of Dress, Body, and Culture* ("The Cloth of Barbaric Pagans: Tourism, Identity, and Modernity in Nepal"), and in *Food, Culture* *and Society* ("The Dangers of Foreign Bodies: Contamination of Travellers in and out of Nepal").

Jennifer Iles is a Senior Lecturer in Sociology at Roehampton University. She has research interests in battlefield tourism, the heritage industry, death studies, and experiential learning. Her PhD examined present-day collective remembrance of the First World War and tourism to the battlefields of the Western Front. Although battlefield tourism remains the focus of her research, Jennifer has recently embarked on research into spiritualism.

Rachel Moffat completed her PhD in English Literature at the University of Glasgow in 2010. Her thesis discusses twentieth-century representations of African countries in travel writing, exploring contemporary developments in the genre. Her publications include the edited volume *Material Worlds* (2007, CSP) and an interview with Dervla Murphy published on the Studies in Travel Writing website in 2009 and referenced in the *Times* (London).

Fiona Murphy is currently working as a lecturer in the Department of Anthropology, NUI Maynooth, Ireland. She has recently finished an IRCHSS-funded project (PI Dr. Mark Maguire) entitled "After Asylum: An Ethnographic Analysis of Refugee Integration." A graduate of University College Cork in 2000 with a joint honors degree in French and English, and an MA in French, Fiona received her PhD in Anthropology from NUI Maynooth in 2009 for her research on trauma and memory amongst Australia's Stolen Generations. Her research interests extend from issues of Indigeneity, trauma and reconciliation to migration and integration studies.

John Nagle is a Lecturer in Anthropology at the University of East London, a Visiting Research Fellow at the University of Exeter, and Research Fellow at INCORE, a United Nations associate department at the University of Ulster. His main books are *Multiculturalism's Double–Bind: Creating Inclusivity, Cosmopolitanism and Difference* (Ashgate, 2009) and *Shared Society or Benign Apartheid? Understanding Peace–Building in Divided Societies* (Palgrave MacMillan, 2010). He has also published over fifteen articles in leading international journals, including *Ethnicities, Political Geography, Nations and Nationalism, Antipode,* and *Ethnopolitics.*

Jonathan Skinner is a Senior Lecturer in Social Anthropology at Queen's University Belfast where he specializes in tourism and dance. His research region is the Caribbean, specifically the island of Montserrat where he has studied the tourist/travel writing projections of a Black Irish ethnicity upon the indigenous population. His key publications are: *Managing Island Life: Social, Economic and Political Dimensions of Formality and Informality in 'Island' Communities* (University of Abertay Press, 2006, J. Skinner and M. Hills, eds.); *Before the Volcano: Reverberations of Identity on Montserrat* (Arawak Publications, 2004); *Scotland's Boundaries and Identities in the New Millennium* (University of Abertay Dundee Press, 2001, J. Skinner, C. Di Domenico, A. Law, and M. Smith, eds.).

Tristram Walker is associated with Nottingham Trent University. He is the presenter of 'Erewash and Beyond,' the weekly news and culture show on regional radio station Erewash Sound. He is also co-writer and co-presenter of the cult podcast *Max Buffer's Media Museum*. He has written for numerous small press publications including the music magazine *Trashpit*.

Index

▶●●◆●●◀